CAMBRIDGE STUDIES

IN

MEDIEVAL LIFE AND THOUGHT

Edited by G. G. COULTON, M.A.
Fellow of St John's College, Cambridge
and University Lecturer in English

ENGLISH
MONASTIC FINANCES
IN THE
LATER MIDDLE AGES

T0381872

ENGLISH
MONASTIC FINANCES
IN THE
LATER MIDDLE AGES

BY

R. H. SNAPE, M.A.
EMMANUEL COLLEGE

CAMBRIDGE
AT THE UNIVERSITY PRESS
1926

CAMBRIDGE
UNIVERSITY PRESS

University Printing House, Cambridge CB2 8BS, United Kingdom

Cambridge University Press is part of the University of Cambridge.

It furthers the University's mission by disseminating knowledge in the pursuit of education, learning and research at the highest international levels of excellence.

www.cambridge.org
Information on this title: www.cambridge.org/9781107455542

First published 1926
First paperback edition 2014

A catalogue record for this publication is available from the British Library

ISBN 978-1-107-45554-2 Paperback

GENERAL PREFACE

THERE is only too much truth in the frequent complaint that history, as compared with the physical sciences, is neglected by the modern public. But historians have the remedy in their own hands; choosing problems of equal importance to those of the scientist, and treating them with equal accuracy, they will command equal attention. Those who insist that the proportion of accurately ascertainable facts is smaller in history, and therefore the room for specu-lation wider, do not thereby establish any essential distinction between truth-seeking in history and truth-seeking in chemistry. The historian, whatever be his subject, is as definitely bound as the chemist "to proclaim certainties as certain, falsehoods as false, and uncertainties as dubious." Those are the words, not of a modern scientist, but of the seventeenth century monk, Jean Mabillon; they sum up his literary profession of faith. Men will follow us in history as implicitly as they follow the chemist, if only we will form the chemist's habit of marking clearly where our facts end and our inferences begin. Then the public, so far from discouraging our speculations, will most heartily encourage them; for the most positive man of science is always grateful to anyone who, by putting forward a working theory, stimulates further discussion.

The present series, therefore, appeals directly to that craving for clearer facts which has been bred in these times of storm and stress. No care can save us altogether from error; but, for our own sake and the public's we have elected to adopt a safe-guard dictated by ordinary business common-sense. Whatever errors of fact are pointed out by reviewers or correspondents shall be publicly corrected with the least possible delay. After a year of publication, all copies shall be provided with such an erratum-slip without waiting for the chance of a second edition; and each fresh volume in this series shall contain a full list of the errata noted in its immediate predecessor. After the lapse of a year from the first publication of any volume, and at any time during the ensuing twelve months, any possessor of that volume who will send a stamped and addressed envelope to the Cambridge University Press, Fetter Lane, Fleet Street, London, E.C. 4, shall receive, in due course, a free copy of the *errata* in that volume. Thus, with the help of our critics, we may reasonably hope to put forward these monographs as roughly representing the most accurate information obtainable under present conditions. Our facts being thus secured, the reader will judge our inferences on their own merits; and something will have been done to dissipate that cloud of suspicion which hangs over too many important chapters in the social and religious history of the Middle Ages.

G. G. C.

October, 1922.

PREFACE

THE following essay was awarded the Prince Consort Prize in 1912. Its publication has been delayed mainly in the hope that it might be possible to remedy, in part at least, its manifest incompleteness, especially by an examination of the methods of monastic estate management, the economic position of the nunneries, the position of the monasteries as regards taxation, and the authority of the Valor Ecclesiasticus as a complete statement of the financial position of the monasteries at the Dissolution. This would have involved, *inter alia*, a rehandling of the monastic accounts already printed, and some inspection of the great number still unpublished, and it has proved impossible to carry out the investigations necessary. The essay is therefore printed in the hope that the collection of information which it contains may, so far as it goes, prove of some interest to other students of monastic history. A few passages have been rewritten, and reference has been made in a few cases to material published since 1912, but the essay remains substantially as originally written.

The main authorities consulted are as follows:

Bond, Sir E. A. *Chronica Monasterii de Melsa.* 3 vols. (Rolls Series.)
Burton, John. *Monasticon Eboracense.*
Capes, W. W. *The English Church in the fourteenth and fifteenth centuries.*
—— *Registrum Ricardi de Swinfield, Episcopi Herefordensis.* (Canterbury and York Society Publications.)
Chapman, F. R. *Sacrist Rolls of Ely.*
Clark, J. W. *The Observances in use at the Augustinian Priory of S. Giles and S. Andrew at Barnwell.*
Coulton, G. G. Medieval Studies.
Delisle, L. *Calendar of Papal Letters.* Vols. I–V.
—— *La Fortune de l'Ordre de St-Benoît.*
Duckett, Sir G. F. *Visitations of English Cluniac Foundations.*

Dugdale, Sir W. *Monasticon Anglicanum*. Ed. Caley, Ellis and Bandinel.

Ely Registers. Summary published in *Ely Diocesan Remembrancer*.

Fowler, J. T. *Extracts from the Account Rolls of the Abbey of Durham*. 3 vols. (Surtees Society.)

—— *Rites of Durham*.

—— *Cistercian Statutes 1256–7*.

Gasquet, F. A. *English Monastic Life*.

Griffiths, Rev. R. G. *Registrum Thome de Cantilupo, Episcopi Herefordensis*.

Heales, A. *The Records of Merton Priory* (Surrey).

Hingeston-Randolph, Rev. F. C. Episcopal Registers. Diocese of Exeter.

Jessopp, A. *Visitations of the Diocese of Norwich*. (Camden Society.)

Kitchin, G. W. *Compotus Rolls of the Obedientiaries of St Swithun's Priory, Winchester*.

Labbé, Philippe. *Sacrosancta Concilia*.

Macray, W. D. *Chronicon Abbatiæ de Evesham, ad annum 1418*.

Matthew Paris. *Chronica Majora*. (Rolls Series.)

Pirenne, H. *Polyptyque et comptes de l'Abbaye de Saint-Trond*.

Rackham, R. B. *The Nave of Westminster*.

Raine, J. *The Inventories and Account Rolls of the Benedictine Houses or cells of Jarrow and Monk-Wearmouth*. (Surtees Society.)

—— *The charters, etc., of the Priory of Finchale*, 1837. (Surtees Society.)

Reynerus, C. *Apostolatus Benedictinorum in Anglia* (1626).

Rigaudus, Odo. *Regestrum Visitationum Archiepiscopi Rothomagensis*.

Rokewode, J. G. *Jocelinus de Brakelonda*. (Camden Society.)

Salter, Rev. H. E. *Eynsham Cartulary*. (Oxford Historical Society.)

Savine, A. N. *English Monasteries on the eve of the Dissolution*.

Stevenson, J. *De Obedientiariis Abbatiæ Abbendoniensis* (Chronicle of Abingdon, Rolls Series, Vol. II, Appendix IV).

Stewart, D. J. *Liber Eliensis*.

Victoria County Histories.

Whitaker, T. D. *The history and antiquities of the Deanery of Craven, in the County of York*.

—— *An history of the original Parish of Whalley, and Honor of Clitheroe, in the Counties of Lancaster and York*.

Wilkins, D. *Concilia Magnae Britanniae et Hiberniae*.

Worcester Account Rolls, edited by J. M. Wilson, C. Gordon, and S. G. Hamilton.

I am under a heavy debt of gratitude to Mr G. G. Coulton both for the suggestion of the subject of this essay, for continual advice as to reading and help in the solution of difficulties, for the use of much material otherwise difficult of consultation (notably the Register of Odo Rigaldi) as well as for the general information on the subject of monasticism given in his various publications, and in the Birkbeck Lectures of 1911. How heavy my debt has been will be readily apparent from the following pages.

I have to thank my colleague, Mr E. T. S. Wheeller, for his assistance in reading the essay in proof.

R. H. S.

October, 1925.

CONTENTS

ENGLISH MONASTIC FINANCES IN THE LATER MIDDLE AGES

INTRODUCTION

To most Englishmen the one great event which the mention of monasticism brings to mind is the Dissolution of the Monasteries. The centuries during which the religious houses stood to the world around as havens wherein it was possible, for some at least, to attain that life which to the mediaeval mind was beyond question the highest, are overshadowed by the moment in which they fell. With that fall questions are connected round which historians have joined in what may seem a battle incapable of ending. Whether the suppression of the monasteries was just or necessary, whether they had degenerated, whether their downfall represents only the achievement of one despotic will, defending itself by purchased lies and winning acquiescence by wholesale corruption, are questions which still bulk large. No student of monastic life and history can ignore them; each is in some measure bound to regard his work as a contribution towards their solution. It is perhaps inevitable that it should be so. Few can contentedly leave it an open question whether, at the beginning of the history of modern England, an institution was destroyed endowed with potentialities of good not otherwise to be attained. Any study of English monasticism, after its earliest ages, is sure to be regarded as in some measure a contribution towards the settling of the problems of the Dissolution. Even from this point of view, not the least promising subject to which research can be directed is monastic finance in the later Middle Ages.

Most historians who deal with the Dissolution have hitherto depended mainly on evidence drawn from the records of the late fifteenth or the early sixteenth century. Here the question is now becoming one rather of interpretation than of discovery. But the period from the twelfth to the sixteenth century, from the time when the last great mediaeval movement of monasticism proper reached England from Cîteaux, to the time when the life of the English monasteries was drawing to a close, still awaits full and adequate treatment. The gap must be filled up to understand fully the conditions prevailing in the sixteenth century. The early stages of monastic movements have been carefully traced. They will always possess the attraction which a noble and unworldly enthusiasm exerts even on those to whom the end does not seem altogether worthy of the zeal with which it is pursued. The conditions of the sixteenth century have been closely scrutinised, if only for polemic purposes. But, for the intervening centuries, though much has been done in the direction of the publication of evidence, comparison and generalisation still lag behind. The workaday life of the monasteries from the twelfth century onward has been taken somewhat too much for granted. Cardinal Gasquet's *Henry VIII and the Monasteries*, for example, deals more adequately with the King than with his victims. Sixteenth century evidence is interpreted without much investigation of the earlier history. Nor does his *English Monasticism* fill the gap. It is based for the most part on Rules, Custumals, and similar documents, and therefore presents a picture in which monastic life is represented without sufficient allowance for the inevitable discrepancies between the ideal and the real. Rules and regulations were not everything. Accounts based on such material cannot be accepted as complete until they have been checked by the examination of masses of material, produced, without much purpose of edification, by the monks themselves, and showing, with varying degrees of clearness, the actual course of their daily life. The gap which too often existed between mediaeval ideals and realities may possibly have existed here as well.

The following pages are an attempt to examine the actual course of monastic life from the twelfth to the sixteenth century, from one special point of view—that of finance. The economic standpoint lacks, perhaps, some of the attractiveness of other methods of approaching monastic history. We cannot concern ourselves with the great leaders of the monastic movement. The exact direction given to the successive waves of ascetic enthusiasm, influencing the mental outlook of the whole of European society, hardly concerns us. We must occupy ourselves simply with the monasteries as holders of property, and try to see something of the day-to-day business in which the monks were thus involved, and of its effect upon the secular world with which they were thus brought into direct contact. A method which, even here, will almost reduce the work of a Matthew Paris or a Roger Bacon to records of the purchase of ink and parchment has very obvious limitations. But the disadvantage is not so great as it seems. The materials which offer themselves are beyond suspicion. They are first hand evidence set down by men with no thought that the records which they left would ever become the objects of historical curiosity. They are, for the most part, mere business documents, compiled in the ordinary run of daily life without any other motive than the enlightenment of those concerned in the business affairs of the religious houses. So far as they can be interpreted, they give an admirable opportunity for inquiry into the normal conditions of monastic life on its material side.

Six main questions are here considered: the population of the religious houses, their organisation, the main features of monastic revenue and of expenditure, the general condition and management of the monastic economy, as shown by the evidence as to debt and the financial expedients adopted to meet it, and lastly a brief consideration of the general tone of monastic life as shown in the material conditions of life within the house.

Complete answers to these questions would not only throw light upon many sides of the social life of the Middle Ages, but would place us in a much better position to deal with the problems of the Dissolution. Completeness, however, is the last thing that could be claimed for the following pages. Much printed evidence exists besides that upon which they are based. In many cases the work which they contain represents little more than a verification of the work of others. Masses of material still remain unprinted; many points of interest and importance are left untouched; the history of the friaries, and in great part that of the nunneries, are perforce set aside, together with the whole question of the relations of both to education. No attempt is made to deal with the wide problems of the management of monastic estates, the decline of villeinage, and the relations between the monasteries and the towns which so often grew up around them.

A few words may be necessary as to the nature of the original authorities followed. They may be ranked in four main divisions. The first consists of legislative enactments, and covers such material as is to be found in the Statute Book and the Rolls of Parliament, the Rules of the monastic Orders, with their various Papal recensions, the Statutes promulgated by the Benedictine Provincial Chapters after the creation of the Benedictine Congregations by the Lateran Council of 1215, and other similar documents. The second group contains the records of visitations held by the bishops or by the visitors of the Orders exempt from episcopal authority, and is valuable as giving the results of an external but friendly criticism. In the third division are such documents as form the staple of Dugdale's *Monasticon* and the various chartularies published; records of the donations of benefactors, of papal or royal grants of privilege, surveys, inquisitions and rentals, regulations for the appointment of the revenues and work of the house, memoranda of rights and dues—records, in short, of all the business documents of the house which were thought likely to be of permanent use in the management of its affairs. Under this head too may be classed the numerous monastic annals and chronicles published in the Rolls Series, most of which have something to say on the varying fortunes of the houses in which they were written, whilst one—the Chronicle of the Cistercian House of Meaux—is practically devoted to that one topic alone. In the last division may be placed the actual account-rolls and balance-sheets of the monasteries, many of which have been published, while many more still remain in manuscript. These accounts are of the first importance. They show the working of the monastic economic organisation in all its complex details, and reflect without any possibility of *arrière pensée* the internal life of the monastery and the actual relations of the monks with the outside world. At the same time it must be admitted that these documents—or such at least as have been published—are disappointing in two respects. In the first place they belong, as is natural, mainly to those great houses which had at their back sufficient endowments to carry them with comparative ease through difficulties under which the accounts of the less wealthy and more numerous houses would have shown greater traces of the struggle, and would therefore have been of greater interest for purposes of generalisation as to the effect of the economic crises through which the houses passed. Secondly, the collection for any one house is usually fragmentary; and this, together with the extreme complexity of curt detail which the accounts present, makes combination and generalisation difficult often to the point of impossibility. Thus, for example, among the accounts of the obedientiaries of Abingdon Abbey, in a collection ranging from 1322 to 1478, the year 1422–3 is the only one for which we have the accounts of more than one obedientiary, and even in that case, the offices represented are of quite minor importance, the refectorer's and the chapel warden's. A similar difficulty is found in dealing with the larger collection of Compotus Rolls of St Swithun's Priory, Winchester. It is often hard, therefore, to grasp the exact relationship between the various officers of the monastery, or to enter into calculations as to the percentage of income spent in alms, on books, and so on. Despite all these difficulties, the value of what we have is inestimable. To quote the editor of the Chronicle of Meaux: "A real obscurity hangs over the actual history of the several monasteries. The knowledge we have of them is mainly confined to their external condition. When the monks wrote of themselves for the edification of the world at large, a great deal was said of their holiness of life, and little of their shortcoming—little too of their indirect influence, good or evil, on the people they were planted amongst." These documents give us an opportunity of making some estimate of what that influence was. Glimpses may be caught in every direction of such parts of mediaeval life as were affected by those monasteries whose accounts we possess; and everywhere we feel that firm ground is beneath our feet, even if we can see only a little way.

CHAPTER I

THE MONASTIC POPULATION

THE monasteries, during the period under consideration, were not inhabited by monks alone: and the fact must be borne in mind in order to understand the claims made upon monastic revenue. As will shortly be seen, it is not going too far to say that in the larger houses at any rate (for which the fullest information is obtainable) from a third to a half only of those dwelling in the monasteries from the close of the thirteenth century onwards were professed monks. Three classes of men found homes within the monastic precincts: the regular monks (with whom may be reckoned the novices), the lay brethren, and the laymen who for one cause or another were admitted to dwell with the monks. Something must be said of the latter classes, and the proportions which at various times they bore to the regulars, in order that the changes which went on inside the monasteries may be made clear.

The lay brethren, or "conversi," were chiefly of importance among the Cistercians: for although other monastic Orders adopted the system of enrolling lay brethren, in the English religious houses, at all events, it never seems to have obtained firm hold. Thus in 1275–6 the delegates of the Cluniac Order visiting eleven of the English houses found in them 254 monks, but only nine lay brethren[1]. But in the early days of the Cistercian Order, the conversi were a large and important class. They represent what may be called an attempt to democratise monasticism, to enlist in its service representatives of those classes in which the Mendicant Orders later found their chief strength and weakness. For the most part, they were of the lower orders, artisans, husbandmen, or labourers, although it is possible to find exceptional cases in which some member of a noble family, eager to enter on the ascetic life, but barred (or in his humility, feigning to be barred) by his illiteracy from obtaining admission to a monastery as one of the religious, was content to accept the subordinate station of a lay brother. The conversi served the

[1] See Appendix A.

monastery to which they were attached, not as the educated monks, largely by service in the choir, but by plying their several crafts, or, it would seem, at a later date by supervising the workers on the estates held in demesne. They undertook the ordinary monastic obligations of poverty, chastity and obedience to their superior, but were subject to less stringent regulations as to attendance in the choir, fasting and vigils. They were definitely regarded as a class of less dignity than the regular monks, and were rarely or never allowed to advance by application to study, to the status of full monachism. In the Cistercian Statutes of 1256[1], which give elaborate details as to the feast days on which the lay brethren should be free from labour, the services at which they should be present, the frequency of their communions and so on, it is particularly enjoined that "no conversus is to have a book, or learn anything save the Paternoster, the Creed, the Miserere and Ave Maria, and the rest which it is decreed that they ought to say, and this not by letter, but by heart." The theory on which the lay brethren were admitted is well illustrated by a passage in the Observances of the Augustinian Priory at Barnwell[2]. "Lay brethren are not to be admitted to the habit unless they are instructed in some craft which is useful to the monastery; for as regular canons ought to be occupied day and night in things spiritual, so lay brethren ought to labour for the profit of the Church in things corporeal."

The Chronicle of the Abbey of Meaux, one of the great Yorkshire religious houses, shows at once, as its editor points out, the importance of this class of semi-monks in a Cistercian monastery, and the ultimate decline of the system even among those with whom it had found its chief strength. It is possible to trace the numbers of conversi at Meaux from the beginning of the thirteenth to the end of the fourteenth century: and these two centuries saw the disappearance of a class originally more numerous than the professed monks. In the Chronicle there is recorded the number of deaths at Meaux during the general interdict of 1214–30[3]. Seven monks and one novice died, as compared with 16 conversi; and the conclusion may be safely drawn that

[1] J. T. Fowler, *Cistercian Statutes*, p. 97.
[2] J. W. Clark, *Observances at the Augustinian Priory of St Giles and St Andrew*, p. 223.
[3] Sir E. A. Bond, *Chronica Monasterii de Melsa*, I, p. 343.

the lay brethren at that date far outnumbered the monks, and indeed that their number was not improbably twice as great as that of the professed. Nor was this proportion unusual: Waverley, the first Cistercian house founded in England, in 1187, or 59 years after its establishment, consisted of 70 monks and 120 lay brethren[1]. The next date for which we have a statement of the number of conversi at Meaux is 1249; 99 years after its foundation, on the death of the eighth abbot, Michael, there were only 90 lay brethren to 60 monks[2]. Exactly a century later, in the year when the Black Death reached Meaux, there were only seven lay brethren actually in the house, as compared with 43 monks[3]; although it is possible, as the editor points out with regard to a later entry, that there were others employed as bailiffs and labourers on the farms of the monastery. Long before this date, however, difficulties had arisen with the conversi; for, about 1230, Abbot Richard of Ottringham found it necessary to put some check upon the arrogance of the lay brothers in charge of the granges and farms, and had to remove them from their positions and set them to menial work—keeping pigs or cattle, ploughing, joinery, stone-cutting, glazing, or plumbing[4]: whilst under his successor, the conversi seriously offended one of the neighbouring landowners, and so involved the house in trouble[5]. These difficulties seem to have continued, for at last, under the eighteenth abbot, William of Scarborough (1372–96), things came to a crisis. "In his time," says the Chronicle, "all the conversi withdrew from the monastery,"[6] and the number of monks was increased to make up for it. Sir E. A. Bond suggests that the meaning of these words possibly may be that the lay brethren who lived within the house—the "conversi claustrales"—ceased to exist as a class, but that they still remained on the farms; he supports his suggestion by quoting from a Rental of 1396 a passage in which the "conversi claustrales" and the "grangarii," are mentioned in such close connection that it is possible to ascribe to the latter word the meaning of "conversi of the granges." But, as he goes on to point out,

[1] *Annales Monastici* (R.S.), II, p. 244.
[2] Sir E. A. Bond, *op. cit.* III, p. 77.
[3] *Ibid.* II, p. 65.   [4] *Ibid.* I, p. 432.
[5] *Ibid.* II, p. 4.
[6] *Ibid.* I, p. 430; III, p. xliii.

in the manuscript documents collected at the close of the four-teenth century by Abbot Thomas Burton, the writer of the Chronicle, there is nowhere any mention of lay brethren. The probability is that in this house at least, this subordinate class of the religious was allowed to drop out of existence before the beginning of the fifteenth century. The relative numbers of another Cistercian house—Whalley Abbey—as given in the record of a visitation by the Abbot of Rievaulx in 1367[1], show a similar absence of lay brethren, although the lack of earlier figures prevents us from tracing the decline. Here there were 29 monks and only one conversus. There is a singular lack of information upon this point, as upon all others connected with the monastic population: but everything points to the conclusion that the English houses were affected to the full by the decline in the importance of the lay brethren which unquestionably showed itself in the Cistercian Order as a whole.

The truth seems to be that in the attempt to introduce the lower classes into the ranks of those leading the ascetic life, much the same difficulty was found as was experienced by the Mendicant Orders. The conversi seem to have been turbulent and unruly, a difficult class to deal with, and, when placed in control of the monastic property—a practice very generally adopted in the granges or manors in demesne—liable to fall into the sin of owning private property, or becoming "proprietaries," as it was technically called. Such was found to be the case at Evesham during the abbacy of John de Brokhampton (1283–1316),

As his predecessors had placed over the manors of the vale certain brethren called conversi, who had nearly demolished every-thing, this abbot, to the great advantage of the house, lest they should become proprietaries any further, had them all recalled, to perform their vows in the monastery by fasting and prayer[2].

While the Benedictines of Evesham and the Cistercians of Meaux found their lay brethren hard to keep in hand, much about the same time the Augustinian canons of the Priory of

[1] T. D. Whitaker, *History of Whalley*, I, p. 98.
[2] *Chronicon Abbatiæ de Evesham* (R.S.), p. 285. The revolt of the Gilbertine conversi against the severity of their life, during the lifetime of St Gilbert, is well known. Miss Rose Graham, *St Gilbert of Sempringham and the Gilbertines*, pp. 19–23. Within a century of its founder's death the Order of Gramont was nearly wrecked by rebellion among the conversi. Hélyot, *Ordres Monastiques*, VI, p. 197.

St Oswald, Gloucester, were on bad terms with theirs. In 1250 Walter Gray, Archbishop of York, as the result of a visitation, besides laying down regulations as to the dress of the conversi, found it necessary to impose a rule that the canons were to have control over the conversi both within and without the monastery, and that no conversus was to have any authority over the canons[1]. The Continental houses were not exempt from similar troubles. Thus the Annals of Waverley note two great crimes committed in foreign Cistercian houses, in each case by a lay brother. In 1197, Reginald, Abbot of Garendon, was stabbed by a conversus in the infirmary of his monastery, and in consequence the General Chapter of the Order decreed that all the conversi of that place should be dispersed. In 1226 a lay brother of the Belgian house of Bodeloa murdered his abbot, and again all the conversi were ejected, thenceforth not to be recalled. The additions to the Cistercian Statutes of 1256 reflect the insubordination of the lay brethren. It had been determined that such men were to be received as conversi as were able to answer for the labour of one hired workman. The General Chapter of 1261 ordered that any conversus who would not perform the labour enjoined upon him was to be reduced to the position of a hired servant at the will of the visitor, and meantime was to be fed on coarse bread[2].

But, as Sir E. A. Bond points out[3], just as the origin of the order of conversi among the Cistercians is to be connected with the revival in that Order of manual, and especially agricultural, labour as a most important element in the monastic ideal and Rule, so its decline must be considered as due to the gradual falling away of the Cistercians from their original insistence upon that importance. The agricultural employments of the Order in its early days brought a large amount of land under actual cultivation by the inmates of the monasteries, while the isolation of the houses in waste places made it necessary for each monastery to be equipped with the crafts required for the repair of buildings or implements. There was room, therefore, for a large class of men willing to take the bulk of this manual labour upon themselves, bearing the main part of the burden of pro-

---

[1] *Register of Archbishop Giffard* (S.S.), p. 205.
[2] J. T. Fowler, *Cistercian Statutes*, p. 122. "Ad familiaris habitum."
[3] *Chronica Monasterii de Melsa*, III, p. xliv.

viding the maintenance of the house, while those qualified by education undertook those other parts of the monastic life which centred round the church of the monastery. Then, as the wealth of the monasteries increased and the reverence shown to the monks raised even the conversi in their own eyes, they were set in positions of authority on the manors and granges, and fewer were required in consequence. When, finally, there came the great changes of the fourteenth century in methods of estate management, and the demesne land was for the most part farmed out, a change largely due to the Black Death and the enormous rise which it caused in the price of agricultural and still more of artisan labour, the conversi ceased altogether to be a necessary class. The lands of the monasteries were now leased out, and but little remained under the actual control of the monks; in this direction little need was then felt of the services of lay brethren, and "for the offices of the house itself, it was found more convenient to employ hired servants than to support a class of half-monks who had not been found very amenable to discipline."

We are thus led on to consider the third class of the inmates of the monastic precincts—the seculars; for of these the servants formed the chief part. The growth of this class illustrates on another side that change in the spirit of the monastic devotees which we have just been considering, and which must have led to a corresponding change in the influence which they exerted upon the world around. The advantage which society drew from the part played by labour in the Benedictine Rule and its later revisions is one of those facts which have been fully recognised.

They were the monks (it has been said of the early Benedictines[1]) who taught, not so much by precept as by example, that lesson of such surpassing worth, namely that in the labour of the hands there is dignity and not degradation. Incalculable was the gain when the Benedictines gave a religious consecration to the cultivation of the earth by the linking of this with prayer and the reading of Scripture, thus effectually and for ever redeeming this labour from the dishonour which slavery had impressed in the old world on an occupation which was there regarded as the proper business of slaves, and relegated to them.

[1] R. C. Trench, *Medieval Church History*, p. 104.

This, of course, is true of every kind of manual labour besides that of agriculture; every association with the ordinary toil of man on the part of that life which had become recognised as the highest possible, was so much to the good; and every revival of this connection in the monastic Rule down to the time of Saint Bernard helped to raise the dignity of labour. But equally we must look on the other side of the shield, and recognise that the connection did not last long, and that every abandonment of labour as a part of their daily life by the religious, meant a diminution of respect for manual toil, the more marked in that their teaching was from the first one of example rather than of precept. In the eyes of the first generation of Cistercian monks labour in the harvest-fields was one of the most meritorious parts of the religious life. The respect felt for this work was expressed in such legends as that which relates how a monk of Clairvaux harvesting with his fellow-monks, saw among them the Virgin with Saint Elizabeth and Saint Mary Magdalene, "visiting her reapers."[1] But even here the decline was rapid. The passage already cited from the Chronicle of Meaux as regards the arrogance of the conversi is significant of the change. Only 80 years after the foundation of the house in all the first flush of enthusiasm—an enthusiasm which led the first abbot to add to the numbers of his monastery until he was forced to clothe the novices with his own tunics and go clad in a frock alone—it was found necessary to check the presumption of the conversi by setting them to menial tasks— "officiis servientium"; and the menial tasks used as a means of correction were everyday employments, ploughing or glazier's work or joinery. In the first quarter of the thirteenth century, then, the Cistercians of Meaux already looked upon the labours which they were originally called on to perform in person, as menial even for this subordinate class of their house. It was through this significant alteration in the tone of monastic life that there arose the great monastic households: the monks ceased from their labours and called in great numbers of servants, kept in employment, not to take part in the outside work of agriculture on the farms, but for actual service in the house. The abbot or prior, where a separate establishment was assigned

[1] Migne, *Patrologia Latina*, vol. 185, col. 1062.

to him, had servants of his own, often in large numbers; others were attached to the monastery in various capacities, and lists of these, sometimes with the payments made to them attached, have come down to us. To speak generally, the servants of these large houses fall under five heads. There is first a class of artisans —smiths, carpenters, tilers, tailors, shoemakers, and so on. Next follow those engaged in the mill, bakehouse, and brewery: in the third class we may include those engaged in work within the convent grounds—gardeners, pig-keepers, keepers of the poultry, and men busied in other such tasks. Then come those engaged in the stables, with whom we may reckon the messengers who, among the wealthy, were the mediaeval substitutes for the General Post. In the last class we may place the servants within the house, who were usually assigned to the various offices of the monastery—the gate, the refectory, the kitchens, the cellarer's department, the laundry, the infirmary and the church. In every department then, the large monasteries paid menials to do the work originally done by the monks.

One or two examples will show how large was the class thus supported out of the monastic revenues. We may begin with a Benedictine house—that of Evesham—at an early date, when the proportion of servants to monks was comparatively small[1]. At some date between 1088 and 1096, the house employed five servants in the church, two in the cellar, five in the kitchen, seven in the bakehouse, four in the brewery, four tailors, two shoemakers, four servants in the bathhouse, two at the great gate, five in the vineyard, four as attendants for the monks when they left the house, four in the abbot's chamber, three in the refectory and two watchmen: a total of 65. The community consisted at this time of 67 monks (of whom however 12 resided in Denmark), five nuns, three clerks, and three poor men "ad mandatum" or maintained out of charity in the house. At this date, therefore, and in this house, the number of servants was not quite equal to the number whom they served: or, if we exclude the artisans and gardeners, there were 52 domestic servants to 66 people actually resident in the house. With this house we may profitably compare a Cistercian house three

[1] *Chronicon Abbatiæ de Evesham* (R.S.), p. xliv.

centuries later. At Meaux in 1393[1], the abbot's establishment in the monastery and that of the monks, combined, employed the following servants: the abbot's squire, his chamberlain, page of the chamber, cook, two pages of the kitchen, his gardener, groom of the stable and stable boy; the cellarer's servant, his page, the servant of the master of the cattle, the bursar's servant, another servant (the marshal of Beningholm) under the bursar, the forester, the wright (or carpenter), the slater and his page, the convent cook, purveyor of food and page of the kitchen, the convent gardener, the baker and his two servants with a page of the bakehouse, and so on down a list of 57 persons ending with the convent laundress. Of these 57, Sir E. A. Bond points out, even excluding "all who appear in the capacity of farmers and mechanics, such as the tiler, the tailor, and the slater, there remain as many as 40 domestic servants; an inordinately numerous household, it would seem, for a family of 26 monks, even after ample allowance for hospitalities."

In the case of other houses for which the numbers of the monks and their servants can be obtained, it is not possible to distinguish in the latter class those engaged in farm-work or as artisans from the domestics, and the comparison is to that extent less valuable. None the less, it is clear that the households were large. At Peterborough, in 1125, there were 67 servants to 60 monks, a slightly higher proportion than at Evesham some 40 years earlier[2]. A compotus of the Augustinian priory of Bolton[3] shows that, in 1298-9, payments were made to 23 servants, "within the close," some being mentioned by their duties, as the smith and the carpenter, but others by name only. There were in the house at the time at least 15 canons. In 1300 there were 24 servants within the close, while in 1304 there are said to have been 53—a rise which on the face of it seems improbable. At Bury St Edmund's, at some date in the reign of Edward I[4], there were apparently 111 servants resident in the abbey, together with 80 monks and 11 chaplains. Croyland Abbey in 1329 was maintaining a less extensive household[5]; there were

---

[1] *Chronica Monasterii de Melsa*, III, p. lxviii.
[2] Dugdale, *Monasticon*, I, p. 351.
[3] T. D. Whitaker, *History of Craven*, p. 453.
[4] Dugdale, *Monasticon*, III, p. 161.
[5] *Ibid.* II, p. 121.

41 monks and 15 others resident in the house, while the servants, including seven artisans, numbered only 37. The Abbey of Eynsham, Oxfordshire, which at the end of 1403 or 1404 consisted of 22 or 23 monks, had a household of 26 servants[1]. At Gloucester, in 1380, there were 50 monks and 200 officials and servants[2].

Other statements of the number of servants maintained are less valuable, as it is impossible to obtain a contemporary statement of the number of monks in the house. Enough has been said however to show that in monasteries of some size and wealth at least, households were maintained which left very little scope for manual work by the monks; a conclusion which may be supported by various incidental references from other sources. Thomas Walsingham, making a list of the monks of St Albans in 1380[3], and noting down against the name of each anything which strikes him as interesting, records of one John de Bokedene that he, together with a lay brother, did much work in stone cutting in the New Gate, the King's chamber, and the Chapel of St James' at Redburn, "et ipse latomus sudavit"—and personally sweated as a stone-cutter. The inference is clear: manual labour on the part of the monks is unusual. One of the account-rolls of Abingdon Abbey for 1383 records a payment made to Brother Nicholas Drayton "pro solicitudine facta circa scripturam que est in fenestris claustri."[4] Whatever may have been the exact part he played in this glazing work, Brother Nicholas was doing a work of supererogation, and something unusual.

This same list of Walsingham's explains no doubt in part this cessation from manual labour. Of the 54 monks whom he mentions, 24 were then holding definite offices in the monastery with more or less onerous duties attached to them, while four are recorded to have written or compiled books. So, in St Benet's at Holme, in 1494, 17 monks out of 24 held office of some kind[5]. The management of the business affairs of the monastery doubtless claimed the attention of many, while others, notably among the Benedictines, turned to intellectual work of many kinds.

[1] H. E. Salter, *Eynsham Cartulary*, II, pp. lxxxi, xciii.
[2] Dugdale, *Monasticon*, I, p. 535.
[3] *Ibid.* II, p. 209.
[4] Kirk, *Account Rolls of Abingdon*, Treasurers' account of 1383–4.
[5] A. Jessopp, *Visitations of the Diocese of Norwich*, p. 63.

None the less, the fact must be remembered that the monastic ideal was abandoned in this respect, even by the Cistercians. Further, it is sufficiently clear that the households maintained in consequence of this change were often extravagantly large. The abbots, as great dignitaries of the Church and of the kingdom, were especially liable to the charge of maintaining over-large numbers of servants; and all through the centuries under consideration, the evil gave rise to attempts to check it, the persistent repetition of which is of itself a sufficient indication of failure. In the constitutions of the Benedictine General Chapter of the province of Canterbury, held at Northampton in 1225[1], it is laid down that whereas some prelates are said to be conspicuous, for certain superfluities and for burdening their monasteries, none is to have servants exceeding what is seemly in number or equipment, "unde ordo monachalis in aliquo posset argui levitatis": and in order to protect the monasteries against claims of the abbot's servants on his death it is ordered that the servants are to receive from their master fixed annual wages.

The warning brings to mind the scene when Abbot Hugh lay on his death-bed at Bury St Edmund's[2];

Ere he was dead, all things were thrown into disorder by his servants, so that in the Abbot's houses there was nothing at all left, except stools and tables which could not be carried away....There was not even some thing of a penny's value, which might be given to the poor for the good of his soul.

However the tenant of Palegrave in the end found 50s. for this purpose. "But those fifty shillings were afterwards again paid to the King's officers, who exacted the full rent for the use of the King."

In 1238, again, when the abbots of the Benedictine houses were summoned to London by the papal legate Otho[3], who laid before them, and got accepted, proposals for a reform of their statutes based upon the Decretals of Gregory IX, one of the articles ran, "numerum vero equorum et familiae praelati studeant in quantum poterunt moderare." The Cluniac Rule as

---

[1] Dugdale, *Monasticon*, I, p. xlvi.
[2] *Chronica Jocelini de Brakelonda* (C.S.), p. 6. I quote from the translation by L. C. Jane.
[3] Matthew Paris, *Chronica Majora* (R.S.), III, p. 499 *et seq.*

revised by Gregory IX[1] shows an effort to restrict the number of attendants on those in authority; the Abbot of Cluny is to content himself with a train of sixteen horses, the other abbots of the order and the Prior of La Charité with eight; the Prior of St Martin is to have six, other conventual priors three or four, and the other minor priors are restricted to two. Moreover, the servants are not to be boys or of noble birth, and are not to be richly dressed. Once again the General Chapter of the Benedictines (meeting at Bermondsey in 1249)[2] repeats that abbots and priors are not to have servants exceeding either in number or equipment what is seemly. Innocent IV in 1253, confirming the statutes of Gregory IX for the Benedictines, fixes the number of horses which an abbot may have in his train at ten[3]. The Benedictine Chapter of Westminster (1422) once more reproves the abbots for their sumptuous and scandalous trains of attendants, both as regards the equipment of their servants and the trappings of their horses, and ordains that the greatest of them is not to have over 20 horses including baggage animals, and those with ungilded bridles[4]. Twenty-two years later, the Provincial Chapter of Northampton repeats the order that abbots and other prelates are not to have with them when they ride, over 20 persons belonging to their own households, except in such cases as the papal Statutes allow, and are to be moderate in their equipment[5]. A tendency also shows itself towards the maintenance of private servants, instead of keeping them in common. Thus Launceston Priory in 1341–2[6] and Bodmin Priory in 1343 were warned to dismiss the private servants of their canons[7]. There are also indications that extravagance in the way of servants was not confined to the monasteries, but touched the nunneries also: the Council of Oxford held in 1222 by Stephen Langton specially warns the nuns to receive into their houses only such servants as are necessary[8]. The analogy of Continental evidence, as represented by the Register of Odo

[1] Leo Marsicanus, *Chronicon Casinense* (1603), p. 836.
[2] Matthew Paris, *op. cit.* Additamenta, p. 175.
[3] *Ibid.* p. 235 *et seq.*   [4] Wilkins, *Concilia*, III, p. 413.
[5] Reynerus, Appendix, p. 113 *et seq.* (cap. ii).
[6] F. C. Hingeston-Randolph, *Register of John de Grandisson*, II, p. 955.
[7] *Ibid.* III, p. 980. Thirteen are named, and there were others.
[8] Wilkins, *Concilia*, I, p. 592.

Rigaldi, Archbishop of Rouen, which covers the period from 1248 to 1269, suggests that this particular breach of the Rule was most frequent among the richer nunneries.

From such evidence as this, it seems certain that the companies of servants maintained by the large monasteries were not far in number from the monks themselves, or even larger, while the endeavours of Popes and Chapters to set limits to the monastic households indicate that extravagance in this direction was a real evil from the thirteenth century onwards. Many of these posts, in fact, as is well known, were valuable means of getting a livelihood, and actually became hereditary possessions handed down from father to son[1]. In other cases, they were sold by the monasteries. Thus, in the chartulary of Eynsham Abbey is a document of January, 1280, recording the appointment of the porter in charge of the abbey gate, John de Iveton. He was appointed for life; every day when the abbot was there, he was to eat with the abbot's servants in his presence. When the abbot was away or when John was not well, he was to receive every day from the cellarer a monk's loaf and a gallon and a half of the "conventual" beer, and also a dish or mess (*ferculum*) from the kitchen; the cellarer was to provide a livery robe like that of the abbot's servants. He was to have forage for one horse like the other servants of the abbot. He was to go as often as required on the business of the abbot and the monks, at their expense, and to pay for any failure in his duties by deductions from his livery duly assessed by "good and lawful men." In the end it appears that for this "donatio" the new porter gave the house 30 marks as a gressum or fine on entry. This sum—£20—may be taken as representing in purchasing power at least £360 of our pre-war money—a sufficiently large sum to be paid by one of the convent's servants[2].

But the servants, however numerous, do not exhaust the list of those who might be found living within the monastery, but not subject to the monastic vows. Other laymen were also maintained out of the monastic revenues; but upon this element of the monastic population information is even scantier than in the

[1] So at Malmesbury the porter's and the cook's position were hereditary. (*Reg. Malmesbur.* (R.S.), II, pp. 318, 337.)

[2] H. E. Salter, *Eynsham Cartulary*, I, p. 300. The preceding porter at some date between 1264 and 1268 paid the same sum (p. 248); and two other servants paid 20 marks each for their places (pp. 268, 305).

case of the servants, and it is difficult to give any satisfactory estimate of its importance. The corrodiers, it is clear, were sometimes numerous. To the exact nature of the corrody, and the uses to which it was put, it will be necessary to return later: it will be sufficient here to say that the corrody was an annual pension given by the monastery for various reasons, paid for the most part in kind, and usually involving the residence of the corrodier as a member of the household. Such a class naturally varied considerably in number, and the same thing may be said of the members of the schools maintained in some of the monasteries and nunneries, the paying guests sometimes found in the nunneries, or the children of noble families attached to the household of the abbot to receive their training there. The illustration or two already given will show the difficulty which the presence of all these classes of lay inmates produces in forming a clear idea of the actual population of a religious house where, as so often happens, the number of the professed only is given. The corrodiers at Evesham between 1088 and 1096 were apparently only three as compared with 72 religious: on the other hand, at Croyland in 1329 there were 15 corrodiers and only 41 monks. As what is probably an extreme instance, we may mention the case of the nunnery of St Mary, Winchester, where the visitors in 1537 found only 26 nuns with the abbess, but the total number of residents maintained by the house was 102, namely, 26 religious, five priests, 13 lay sisters, nine women servants, 20 officers of household and waiting servants, three corrodiers, and 23 children of lords, knights and gentlemen being brought up[1]. Professor Savine has calculated from the Valor Ecclesiasticus that the general proportion of monks to lay inmates in the sixteenth century was one to three. It is difficult to make a definite statement as to earlier times: but the estimate given at the head of this chapter, that the religious themselves formed only from a half to a third of the numbers actually living in the monastery, seems to be well within the mark.

On turning to the religious themselves, we are met by a question difficult of solution. That by the time of the Dissolution the number of professed religious was much lower than it had been is an unquestioned fact: the problem is to account for the decline. The solution usually offered by monastic apologists, stated

---

[1] Dugdale, *Monasticon*, II, p. 456.

briefly, is that it was due to the Black Death, whether by reason of the reduction of the "number of vocations in the diminished population," to quote the words of Cardinal Gasquet, or by reason of the general decline in the purchasing power of money, which affected especially those who, like the monks, found that they required to employ labour to any great extent when its price had undergone a great rise. In so far as the decline really occurred after the Black Death, both reasons are valid: but if the decline can be shown to have been in progress before the plague year, other causes must be sought for. It must be admitted that here the authorities at our command are somewhat disappointing: the information given is full enough to suggest grave doubts as to the completeness of the solution offered, yet not enough to put the matter beyond all dispute. It was not to be expected that it would be possible to determine the total number of the religious and to compare it with the total population of England at any date other than that of the Dissolution, when, according to Cardinal Gasquet's calculations, the number of monks, nuns, and friars expelled, was about eight thousand, the population at the time being between two and three millions. But it should be possible to get sufficient information about individual houses to give a rough estimate of the total decline in numbers, and the proportion of that decline which took place after the Black Death: and it is here that the figures available are scanty and tantalising. In order to give a satisfactory answer to these questions, three sets of figures at least are necessary; one showing the number of monks in a large number of houses at some date well before the first half of the fourteenth century; a second at some date within the first half of the fourteenth century, before the Black Death; and a third for the period of the Dissolution. All too often the only statement of the numbers in any given house is that of the sixteenth century: rarely does it happen that two of the required set are attainable, and very rarely that all three can be found. The result is that the data leave some doubt as to whether they are sufficiently wide to make negligible the peculiar conditions of individual houses, and to neutralise the merely temporary oscillations which are to be noticed in various cases.

The following table, however, compiled on the lines indicated above, deserves careful consideration. Column A contains the number of inmates in the houses named, at some date between 1100 and 1300, the higher figure being taken if, as sometimes happens, there is more than one statement of the number of the monks between the limits named. Column B comprises the figures for the same houses at any date between 1300 and the outbreak of the Black Death in 1349; and Column C the number of inmates at some date sufficiently near the Dissolution, which date is taken wherever possible. The table represents professed monks or novices only, lay brethren not being included[1].

	A	B	C
Bath	40 (1206)	30 (1344)	21 (1539)
Bermondsey	32 (1262)	13? (1331)	13 (1536)
Bolton	—	15 (1311)	15 (15—)
Boxgrove	19 (1230)	—	9 (1536)
Bromholme	16 (1275)	—	11 (1446)
Bury St Edmund's	80 (c. 1300)	—	44 (1539)
Canterbury, Christ Church	140 (c. 1190)	77 (1207)	53 (15—)
Carrow (nuns)	21 (1287)	—	13 (1532)
Coventry	26 (1292)	—	13 (1538)
Croyland	—	41 (1329)	31 (1534)
Evesham	58 (1096)	—	38 (1418)
Gloucester	100? (1104)	37 (1348)	34 (1534)
Great Malvern	26 (c. 1300)	—	12 (1539)
Lewes	50 (1279)	—	24 (1538)
Meaux	60 (1249)	43 (1349)	25 (1538)
Milton Abbas	40 (933)	—	13 (1539)
Montacute	28 (1279)	13? (1331)	14 (1536)
Norwich	60 (1101)	—	47 (1449)
Pershore	17 at least (1288)	—	15 (1539)
Peterborough	80 (1219)	—	39 (15—)
Romsey (nuns)	—	90 (1333)	25 (1539)
St Albans	75 (c. 1200)	—	39 (15—)
St Neot's	60 (1078)	12 (before 1339)	12 (1534)
Tewkesbury	57 (1105)	—	36 (1539)
Upholland	—	13 (1319)	5 (1536)
Westminster	—	49 (1303)	25 (1540)
Winchester, St Swithun's	—	64 (1325)	40 (1500)
Wymondham	36 (1260)	—	11 (1539)

This list shows that the decline in the number of the religious during the three centuries preceding the Reformation had indeed been considerable: the 22 houses which appear in both A and C

[1] The table has been compiled from various sources, mainly Dugdale. The figures marked [?] in column B are from the petition of the Cluniacs cited on p. 22, and rhetorical exaggeration may be suspected. The editors of Dugdale apparently have doubts as to the correctness of the figure for Gloucester in A. I am indebted to Mr G. G. Coulton for some of the references.

show a decline in their aggregate numbers from 1121 to 536, or a little over 52 per cent. But it will be observed that the diminution represented by the difference between B and C, which covers the period during which the Black Death's effects should be seen, by no means covers the whole of this decline. The aggregate number in the 13 houses which occur in both these columns declines only from 497 to 313—a decline of a little over 38 per cent.: while the seven houses represented in A and B show a decline from 460 to 225, or over 51 per cent. The difference between the two figures thus obtained for the decline previous to the Black Death is extreme, and shows the difficulty of making any generalisation as to proportions[1]. None the less, the table suggests that the number of monks had begun to diminish well before the Black Death. Confirmation of this view may be found from other sources. Thus, one of the constitutions of the legate Ottobon[2], promulgated in the Council of London of 1268, ordains that the ancient number of monks is to be maintained, and Benedict XII in his reformation of the Augustinian Statutes gives a similar order[3]. In the alien priories, or priories directly subject to religious houses abroad, the tendency had undoubtedly shown itself before the close of the thirteenth century; for in 1331 certain of the English Cluniacs presented a petition to Edward III, then in Parliament at Winchester, in which they asserted that in some Cluniac houses, notably Montacute and Bermondsey, where there ought to be 30 or 40 monks there were not a third of the number[4]. These alien priories, however, were in the difficult position of being subject to exactions by their mother-houses abroad, and of finding their revenues confiscated by the crown in consequence, when war was in progress with France. The Register of Odo Rigaldi, however, shows distinct traces of a decline in the number of monks in Normandy before 1268; thus there are 18 cells mentioned as having no residents at all, and frequent complaints are made that the statutory number is not maintained.

---

[1] In the four houses where the figures in all three columns are beyond suspicion, over 73 per cent. of the decline occurred before the Black Death. At Christ Church, Canterbury, with its elaborate drainage system and water supply, only four monks died of the plague (J. B. Sheppard, *Literae Cantuarienses*, R.S. vol. II).

[2] Wilkins, *Concilia*, II, p. I.   [3] *Ibid.* p. 629.

[4] Dugdale, *Monasticon*, v, p. viii.

CHAPTER II

THE MONASTIC ORGANISATION

THE elaborate structure of the monastic household, the careful ordering of its everyday life, the division and subdivision of responsibilities and duties, form perhaps the most striking of all the remarkable features of mediaeval monasticism. What Dean Kitchin says of Winchester applies in greater or less degree to all the larger monasteries. The monastery, he says,

was a well-ordered peaceful community, which on the one side kept up a perpetual protest against the rude vices of the age, and on the other showed to the King's nobles and prelates who thronged our city, the pattern of an organisation for the conduct of life and business which could hardly have been found elsewhere in mediaeval times.

Undoubtedly there was a time when this was true, and the causes of this pre-eminence may be sufficiently clearly discerned. The life of the mediaeval monastery, however individual the object aimed at, was for the most part social, so far at least as the monastery was concerned: the individual end was sought in company and the pursuit of it lay along one common path. Life within the monastery, speaking generally, was absolutely public: the Carthusians alone of the great Orders in the Middle Ages introduced into their system the eremitic principle by combining a life of seclusion in a private cell with one of participation in common devotions; and of these houses there were never more than nine in England. The necessity for permanent organisation inevitably felt among those who recognise themselves as members of an undying corporation, the need of preventing the complete absorption of any member of the brotherhood in worldly business, and the complexity of duties which the increasing wealth of the religious houses laid upon those in whose care the material well-being of the community was placed, must all have tended towards the development of a complicated yet orderly domestic system, running along definite lines, bound in every direction by rule and custom. The peaceful life which, on the whole, the religious houses sought and were allowed to enjoy offered an opportunity for regular and lasting organisation such as was open to few other groups of men during the Middle Ages. With this organisation, having touched briefly on the character and development of the population which it was intended to serve, we are next concerned. In every case the general features are much the same, although variations naturally occur. The system, however, is known mainly as regards large and important houses; it must have been much simpler in the smaller and less wealthy monasteries which abounded.

The plan on which the monastic household was arranged and its business distributed, will best be realised by a consideration of one of the simpler documents dealing with the question—one in which multiplicity of detail may be conveniently ignored with the object of making the main features more salient, and leaving variations and difficulties to be considered later. Perhaps the best example to take is a document of the Benedictine Abbey of Bury St Edmund's[1]: this is a mutual agreement entered into by Abbot John de Northwood and his monks, and approved by Edward I in the ninth year of his reign. Its contents, abridged, are as follows:

The Abbot and convent of St Edmund, for themselves and their successors for ever, enter into the following agreement. Of the possessions pertaining to the monastery of St Edmund, there are assigned to the Lord Abbot certain portions and manors, "cum omnibus suis exitibus, consuetudinibus, fortunis, et perquisitis ad ipsa regaliter spectantibus," and also the payments called hidage and foddercorn, together with the suit of freemen at the hundred-court, and in pleas of the great court of St Edmund, of those, to wit, who by ancient right are bound thereto by reason of their tenements; and their homages and reliefs, together with the homages, reliefs, wardships, marriages and escheats of military fees, advowsons of and presentations to churches, and collations to sergeanties "infra curiam St Edmundi." All else pertaining to the portion, barony and dignity of the said Lord Abbot is to remain his, free from any claim on the part of the convent. So also certain manors, "cum omnibus suis exitibus, proventibus et emolumentis," and so forth, are assigned as freely and entirely to the convent as are the Abbot's to him. Then follow the details of this latter assignment.

---

[1] Dugdale, *Monasticon*, III, p. 156.

To the use of the cellarer's office are assigned "for the food of the convent, the reception of guests, certain annual pittances" (i.e. additional dishes for the monks' table provided at certain appointed seasons) "liveries of servants and other business of the convent," in the county of Suffolk the cellarer's grange at St Edmund's, with the lands, rents, woods, meadows, pastures, mills, waters, fortuitous revenues and all else appertaining thereto. "In the vill of Rosseby, two carucates of land with all appurtenances...also the manor of Magna Berton near St Edmund's, with its lands, the church granted to the convent 'in proprios usus' and all its appurtenances....Moreover in the county of Suffolk 4s. annual rent in the vill of Westle....From the church of St Peter in Parva Hornegewelle 13s. 4d." And so on.

To the use of the sacristy, for lighting the church, and the provision of the sacramental wine and bread in the church itself and through the liberty of St Edmund; and for the livery of wax every week to the abbot and others according to custom; and for the repairs of the church and other buildings, especially some standing within the close and belonging to the abbot; and for the construction of all other houses for the future; and for the liveries of the servants of the church; and the repair of the church ornaments; and for pittances and presents and other burdens according to the customs of the church; there is appointed "the town of St Edmund's with its lands, meadows, fairs, markets, rents, 'fortunae,' reliefs, escheats, etc., together with the mint and its profits." Also, in the county of Norfolk, Therlham in Aylesham, "which was granted by King Richard of happy memory for the provision of four candles burning day and night about St Edmund": and so on down a second list of sources of revenue.

To the use of the chamberlain's office, for the clothing and shoeing of the brethren, is given the manor of Brock with the appropriated church and other appurtenances: two mills at Hemenhall, one a windmill, the other a watermill: a pension of 6 marks from the church of Rutham, etc.

For the uses of the almonry, that which is appointed for the maintenance of the poor and needy; in Bury St Edmund's, the almoner's grange with its tithes, lands and rents; from Redgrave (in Suffolk) 2s. annual rent and the third sheaf of the tithes from the abbot's ancient demesne; and so on.

To the uses of the pittancer's office, for divers pittances throughout the year, other sources of income are assigned. For the infirmary, to be applied to the needs of the sick brethren, rents are appointed to the extent of £11. 13s. 2d. and an annual pension of 9 marks from the church of Woolpit. To the guest chamber is appropriated £4. 13s. 3½d. from the town of Bury St Edmund's and elsewhere, and an annual pension of 2 marks also from the church of Woolpit; this for necessary utensils of the guest chamber and the provision of fuel, napkins, towels and cloths for the use of the guests. To the precentor are granted two watermills in Westowe for the provision of the monastery's parchment and ink; and to his care are assigned four hospitals outside the gates of the town, with their endowments. Lastly to the refectory is granted, for the repair of cups and the necessary utensils, 14s. to be received from the town of Bury St Edmund's.

Then follow certain other arrangements. When a newly elected abbot has to go to Rome for the confirmation of his election and to receive the papal benediction, his own expenses and those of his attendants are to be borne by the monastery. The abbot is to defend the manors assigned to the monastery in courts both civil and ecclesiastical: if the abbot thus pleads or is impleaded in an ecclesiastical court and a condemnation is made, the monastery is to bear the loss, the abbot being responsible for the expenses "pendente lite": but if the suit is in a secular court, the whole expense is to be borne by the abbot. But if anything is done on the manors of the monastery whereby the abbot is placed "in misericordia domini regis," the house is to pay the fine. Then the question of receiving guests is settled: when the abbot is staying in Bury St Edmund's with his household, all guests whether on horse or foot are to be entertained by him, except the religious and their servants, whom the monastery is to receive. When the abbot is away, all seculars on foot or with thirteen horses or fewer are to be received by the monastery: those with over thirteen horses are still to be entertained at the abbot's expense, unless specially invited by the prior. Finally there comes the royal assent to these arrangements, saving to the crown the custody of the barony and all the lands of the abbot and his succcessors during the periods when the abbacy is vacant.

This agreement marks out sufficiently plainly the main lines on which the business side of things was worked in a great abbey; and something must be said of each of the great facts so disclosed. First, then, for the distinction between the lands and possessions of the abbot and those of the house over which he presided. This division was very common but not universal. It had two advantages from the monastery's point of view. To begin with, the abbot as one of the magnates of the land was liable to find himself called upon to bear heavy expenses of one sort or another; and an arrangement of this sort settled definitely what income he might usually expect, and what must be left untouched for his convent. It set some barrier in the way of an abbot inclined to personal extravagance and prevented undue claims for the support of his household. The second advantage appears from an earlier charter of Bury St Edmund's, granted by Henry I, when Abbot Robert (1107–1112) for the first time made this division of the abbot's endowments from those of the monastery[1]. The King warns the Bishop of Norwich, the sheriffs, all barons and liegemen, and all his ministers of Norfolk, Suffolk and elsewhere where St Edmund has lands, of his approval of this new arrangement.

And the King's ministers, at the time when the abbacy is vacant, shall take to themselves no power in the manors of the aforesaid convent, save for those dignities and liberties which belong to the crown, which St Edmund has and ought to have...of all which I found St Edmund seised on the day when my brother William was alive and dead.

The Chronicle of Jocelin of Brakelond explains the exact effect of this. The cellarers of the house had been mismanaging their business, and Abbot Samson stepped in and associated a clerk of his own with the cellarer. The indignation of the monks is vividly described. By one warning, Jocelin, despite his hero-worship, was clearly impressed.

There is one thing that will prove dangerous after the death of Abbot Samson, such as has never come to pass in our days or our lives. Of a surety, the King's bailiffs will come and will possess them-

[1] Dugdale, *Monasticon*, III, p. 153.

selves of the abbey, I mean the barony, as was done in the past after
the deaths of other abbots. As after the death of Abbot Hugh, the
King's bailiffs likewise desired to appoint new bailiffs in the town
of St Edmund alleging as their warrant that Abbot Hugh had done
this, in the same way the King's bailiffs will in course of time appoint
their clerk to keep the cellary, in order that everything shall be done
by him and under his direction....Thus they will have the power of
intermixing and confusing all the concerns and rents of the abbot
and of the convent[1].

The lands which, on the death of the abbot of this house, the
King had the right to take into his custody and take revenue
from, were those lands assigned to the abbot alone; the house,
although deprived of its head, still enjoyed undisturbed possession of its own income. The advantage thus secured was no mean
one: some difficulty was found however in maintaining it. On
the death of Abbot Hugh, the monks of Bury, despite their
possession of Henry I's charter, took the trouble of sending
Master Samson and Master Robert Ruffus across the sea to the
King, to obtain from him letters directing that the monastery's
possessions should remain in the monks' hands[2]. At Abingdon
in 1189, the monastery was involved in a great law-suit by an
attempt to ignore this right[3]: and at St Albans in 1290, the
chronicler complains, the royal escheator, despite a special writ
obtained from the King, did not observe the distinction but
took over with the abbot's barony revenues which of right
belonged to the monastery[4].

It will be observed that the different treatment accorded to
the lands of the Abbot of Bury St Edmund's and of the monastery of Bury St Edmund's involves on the part of the temporal
courts some legal recognition of the convent as a separate entity,
while at the same time the very document embodying this
recognition shows how incompletely the idea was worked out.
In all law proceedings, it is not the monastery which brings or
defends the action, even where the suit arises in connection with
the property recognised as being the convent's, and not the
abbot's; the abbot has to defend the manors assigned to the

---

[1] J. G. Rokewode, *Chronica Jocelini de Brakelonda*, p. 59.
[2] *Ibid.* p. 6.
[3] *Chronicle of Abingdon* (R.S.), II, p. 297.
[4] *Gesta Abbatum* (R.S.), II, p. 5.

monastery. The question of bearing the expenses of litigation and paying the fines is one for private arrangement between the abbot and his convent. This is typical of the general attitude of the English law.

The ecclesia or abbacy (it has been said) succeeded the saint as the subject of proprietary rights. But, at least in the view of the King's courts, the abbot's power was that of an absolute owner.... Already in Domesday Book we see that it matters little whether one says that the land is held by the church of Ely, the abbey of Ely or the abbot of Ely. True that when lands are given to an abbey it is rare to find no mention of "the convent" or the monks as well as of God, the saint and the abbot. True also that when the abbey lands are alienated, the feoffment is usually said to be made either by the abbot and convent, or by the abbot with the consent of the convent. For all this, the temporal courts are apt to treat the abbot as the one and only natural person who has anything to do with the proprietary rights of the abbey. To the complete exclusion of the convent or the monks, he fully represents the abbey before the law: he sues and is sued alone....In short owing to the legal deadness of the monks, the abbey property seems to be administered by, and represented by (and we may easily pass thence to possessed by and owned by) the series of successive abbots[1].

Given this distinction between the abbot's possessions and those of the monastery the next matter which claims attention is the well-known system whereby the duties of the monastery and the management of its property were divided among certain officials, known as the obedientiaries, and definite portions of the income of the house granted, if not to all, yet to the most important of the offices thus created. The document of Bury St Edmund's which we have taken as our text gives the main officials to be found in most monasteries and some general idea of their duties: the system, however, was one which developed greatly, and the simplicity of the arrangements shown in this document of the thirteenth century may profitably be compared with the complexity shown in the arrangements of other great monasteries at a later date. Dean Kitchin, in his introduction to the Obedientiary Rolls of St Swithun's, Winchester, shows us the system as it existed there.

He groups the obedientiaries according as their duties centre round the Prior, the Church, and the House. St Swithun's, it

[1] Pollock and Maitland, *History of English Law*, I, p. 504.

must be pointed out, was one of the English cathedrals with monastic chapters, and although in these cases the bishop was theoretically looked upon as taking the abbot's place, in point of fact the duties which the abbot would have performed fell to the lot of the prior. We may therefore regard the Prior of St Swithun's as equivalent to the abbot of an ordinary monastic house. Round him there stood the first group of obedientiaries, consisting of the Sub-Prior, the Third Prior and the Fourth Prior, who assisted him in his duties, more especially taking his place in case of illness. The second group—that centring round the Church—consisted of (1) the Sacrist, who with a Sub-Sacrist had charge of all the material equipment of the church, the vessels, vestments, relics and all books except the singing-books, and who, as at Bury St Edmund's, was responsible for the lighting of the church; (2) the precentor, who was in charge of the actual services, and of the singing-books; we may notice that in many cases, as at Bury St Edmund's, the precentor was also responsbile for the ink and parchment of the monastery, and in general for the scriptorium and library; (3) the Anniversarian, who saw to the observance of the obit-days, and the various payments connected with them; and (4) the Custos operum, who had charge of the repairs of the church, and of the conventual buildings as well. Another obedientiary often found, Dean Kitchin points out, is not represented at St Swithun's —the Circa, who was responsible for the preservation of order in the church. Lastly comes the third group—the officers of the House. Here are found (1) the Receiver, of whom Dean Kitchin says that he received all the rents of estates, and other revenues, not assigned to the support of other obedientiaries' offices; his duties will need a rather detailed consideration later: (2) the Hordarian, who received the food which came to the monastery from its own lands, and "had charge of the home or material resources of the convent; providing bread and beer, fish and meat for the Refectory"; (3) the Refectorian, who received the eatables from the hordarian and passed them on to the kitchener and cooks who were under his charge; (4) the Chamberlain, who at St Swithun's seems to have had a varied assortment of business on his hands, but, curiously enough, not that which generally was one of his chief duties, the provision of the monks' clothing and shoes; (5) the Cellarer, who had to care for all things necessary for the brethren in bread and drink and divers kinds of food; (6) the Curtarian, who had charge of the out-buildings of the house, and had to give out bread, beer, and so on for consumption at table, to find the bread for doles, to look after visitors and find their food; (7) the Almoner; (8) the Infirmarian or Keeper of the Infirmary; (9) the Master of the Novices; (10) the Hortulan or Gardener; (11) the Custos Operum (mentioned again to complete the list of those engaged in the house); and lastly (12) the Porters and (13) the Guestmaster.

Such was roughly the system of obedientiaries and their duties at St Swithun's. It is, on the whole, fairly typical. The exceptional position of the prior is of small importance: the prior was head of the house, not only in cathedral churches with monastic chapters, but in priories "without an abbot of their own"; that is to say, in the case of the cells of great monasteries, and such houses as were in a measure subject to some one central abbey, as was the case with the Cluniac houses. Many of the houses of regular canons were also subject to priors only. Where both prior and abbot are found, it may be said that the prior was the abbot's vicegerent, watching over the affairs of the house and responsible for its discipline during the not infrequent intervals of absence of the abbot, either on business or when, like other great lords of the Middle Ages, he moved his household from point to point of his estates, living on the produce now of one manor and now of another. For the rest, apart from the appearance of the Hordarian, most of the Winchester obedientiaries found their parallel in other great houses, as will be seen by a comparison with three other monasteries. The following lists contain the obedientiaries of St Albans (1380)[1], Abingdon[2], and Durham (both as during the fourteenth century)[3]. The first three groups of names follow Dean Kitchin's method of distinction: the fourth covers a set of officials with miscellaneous duties outside the monastery, who

---

[1] Dugdale, *Monasticon*, II, p 209: a list of monks and their offices compiled by Thomas Walsingham.

[2] From G. G. Kirk's edition of the account-rolls, and the treatise "De obedientiariis Abbendoniae" printed as an appendix to the *Chronicle* (R.S.), vol. II.

[3] J. T. Fowler, *Account Rolls of Durham*, and *Rites of Durham*.

were not necessarily monks, but whom it is necessary to include for the sake of completeness.

St Albans.
  I. [Abbot], Prior, Sub-Prior, Third Prior.
  II. Sacristan, Sub-sacristan, Precentor, Succentor, Keeper of St Alban's Shrine, Archidiaconus, 3 Scrutators (or Circae).
  III. Bursar, Cellarer, Sub-cellarer, Chamberlain, Almoner, Kitchener, Refectorer, Sub-refectorer, Infirmarer, Forestarius, Guest-master.
  IV. Prior of Redburne, Warden of St Mary's Chapel.

Abingdon.
  I. [Abbot], Prior, Sub-prior.
  II. Sacristan, Sub-sacristan, Precentor, Succentor.
  III. Treasurers (2), Cellarer, Curtarius, Refectorer, Kitchener, Chamberlain, Sub-chamberlain, Almoner, Infirmarer, Pittancer, Custos Operum, Lignar, Gardener.
  IV. Warden of Chapel of St Edmund, Keeper of Cuddesdon.

Durham.
  I. [Bishop, Prior], Sub-prior, Third Prior.
  II. Sacristan, Sub-sacristan, Feretrar, Vicars.
  III. Bursar, Cellarer, Guest-master, Terrar (probably identical with Guest-master), Almoner, Chamberlain, Infirmarian, Master of the Common House, Master of the Novices, Master of the Garners, Master of the Song-School, Schoolmaster of the children of the Almery.

It is unnecessary to attempt to trace in detail the work of all the officials mentioned in these lists: a glance will show both the presence of local variations, and the underlying uniformity in essentials. The origin of this elaborate system is of unknown date. The Rule of St Benedict speaks only in general terms, except as regards the infirmarian, the guestmaster and the porter. Its development must have been begun before the eleventh century, for the main officials are already to be found in Lanfranc's Constitutions[1], where, in function, though not actually in name, there appear the abbot, the prior, the sub-prior, the circae, the precentor or cantor, the sacristan, the chamberlain, the cellarer, the guest-master and the infirmarer. The development was doubtless affected by local circumstances, and the actual subdivision of the work of the monastery was a matter of

---

[1] Pointed out by Canon Fowler in his edition of the Durham account-rolls.

convenient arrangement rather than of any hard and fast rule; it varied not only in different houses, but at different times in the same house. Thus when Thomas de la Mare (1349–1396) was reorganising the affairs of his abbey of St Albans, he altered the duties of the bursar, releasing him "a sumptibus placitorum et solutionibus feodorum, et officio hundredarii, oneribus aliisque nonnullis...."[1] But although these variations occur, the main needs of the monasteries were all fairly alike, and the main officials and the main lines of their work remained much the same in all the large houses. If to the list of obedientiaries given in Lanfranc's Constitutions we add the almoner, only one other obedientiary of importance makes his appearance, the bursar. Other officials arise simply from a further subdivision of functions. Thus the custody of some great shrine in the church would be withdrawn from the care of the sacristan and handed over to a new obedientiary, the feretrar: or in place of a pittance being due from one obedientiary and one from another, a special official, the pittancer, would be instituted to receive and spend all the pittance money. One result of this subdivision of functions was that a fair proportion of the monks in one of these larger monasteries had some definite work to do in connection with it. Attention has already been called to the case of St Albans where, in 1380, out of 56 monks and novices 24 held some office, one combining the duties of kitchener, refectorer, and infirmarer. An inquisition of 1517 at a smaller Benedictine house, the Abbey of Eynsham[2], where 15 monks (presumably the whole convent) were examined, mentions the offices of the precentor, of the sub-prior, kitchener and chaplain, all held by one man, the third prior and the sub-sacristan so that at least six (including the prior and the sacristan, who are not mentioned) held office in the monastery.

The most interesting feature of this system for our present purpose—the comprehension of the business management of the monasteries—is the endowment of the obedientiaries' offices. The practice of assigning definite sources of revenue to various departments of the monastery, already illustrated by the agreement between the Abbot and the monks of Bury St Edmund's,

[1] *Gesta Abbatum* (R.S.), II, p. 411.
[2] H. E. Salter, *Eynsham Cartulary*, I, p. 433.

was the general system adopted. Not all of the obedientiaries' offices were thus endowed, for some of the minor posts involved neither receipt nor expenditure of money. But to all the more important offices of the house special manors, mills, churches, or other sources of income were granted for the performance of the duties attached to them. The motives for this division of property were doubtless mixed. It was probably in part due to a certain scrupulosity in applying the donations of benefactors to the purposes for which they were granted. When a piece of land was bestowed on the monastery for pittances, if it was handed over to the care of the pittancer, the monastery had the satisfaction of knowing that the income, however it varied, was then most likely to be spent on pittances[1]. But at bottom the original motive was doubtless the same as that which played its part in the separation of the abbot's estates from those of the abbey. The endowment of the obedientiaries secured for the abbey a reasonable certainty that its main needs would be met, and that the abbot's control over the business affairs of his house would not end in the complete absorption of the available income in satisfying his own requirements. Such arrangements, Pollock and Maitland have pointed out, were only matters of internal economy, "and at least as regards the outside world, had no legal effect."[2] None the less they were "solemn and permanent." They gave a moral security against interference, whilst in addition the actual independence of the obedientiary in the control of the revenues of his office placed them to some extent beyond the abbot's reach.

It will be observed that the endowment of the obedientiary's

---

[1] Mr I. S. Leadam (*Select Cases in the Star Chamber*, I, p. cxxx) has pointed out in this connection that, until recent times, it was the practice in the Colleges of the Universities to keep separate the accounts of the various foundations, the revenues being allotted to their respective beneficiaries. One of the steps taken by Archbishop Baldwin which led to his great quarrel with the monks of Canterbury Cathedral was to divert to other uses the churches of Easting and Monkton, which one of his predecessors had granted for the uses of the poor, and the oblations offered by pilgrims in honour of St Thomas and the other saints whose relics lay in the church, which had been set apart perpetually for lighting, vestments and repairs to the church. In 1187 Urban III ordered Baldwin to restore these sources of revenue to the uses for which they had been solemnly set apart. F. W. Maitland, *Collected Papers*, II, p. 414; *Epistolae Cantuarienses* (R.S.), pp. 5, 38.

[2] *History of English Law*, I, p. 506.

office need not of necessity have implied any actual close connection between the obedientiary and the sources of his revenue:
the obedientiary, that is to say, need not necessarily have been
responsible for the collection of the rents or the general supervision of the manors in demesne from which his revenues were
derived. In fact, according to modern ideas of business, the
most natural system would be the establishment of one central
office for the management of the whole of the monastic estates,
and for the distribution of the income thus obtained among the
obedientiaries according to the arrangements prevalent at the
monastery in question. But as a matter of fact, during the earlier
portion of our period, at any rate, exactly the opposite practice
prevailed: the obedientiary received his income direct from its
sources, and was responsible not only for the way in which he
expended the money he received, but also for the management
of the property from which he received it. His individual
responsibility was at times pushed so far that he was even allowed
to raise money by loan for the use of his office. It may perhaps
be suspected that even the law's disregard of anybody but the
abbot as representing the proprietary rights of his house was
ultimately weakened a little by the independent responsibility
of the obedientiary. In the Star Chamber of the fifteenth century, at any rate, it was possible to bring an action against the
obedientiary. About 1494, John Culford of Brynkworth, a copy-
holder of the Abbey of Malmesbury, lamentably showed and
grievously complained, in due form, to the King, how he had
been outrageously treated by "oon Dane John Wootton Monk
& Kychener of the said Abbey to whom the forsaid Messuage
and landes with thappurtenaunces ben limited for his parte to
have and receyve the rentes of the same as is accustomed." The
writ issued in consequence by the Star Chamber was indeed sent
to the abbot, from whom, and not from the kitchener, Culford
legally held his land. But it was on Dan John's behalf that
the written reply was put in denying point-blank all the
alleged notorious proceedings, in the course of which it was
said a child in the cradle was cast into the fire "in evill
example to others in that country"; and it was Dan John
himself who swore upon oath that the counter-story was
correct, and that, as Culford refused to pay pannage for his

swine, the bailiff of the manor evicted him "as wos lawfull for hym to doo."[1]

The obedientiaries' account-rolls which survive make quite clear the way in which the system of endowing the obediences usually operated. Let us take an example from Abingdon—the sacristan's account for 1396–7. The receipts here include firstly a sum of about £9 "by allowance of the convent." Then under the heading "Receptio redditus" comes a series of entries such as "Et de lvij *s*. ij *d*. de redditu terrarum et tenementorum Sacriste in Merchame et Gareforde per annum....Et de vii *s*. vi *d*. de operibus in Merchame et Gareforde." Next follow the "porciones et pensiones" from various churches, then the oblations on various feast-days, and then the "receptio de Mercham," a church apparently assigned entirely to the sacristan. This concludes the receipts. On the other side occurs first a payment of the office's debt of the last year; next come rents, paid to other obedientiaries for various lands belonging to their offices, but apparently in the sacristan's hands. Then follow the expenses of the church, including such items as the wages of a servant in the church, and a laundress of the vestments. Then comes a miscellaneous list of payments in the convent, of which the most interesting for our present purpose runs: "In medicina nostra, v *s*." The identification of the sacristan and his office is pushed so far that even personal expenses of this kind, which we should naturally expect to come from the infirmary account, are borne out of the income of the sacristy. Next follow "necessary expenses," which include such items as "In the mowing and tossing the meadow of Cherchewardeseyte, with cartage of the same, iij *s*. iv *d*." Next come various expenses at Mercham, and finally "expense pro Aula et Camer' de novo reparatis." The account is then balanced: and on the dorse of the roll is the grange-account of Mercham, giving the corn in store there, and the stock of horses, cows and so on. Finally comes a statement of the debts owed to the office, and those owed by it to others.

All this, it is sufficiently clear, points directly to the conclusion that the sacristan was occupied in the closest possible way with

---

[1] I. S. Leadam, *Select Cases in the Star Chamber* (Selden Society), pp. 45 *et seq*. The question of riot and violence was no doubt prominent, but Culford was petitioning also for restitution of his holding.

the estates whence his revenues were drawn: that he was personally responsible, through the bailiffs, no doubt, for the collection of rents, of the payments in commutation of tenants' services, the sums due from the various churches, etc.; that the cash actually passed through his hands without interference by others, and that in short he had charge of the business of his office to the fullest extent. This being so, it follows that in a house so organised there could be no one central business office concerned solely with the collection and distribution of revenue; there could be no one office through which all the income and expenditure of the house would pass, and which therefore would give in its accounts a complete statement of the finances of the house for the year. To obtain a complete statement of what such a house possessed and how it spent its income, it would be necessary to have full accounts of all the obedientiaries, and to disentangle the complications introduced by cross-payments from one office to another. The difficulties of obtaining a clear understanding of the financial position of the house at any given moment would consequently be very great.

There is evidence, however, which would appear at first sight to show that, sometimes spontaneously, sometimes under the stimulus of external criticism, many monasteries came to recognise the advantage of having a central office through which all receipts, if not all detailed payments, should be made, and established a common exchequer for the whole house. This evidence centres round the official known as the bursar, the treasurer or the receiver, whose office would seem to make its first appearance towards the close of the twelfth century, and became common during the earlier thirteenth century.

Originally, no doubt, the bursar was merely the keeper of the convent chest or treasury in which the cash in hand and other valuables of the house were deposited. As this was originally part of the cellarer's business[1], the new office may be regarded

---

[1] A close connection between the bursary and the cellarer's office was frequently maintained. At Worcester, for example, the earliest rolls show that both offices were in the hands of the same man; and in the later rolls, the bursary seems to have been reabsorbed into the cellarer's office, and the two accounts, originally distinct, fused into one. At Clairvaux, again, in the fifteenth century the same official was both bursar and cellarer. D'Arbois de Jubainville, *Études sur les Abbayes Cisterciennes*, p. 236.

as carrying yet a stage further the differentiation of functions which led to the establishment of many of the obediences. Thus in 1199 Innocent III intervened to compel the Abbot of Waltham to observe the constitution agreed upon between himself and his monks, and confirmed by the Apostolic See, whereby it was determined that the money of the abbey was to be kept in a bag in the custody of two or three canons, who were to be appointed only in consultation with the Chapter, and whose accounts were to be audited in the presence of the Chapter[1]. At Clairvaux, the bursary, in this sense, dates back to the early thirteenth century[2].

It is probable that this function always remained attached to the bursar's office; in some cases, it possibly remained the only function. In 1423, Bishop Flemyng, after a visitation of St Frideswide's, Oxford, ordered the prior to collect all debts due to the house, pay off everything that it owed and "deliver without abatement to the two bursars for the time being, that which shall remain over and above such debts when they have been thus paid." The prior was to provide the bursars with an inventory of all the moveable goods belonging to the house, to "certify thereof the sounder and elder part of the convent, and present the same moveable goods to be seen by the eyes of the said bursars." He was also to give notice to the bursars and the elder and sounder part of the convent of the whereabouts of his jewels and archives, and by whom they had been pawned or taken in pawn, and to deposit with the bursars indentures of the jewels and archives. The bursars were to be given a special seal for their office, kept under a lock with two keys of different shapes, one in the hands of each bursar[3]. It is possible that this duty of keeping the convent's surplus cash and assuming responsibility for all moveable property exhausted the bursar's functions at St Frideswide's.

But at Canterbury, where the treasurers' office appeared at

[1] Migne, *Opera Latina*, I, p. 679.

[2] D'Arbois de Jubainville, *Études sur les Abbayes Cisterciennes*, p. 236. In some Continental houses, as for example, Mont-Saint-Michel, the bursar seems to have remained of minor importance even in the fourteenth century. L. Delisle, *La Fortune de l'Ordre de St-Benoît*.

[3] A. Hamilton Thompson, *Visitations of Religious Houses in the Diocese of Lincoln*, I, pp. 95 and 98 (Lincoln Record Society).

least as early as the closing years of the twelfth century, their duties were of much greater importance. The arrangements here come to light in the records of the great quarrel, lasting from 1187 to 1189, between the Cistercian archbishop, Baldwin, and the Benedictine monks of the Cathedral Priory[1]. The struggle centred chiefly round the Archbishop's attempts to interfere with the management of the property assigned to the convent. This property, as Stubbs explains,

was apportioned partly to the cellarership...partly to the chamber-lainship...and partly to the sacrist....The manors appropriated to these purposes were not, however, managed by the obedientiaries themselves, but by three stewards, bursars or treasurers who received the whole revenue and divided it in proper proportions.

Baldwin wished that the obedientiaries should hold the manors themselves, should receive them from him and not from the convent, and should send their accounts to him alone. An appeal made by the convent in September, 1187, to Henry II protested emphatically that the Archbishop's design was an innovation. "The cellarer and the sacristan never held the manors as the Lord Archbishop now wishes." By common counsel three of the brethren, acting as treasurers, received all the income from the manors, and all the rents and casual income of the church, by tallies and writing, and "distributed them to those three obedientiaries and to all the others as each had need." This arrangement, it was said, Baldwin had himself approved[2]. The quarrel was at last patched up, and the Archbishop did not get his way.

Canterbury, from this account, would seem to have possessed from an early date a treasury in the modern sense. The accounts of the treasurers would present a complete statement both of the house's revenues—"omnia quae de maneriis proveniebant simi-liter et omnes redditus ecclesiae et obventiones"[3]—and, in its broad outlines at least, of the expenditure also. The accounts of the obedientiaries receiving their revenues from the treasurers would be necessary to complete the statement of expenditure. But under such a system, a broad view of the financial position of the house would be fairly easily obtained. There is a con-

---

[1] Stubbs, *Epistolae Cantuarienses* (R.S.), p. li and references.
[2] Stubbs, *op. cit.* p. 93.   [3] Stubbs, *op. cit.* p. 93.

siderable amount of evidence to show that bishops and others in authority set themselves during the thirteenth century to develope a less complicated financial system, in the houses under their supervision, by the institution of bursaries of this character. Thus in 1261, the Augustinian Priory of Newstead was visited by the Priors of Nostell and Guisbrough who drew up regulations for the control of the monastery's affairs[1]. Certain of the canons were to be chosen to receive all the income of the house, and distribute it, by tally, to the cellarers and the other obedientiaries as need demanded. Twice a year, or one at the least, these receivers (*receptores*), as well as the cellarer and the chamberlain, were to give full accounts.

Archbishop Peckham, as his register shows, was especially active in ordering the establishment of bursaries, considering them, as he said, well fitted for the common good of the monastery, "as we have learned by example in all well-ordered monasteries."[2] He enjoined the appointment of bursars or treasurers[3] at Reading, at Rochester, at St Martin's Priory, Dover, at Lesnes Abbey, at Southwark Priory, at Glastonbury, at Mottesfont Priory, at the Augustinian Priory of Haverfordwest, at Llanthony Priory, at the nunnery of Usk, at Ewenny Priory, at Goldclive Priory, and at Bardney Abbey. In addition, he ordered the Bishop of St David's to establish treasurers in every house in his diocese, from whom, and from no other source, priors and prioresses, abbots and abbesses, as well as all other persons of the monastery were to receive the money which they expended. Breach of this rule was to be punished as proprietarism[4]. In 1338, to give another example, Bishop Grandisson, finding Tavistock Abbey in a bad state, appointed a common receiver (*receptor*), with a coadjutor, to receive, distribute and conserve all the rents and income of the house, and to provide the cellarer (*dispensator*) with the sums appointed for the necessities of the convent[5].

[1] *Register of Walter Giffard* (S.S.), p. 213.
[2] C. T. Martin, *Registrum Epistolarum Fratris Johannis Peckham* (R.S.), II, p. 622.
[3] The name is not definitely attached to the office in all cases, but the functions are parallel with those of the officials whom he actually names "treasurers."
[4] C. T. Martin, *Registrum Epistolarum Fratris Johannis Peckham* (R.S.), III, p. 794.
[5] *Exeter Registers: John de Grandisson*, II, pp. 889 et seq.

It would seem, however, that this simplification of the monastic economy was not usually pushed to its full extent. Prof. A. Hamilton Thompson, in a brief summary of the duties of the convent officials, restricts the receiver, treasurer or bursar to "collecting rents in money."[1] In a community receiving a considerable part of its income in kind, this would in itself be a serious limitation; and although, as in the case of Canterbury[2], the terms applied to the income which the bursar received are sometimes very broad, the general evidence supports the theory that this limitation was frequently imposed. Benedict XII, in 1335, reforming the statutes of the Cistercian Order, directed two bursars to be appointed in every house

to receive in every case all the moneys (*pecunias*) of the monastery... from whatever source, and to distribute them by command of the abbot, to the other officials and the rest, as shall be opportune[3].

Bishop Gray, in his injunctions of 1421–2 for the nunnery of Elstow, gave instructions that two nuns of high repute were to be chosen as treasurers or bursars,

to whom we will that all moneys to the said monastery forthcoming be paid faithfully without any sort of subtraction, to be laid up and safely guarded in a common chest under three keys, whereof the abbess shall have one and the same treasurer the other two[4].

From this fund payments were to be made for the uses of the monastery by direction of the abbess and the "sounder part" of the convent. The "collectors and receivers of the rents and profits" of the house were to take a corporal oath that they would faithfully levy and collect the money forthcoming from such rents and profits and pay it to the abbess and the treasurers by indentures and tallies. Similar injunctions were laid down for Huntingdon Priory[5], a house of Augustinian canons. In none of these cases, it will be noted, is any mention made of income in kind.

A further limitation, however, may be detected even as regards the cash income. Monastic conservatism seems to have resented

[1] *English Monasteries*, p. 136.   [2] See p. 39 above.
[3] So quoted by the General Chapter of 1402. Martène-Durand, *Thesaurus*, IV, 1539.
[4] A. Hamilton Thompson, *Visitations of Religious Houses*, I, p. 49 (Lincoln Record Society).
[5] A. Hamilton Thompson, *op. cit.* p. 73.

the attempt to pool the money assigned to the various obediences, especially where the arrangement rested upon some solemn donation. The institution by Archbishop Peckham, of a bursary at Reading Abbey, in 1281, will serve to illustrate the point[1]. He found the house grievously in debt. Two monks, together with the abbot's chaplain, were to receive all the rents and income of the house to whatever use they were assigned, whether to the table of the abbot, or to the table of the convent, or to the obedientiaries. The cash was to be kept under three locks. Each of the treasurers was to keep an account of the income and the expenditure, and no one was to receive any part of the money except in their presence. All were to receive from the common purse, the abbot according to his dignity, and the obedientiaries according to necessity, the providence of the abbot and the counsel of others. But Peckham clearly expected opposition to such an arrangement. He warned the obedientiaries, especially, not to murmur at this decree. He expressly disclaimed all intention of evading the wishes of benefactors who had assigned manors to the infirmary, the cellar or other obedience, and claimed that, in thus "excluding fraud and the abuse of super-fluity," his action was in full agreement with their intention; nor, he said, was it to be believed that these benefactors wished their property to be dealt with otherwise, since this was the best and most fitting way of securing the wellbeing of the house. Finally he professed himself ready to mitigate the rigour of this arrangement at any time when the debts of the house had been paid.

In this case, then, the pooling of the obedientiaries' incomes was intended only as a temporary expedient. The archbishop's instructions at Glastonbury were to the same effect[2]. In all other cases Peckham either passed over the question of the

[1] C. T. Martin, *Registrum Epistolarum Fratris Johannis Peckham*, I, pp. 224-5.

[2] C. T. Martin, *op. cit.* I, p. 259. A "celerarius forensis" was to be appointed, who, together with the seneschal of the house and the wardens of the manors, was to receive and transfer to the exchequer all the rents and income, whether of the barony, the lands and rents assigned to the obedientiaries, or the appropriated churches to whatever use they were assigned. The exchequer was to be in charge of the sub-cellarer and two colleagues (one appointed by the Abbot), the co-operation of all three being necessary for both receipts and payments. The arrangement again was apparently intended to be temporary.

obedientiaries' income in silence or expressly stipulated, as at Rochester in 1282[1], that the treasurers were not to receive such revenues as were of old assigned by their donors to special offices such as the almonry, the kitchen or the sacristy. The ordinance of Bishop Grandisson for Tavistock, already cited[2], may be read in the light of another injunction laid on the same house in 1373 by his successor, Thomas de Brantyngham, who ordered that a monk should be appointed to receive and expend, by tally and indenture, all the money arising from all churches, manors and other places belonging to the monastery, outside the offices and obediences[3].

Such limitations as these must often have interfered with the simplification of accountancy which, in at least one case, was put forward as the main reason for the establishment of the bursary[4]. Instructions were given by the visitor for the appointment of two treasurers or bursars, to receive all the money and to answer for it before the prior and the elder members of the Chapter, and so "the account be entire and split up as little as possible, and, when the account is heard, the position of the house be set forth truly."[5] If this visitor had been confronted with the accounts of Durham, Winchester, Worcester or Abingdon, he would certainly not have found in the bursars' or treasurers' rolls what he expected. In the case of Durham, this is all the more remarkable in that there is evidence, though not strictly contemporary, that through the bursar's hands there passed the whole incomings and outgoings of this great monastery.

According to the Rites of Durham[6], as Canon Fowler points out in his edition of the Durham accounts, the bursar's office was to Receive all the Rents that was pertaining to the house

[1] C. T. Martin, *op. cit.* II, p. 622. At Haverfordwest the only exception made is the almoner's office; at Bardney the rents assigned to the abbot's alms or those of the convent. *Ibid.* III, pp. 782, 823.
[2] See p. 40, above.
[3] F. C. Hingeston-Randolph, *Exeter Registers, Thomas de Brantyngham*, p. 312 *et seq.*
[4] Apparently the house was Felley Priory, and the date 1276, but neither point is quite clear. W. Brown, *York Registers* (S.S.), p. 317.
[5] "Ita quod compotus sit integer et minime dividatur, [et] quod audito compoto manifestetur status domus veraciter in conventu."
[6] This description of the monastic organisation at Durham was written, it should be remembered, in 1593.

and all other officers of ye house mayde there accoumptes to him, and he discharged all ye servants' wages and paid all the expences and somes of money as was laid forth about any work appertaining to ye said house.

"We should expect," says Canon Fowler, "that the Bursar's Rolls would simply be extracts from those of the other officials." But, as a matter of fact, they are not. The bursar, emphatically, was not the convent accountant making out the year's balance sheet. The obedientiaries, Canon Fowler continues,

may have rendered their accounts to him, and their receipts and spendings may have passed through his hands, but he kept an account of his own, independent of the rest, and concerned with many different matters.

But that the obedientiaries' revenues should so have passed through the bursar's hands without leaving a trace in his accounts seems almost impossible. The instructions of visitors instituting bursaries are, almost without exception, emphatic on the duty of presenting accounts. Many of them insist that payment into or out of the bursar's funds shall take place "by tally and indenture." That the Durham bursar should have passed on very considerable sums without accounting for them is practically incredible. Equally so is the alternative theory that he kept separate accounts of the obedientiaries' endowments, which have vanished without a single example remaining.

That the bursar's roll is not a summary of the other officers' accounts may be shown clearly by summarising the expenditure side of the largest and most complete example which is printed —that for 1536–7. The expenditure falls into the following groups: (1) the "special wardrobe" of the obedientiaries, the prior[1] and his household; (2) the purchase of wine, (3) of horses; (4) of wheat, (5) of barley, (6) of oats, (7) of peas and beans, and (8) of iron; (9) gifts and presents; (10) the prior's *ludi*, or annual holiday; (11) the bursar's personal expenses; (12) customary alms; (13) necessary expenses—a long and miscellaneous list of payments connected either with agriculture or the purchase of stores; (14) repairs to buildings in various parts of the monastic estates; (15) fuel; (16) soul-silver—that part of the servants' wages given in food, or a money payment in lieu of it; (17) pen-

---

[1] Here practically equivalent to the abbot of an ordinary house.

sions—payments to various persons from the Archdeacon of "Estrydyng" down to the launderers of the prior's napery; (18) stipends, again a varied list "from the sub-prior to the plumber"; (19) and (20) rents for various pieces of land; (21) contributions paid to the Pope and the King; (22) allowances to various persons; and, finally, (23) payments to the cellarer for the expenses of the kitchen "by tally and indenture."

In spite of its varied character and its wide extent, this roll does not cover the whole range of monastic expenditure. It lacks, for example, any account of payments for the infirmary; it includes no such items of expenditure within the church as appear in the sacristan's roll of 1535-6. Nor was the bursar transmitting from a central fund to the obedientiaries the revenue which they received, though to some extent this was done. The cellarer was receiving money for the kitchen account by tally and indenture. It does not follow that he had not other funds at his disposal. The cellarer's account for 1536-7 is unfortunately not available for comparison. But from 1307 to 1333-4 at least, when the cellarer was receiving the greater part of his income in the same way, there was still a part which he did not receive from the bursar. Under the heading of "rents paid," in the bursar's roll of 1536-7 occur also such items as, "Paid to the Sacristan of Durham for three acres of meadow in Bellacis, 7d.... To the Almoner of Durham for Ferthingcroft in South Street, 14s." But such payments to the sacristan amounted only to £5. 13s. 2d., whereas, in the previous year, he had £131. 13s. 1d. at his disposal. The bursar's contributions of this kind did not make up the whole revenue of the obedientiaries. They represent rather the "farming" by the bursar of income appropriated to the other obediences.

The position at Winchester was much the same. The Receiver of the Treasury in this house has left accounts which present much the same complex appearance as the Durham bursar's.

The great sums of money which passed yearly through his hands, the heavy liabilities which he was obliged to meet, the loans he was compelled to contract with foreign merchants; the vast variety and extent of his purchases in wines, spices, furs, robes and a miscellaneous multitude of articles; the large quantities to be provided for the use of the convent kitchen; the fees, stipends, gratuities, repairs, refurnishing of buildings, etc.; the heavy payments of tenths and procurations,

which Dean Kitchin notes as characteristic of the receiver's account, are all paralleled by the expenditure of the bursar at Durham. But the full tale of the priory's spending is not told by the receiver. Nor did he transmit the obedientiaries' income to them from any central fund[1].

The explanation which Dean Kitchin gives of the receiver's function is that he received all the rents of estates and other revenues not assigned to the support of other obedientiaries and offices. This agrees with Blomfield's view of the bursar's position in the Augustinian house at Burcester[2]. It meets the facts of the case for Durham. Peckham's semi-apologetic attitude when, at Reading, he pooled the obedientiaries' revenues under the bursar goes to strengthen the impression that, in general, some such limitation existed even where the bursar is said to receive all the income of the house. The original obedientiaries, it may be said, were entrusted only with the ordinary routine work of the monastery; the endowments of their offices were intended, in general, only to cover everyday expenses. For what may be called the extraordinary business of the house, for any extensive building operations, for any especially heavy outlay involving large sums of ready money, responsibility originally lay, not on the obedientiaries, but on the abbot; and for meeting these expenses there remained revenues unassigned to any of the obedientiaries[3]. It was these revenues only, it would seem, which the bursar usually received when his office was instituted,

---

[1] Three of the manors attached to the hordarian's office in 1334 occur among the sources of the receiver's income for 1334-5; and the hordarian was then receiving most of his income by tally. But the office was at the time administered by the prior's receiver (not to be confounded with the receiver of the treasury). The circumstances were exceptional. The hordarian's revenues were probably passed through the treasury because the convent desired to have some check upon the prior's officer who had been placed in charge of this obedience.

[2] J. C. Blomfield, *Deanery of Bicester*, II, p. 135.

[3] Under arrangements made at Evesham in 1206 the cellarer was to have "the whole care of the Abbey, except the incomes assigned to the offices of the monks." In this case the cellarer may be regarded as bursar in all but name. The connection between the bursar's office and that of the cellarer was always close. *Chronicon Abbatiæ de Evesham* (R.S.), p. 207.

and for the expenditure of which he was called to account. The income of the house, in short, was a distinct thing from that of the obedientiaries.

This general conclusion may be supported by other evidence. The truth seems to be that there was a growing tendency for the obediences to be treated almost as distinct corporations. We may notice, for instance, the method of valuation adopted in the inquisition into the property of the Benedictine houses in France, held early in the fourteenth century by command of Benedict XII. The general form of the returns is much after this fashion:

> The monastery has so much in annual rents, in tithes, in meadows, in vineyards: sum total, so much. The almoner's office has so much income, the infirmarer's office, so much.

The income of the monastery and of the endowed obediences is not added together; the house is one thing, the obedience is another[1]. A certain sense of private interest in the office funds may even be detected. The account rolls show that the obedientiary was entitled to apply certain portions of his official revenue to his own purposes. When ill, he pays for his own medicine[2], which it would be expected the infirmarer ought to provide. Frequently he pays for his own clothing and that of his servants, in spite of the chamberlain's responsibilities. He pays for the entertainment of his friends and visitors. There are even cases in which the obedientiaries are regarded as personally responsible to the convent for the debts incurred by the offices under their charge, even where substantial sums are involved. The treasurer at Abingdon, in his accounts for 1383–4, records the receipt of £1. 6s. 4d. from Peter Crundon in part payment of his debt "in respect of the Kitchener's office, for the time when the same Peter held that office." The list of debts owing to the house, given at the end of the roll, shows that Peter also owed £16. 15s., "for the debt at the foot of the compotus for the time when he was cellarer," and that John Mercham owed £2. 10s. "for the time when he was custos operis." At Winchester in 1404, when a disastrous fire occurred on the almonry property, the almoner

---

[1] See, especially, the valuation of Mont-Saint-Michel: L. Delisle, *La Fortune de l'Ordre de St-Benoît*, pp. 16–25.

[2] "In medicina nostra, v s." See p. 36, above.

himself paid off the debit balance of his account. The frequent transference of money from one obedientiary's account to another for the purpose of paying off an adverse balance is a warning not to regard the obedientiary as generally responsible for the debts of his office; he was probably called on only to pay some loss to the monastery caused by his own fault or neglect. But that, even under exceptional circumstances, the obedientiary should be under such an obligation is sufficiently indicative of the independence of these obediences, and the definite separation of their endowments from those of the monastery.

Where such an attitude prevailed, the need for a central fund goes far in itself to explain the anxiety of the bishops and other visitors to institute a bursary, even though the obedientiaries' income could not be brought into the common stock. The duties of the obediences were clearly defined by custom; the obedientiary's credit as an official rested upon his ending the year with a credit balance. There was a risk that, when some heavy or unexpected expenditure was necessary, especially if large sums of ready cash were necessary, none of the obedientiaries would be very willing to bear the burden. All the convent's resources might be divided out for everyday purposes, and nothing in the nature of a reserve fund left. In the smaller houses, where the special endowments of the obediences were not large, the risk was not so great[1]. But in the larger houses, it might even be necessary to retrieve considerable sums from the obedientiaries' hands. The accounts of the treasurers of the Convent at Abingdon show that such a process had been necessary there. These officials make no appearance in the treatise *De Obedientiariis Abbatiae Abbendonensis*, written late in the

---

[1] In such cases, the cellarer's office, which was usually the most important, might serve the purpose of the bursary well enough. Thus at Eynsham, in 1406, the kitchener, chamberlain and infirmarer received sums by tally from the cellarer; and as the amount so received by the chamberlain corresponds roughly with the income shown in his account of 1403–4, it is probable that these officials had nothing but what they received from the cellarer. The sacristan and the almoner had some independent income, but, as the Rev. H. E. Salter has pointed out to me, the amount probably did not exceed £12 for the sacristan and £2 for the almoner (*Eynsham Cartulary*, II, p. lxxvi). The cantor may have had some small funds as well; the cellarer in 1390 received no income from a mill because the cantor computed for it. It is therefore not strictly accurate to represent the cellarer's account as covering the whole income of the house, but the amount excluded is small.

thirteenth century[1]. The first of the three remaining examples
of their accounts dates from 1375–6[2]. The office, therefore, was
probably instituted in the first half of the fourteenth century.
The income of the office was partly derived from tenements in
Abingdon, and partly from payments by the abbot for provisions
supplied by him to the convent. But the main part of the treasurers' fund was formed by contributions from the other officials.
The obedientiaries did not hand over the balance of their accounts
at the end of the year[3]; they made fixed customary payments.
In 1440–1 the sums are entered under the heading, "Recepcio
consueta," and the formula used is, "De liiij s. iij d. receptis de
consuetudinibus Precentoris prout patet in providentia hujus
anni...Et de x li. pro consuetudinibus Lingnarii per annum."
The amounts to be placed in the central reserve fund seem to
have been mapped out beforehand for the year. The treasurers'
funds in 1375–6 and 1383–4 went mainly in building expenses.
Part went to pay off the debit balances of other obedientiaries.
Thus in 1375–6 payments were made for this purpose to the
lignar, the infirmarer, the Trinity warden and the chamberlain.
In 1383–4, £6 was handed over to the sacristan for the relief
of his office. But, as the editor of the accounts points out, this
latter duty was not more incumbent on the treasurers than on
any other obedientiary fortunate enough to have a balance in
hand[4]. Among the officials who drew heavily on this reserve
fund was the abbot[5]. At the beginning of 1375–6 he owed the
house, through this account, £1374, to which at the end of the
year he had added £94 more. It appears highly probable from

[1] Printed in the appendix to the *Abingdon Chronicle* (R.S.), vol. II.
[2] R. E. G. Kirk, *Accounts of the Obedientiaries of Abingdon Abbey.*
The second account is for 1383–4; the third for 1440–1, in which the
treasurers deal with a much smaller sum, is unfortunately incomplete.
[3] The cellarer did so in 1375–6, but this is the only example. It is most
likely, as Mr Kirk suggests, that the treasurers, for the time being, were
superintending the cellarer's office.
[4] So, at Evesham, the agreement of 1206 (p. 46, above) provided that if,
through a bad season, any officer ended the year with a debit balance, it was
to be made up from the surplus of another office, if any had a surplus, and,
if not, by the abbot through the cellarer's hands.
[5] In the fifteenth century the abbot himself acted as one of the two joint
treasurers. At Burcester also, in the fifteenth century, the prior and sub-
prior in person were bursars. J. C. Blomfield, *Deanery of Bicester*, II, p. 161
(account of 1409), p. 167 (1412), p. 171 (1425, prior and a canon), p. 177
(1433–4, prior and a canon). After this the bursars are canons only till 1481.

the treasurers' roll of 1440–1 that much of this had eventually
to be written off as a bad debt.

The treasury at Norwich also seems to have been designed as
a reserve fund of this kind, kept up, at least in part, by contributions from the obediences. Bishop Nicke, in 1514, finding
the church, the dormitory and the chapter-house in a dilapidated
state, and a good deal else in the financial management which
needed reform[1], ordered the prior and monks to collect "half a
whole tenth" from all the offices of the monastery, and another
half after a short time. The proceeds were to be placed in the
treasury of the monastery, for the protection of the house[2].

To sum up, the bursar would appear in general to have been
in much the same position as any of the other obedientiaries,
with his own special duties to perform and his own revenues
to bear the burden. His office was one of great importance; at
Durham, the burden of complex duties laid upon his shoulders,
as the increasing length of his successive accounts shows, was
growing from his appearance in the thirteenth century down to
the period just before the Dissolution. He was the "handy man"
of the monastery, in charge of that portion of the revenues of
the house which had never been solemnly set aside for any of
the older obediences, or which had been specially detached from
their claims, and, therefore, could readily be turned to meet any
of the changing needs or purposes of the time. The other obedientiaries on occasion might find their funds supplemented by
the bursar. But in general they were left unaffected by the
development of the bursar's office, with a large measure of independence in the management of their revenues, and drawing
them, not from any central fund, but directly from the sources
assigned to their offices[3].

"The bearings of these observations lies in the application
of them." In the first place, doubt is thrown upon the validity
of certain arguments about the amount of revenue enjoyed by

---

[1] A. Jessopp, *Visitations of Norwich Diocese* (C.S.).

[2] "Ad defensionem ejusdem" (*sc.* monasterii). At Westacre the treasury
also received contributions from the obediences. Complaint was made in
1494 that the sub-prior had administered the office of the cellarer for three
years and paid nothing into the treasury, whereas when one Master Geoffrey
held the office, he paid in 100 marks in four years. (A. Jessopp, *op. cit.* p. 50.)

[3] See also Appendix C.

particular houses, and the purposes to which it was applied. Dr Whitaker, for example, in his History of Whalley takes it for granted that two accounts of Whalley Abbey which he prints, one for 1477, the other for 1521, contain a complete statement of the year's income and expenditure. Both these accounts are those of the bursar: and although, as we have seen, the directions of Benedict XII for the institution of bursars in the Cistercian Order lend some colour to Dr Whitaker's assumption, if the account given above of the functions of the bursar is accepted, his view must be abandoned. If so, it is impossible to argue from these accounts on the proportion of the monastic income spent, say, on alms: for the almoner in all probability had special revenues of his own, which would make no appearance in the bursar's rolls.

It would even appear possible that the arrangements at Canterbury were not quite so simple as was represented by the monks in the contest of 1187[1]. The treasurer's accounts of the thirteenth and fourteenth centuries are examined by Dr J. B. Sheppard in the introduction to the second volume of the *Literae Cantuarienses*, and an outline of the credit side is given for two years. It is apparently assumed that the entire income of the house is covered. It is true that the obedientiaries drew by tally upon the treasury funds freely. But on the receipts side of the accounts occurs the heading "De arreragiis obedientiorum"; and in this connection Dr Sheppard himself explains that the sacrist, the keeper of the barton (custos berthonae), the cellarer and the other chief officers had rents annexed to and settled upon their offices for the proceeds of which they were bound to account. Moreover, a formula of a certificate to be given by the rector of a pensionary church to the patron[2] shows John de Ros as "rector of the church of the Blessed Mary which is called Aldermaricherche in London," and presented thereto by the prior and Chapter "saving an annual portion of six marks to the sacristan" and "an annual portion of 8s. 4d. to the treasurers." He certifies that he has paid these sums every year to the sacristan and the treasurers. The assumption that the treasurers' accounts give a complete statement of the revenues of the cathedral priory seems hazardous.

---

[1] See p. 39, above.   [2] J. B. Sheppard, *Literae Cantuarienses*, I, p. 20.

Care must be exercised, then, in dealing with the position of the obedientiaries, and especially of the bursar, in respect of the interpretation of their accounts. More interesting, however, is the light which the establishment of the bursary, and the duties associated with it, throw upon the whole history of this business organisation, the motives underlying it, and the difficulties which it was intended to meet. We see the monastery, on the horns of a dilemma, meeting one difficulty with a remedy which ends only in another difficulty. If the duties given to the bursar have been correctly interpreted, his office represents, in general, the completion of the system of obediences. A new official was interposed between the abbot and the last unassigned portion of his house's revenues. A representative of the convent was to place some check upon his administration of those funds reserved for exceptional needs, or, at least, to give some account of how they had been spent. In most of the instances of the establishment of bursaries which have come beneath my notice, maladministration has been the evil attacked. Probably, therefore, it is not far wrong to see in the whole system of the endowment of the obediences, of which this is the last development, evidence, in the first place, of a persistent attempt to secure the convent against the danger of an extravagant or dishonest abbot. The independent incomes assigned to these offices which supplied the daily needs of the monasteries were to some extent beyond the control of the abbot. But, on the other hand, such cases as that of Abingdon, where the bursars (and one of them the abbot) were in charge of a large fund retrieved in the main from the obedientiaries' revenues, and still more that of Reading, where (at least for a time) the whole revenues of the house were once more concentrated in one fund and distributed among the obedientiaries "according to the providence of the abbot and the counsel of others" show that the remedy was not over-successful. The individual control of the obedientiaries over their revenues was liable to prove as dangerous as the individual control of the abbot over the whole of the house's possessions: and the only course which remained was to return in a vicious circle to "the providence of the abbot and the counsel of others."

Indeed none of the internal checks upon the abbot which we have yet seen were really effective, whether he interfered for good or for evil. His autocratic authority as guardian of the morals of his monks finds to the end a reflection in his power of interference in the management of the monastic revenues. He was responsible both for the moral and for the temporal welfare of the house over which he presided: and if he chose to exert his power there was no solemn arrangement which could bind him, no man or body of men who could really resist him. That this was the case may easily be shown. The claims of the abbot upon the property of the house were not really barred by that division of the abbot's revenues from those of the convent which, as we have seen, even the temporal courts recognised. It was not merely the case that even where such a division existed, many payments were due from the monastery to its head. The division was really no protection against the laying of the burden of the abbot's extravagance or debt, not upon his successor, but upon his abbey. We have already seen how in 1375–6 the Abbot of Abingdon owed his house over £1400, and how in the end most of it proved a bad debt. A passage in the *Gesta Abbatum S. Albani*[1] also shows how closely the monastery was concerned in the abbot's management of his own revenues. The Bishop of Lichfield demanded from Abbot John (1302–8) a pension for three lives, in settlement, apparently, of a debt of £900. The abbot laid the matter before his Chapter, and after a private protest made to him by one of the brethren, got the bishop to meet the Chapter. The convent showed great unwillingness to let the agreement (for the fulfilment of which it was clearly expected to make itself responsible) take effect: and when the bishop explained that the convent would not be aggrieved, for the burden would fall upon the abbot, "the prior prudently and truthfully made answer that whenever the abbot was burdened with heavy debts, it was absolutely necessary for the convent to give him assistance." On the other hand, as has been noticed of Evesham, the abbot was often held responsible for making up the deficiencies of the obedientiaries' offices from his own estates[2]. The separation of the two incomes was not rigorously observed: and it is clear that it was no safeguard against an abbot's masterfulness, be it good or bad.

So also the obedientiaries were powerless in the face of an

---

[1] Vol. II, pp. 90–94.   [2] See p. 49, above.

abbot who chose to defy custom and to combat the essential conservatism of monasticism. He could intervene where things were going badly, or take into his own hands any of the monastic offices which gave evidence of perpetual mismanagement. The best known example is, of course, that of Abbot Samson of Bury St Edmund's, who, after setting a clerk of his own as "socius" by the side of the cellarer, at last took the offices both of the cellarer and of the guest-master under his own care, putting in clerks to manage the affairs of the obediences, greatly to the disgust of many of the monks. So, too, at St Swithun's, the hordarian's office was in charge of the prior's receiver from 1331 to 1337[1]. But even without taking this extreme step, the abbot could interfere with the spending of the income assigned to the obedientiaries. At Bury St Edmund's, it was one of the complaints levelled against Abbot Samson that "he resorted to the sacristy at his own pleasure, sparing his own purse," and Jocelin's defence is simply "that if he took anything from the sacrist, he turned it to the good account of the church." Despite the institution of the bursary, it is clear that it was with the abbot that there lay the initiative in what we have called the extraordinary business of the house; it was the abbot's policy which decided on any extensive building operations, any purchases of land, the raising of loans, or the conduct of the lawsuits of the house.

One other check, indeed, there existed within the house—the monastic Chapter. In all things of importance, the abbot was bound by the Rule to consult the Chapter: the obedientiaries were elected in the Chapter, the consent of the Chapter was held to be necessary before any important agreement was entered into. But it is clear that there was no true constitutional division of powers, and no means of checking the designs of the abbot if he was really bent upon them. A strong-minded abbot naturally could impress his will upon the Chapter. Jocelin of Brakelond's account of the election of a new prior at Bury St Edmund's shows that even in such a matter as the election and dismissal of obedientiaries, the abbot could be practically certain of getting his own way. But the abbot's control went much further. The deference which the abbot owed to the Chapter was usually

[1] See the hordarian's rolls between these dates: G. W. Kitchin, *Compotus Rolls of Obedientiaries of St Swithun's.*

limited to the older (*seniores*) or sounder (*saniores*) members of that body. In business affairs, especially, the Chapter might be shut out entirely from all effective consultation. At Westminster, in 1234, the Papal visitors gave instructions that matters discussed in the Chapter were only to be such as pertained to "the welfare of souls and the great advantage of the church." The business management of the house (*extrinseca negotia*) was to be discussed outside the Chapter by its "more discreet" members, and the full body was only to be informed of their decision[1]. The decision as to which of the community were sufficiently "sound" or "discreet" seems to have been left to the abbot.

If the abbot chose to disregard the Chapter utterly, it could make no effective protest without calling in outside help. Its functions, speaking broadly, were purely consultative. The spirit of the Rule of St Benedict remained virtually unchanged in all later recensions: and this is how St Benedict defines the relations of the abbot and the Chapter:

Whenever any weighty matters have to be transacted in the monastery, let the abbot call together all the community and himself propose the matter for discussion. After hearing the advice of the brethren, let him consider it in his own mind, and then do what he shall judge most expedient.

The abbot's will, in short, prevailed wherever he chose to insist upon it: and so far as the monastery, standing by itself, was concerned, practically the only limit was the breaking-point reached sooner or later even in monastic obedience. Abbot Warin of St Albans (1183–95[2]) ordained that the monks should be buried in stone coffins: and although some at least believed that this was a piece of spite against the sacristan, who had objected to the abbot's election, and, on whose office the extra expense would fall, the abbot's will was done. The same abbot, founding the hospital of St Mary des Prez for leprous nuns, endowed it from the revenues of the monastery[3], although many, while applauding the piety of the deed, objected to it on the score of the temporal welfare of the house. But it is needless to insist on a point so obvious as this. To see the lengths to which

[1] *English Historical Review*, 1912, p. 739.
[2] *Gesta Abbatum* (R.S.), I, p. 198.
[3] *Ibid.* I, p. 202.

the control of the abbot over the finances of the house could go, we have only to take the well-known case of Abbot Roger Norreys of Evesham (1191–1213)[1]. This man, according to the account given by the monks, reduced the house to the deepest penury. The only food which the monks often obtained was bad bread and water: they were not properly clothed, and had to support themselves by begging. The church was allowed to fall into ruin, the abbot appropriating the rents assigned to keep it in repair. He took away the revenues from the cellar, the kitchen, and other offices. He wasted the property of the abbey, bestowing it upon his nephew and others. He transacted all the business of the house in his own private chamber instead of in the chapter-house, and instituted and deprived the obedientiaries at his own pleasure. By a secession and an actual skirmish in arms the monks obtained an agreement settling the disposal of the revenues of the house: but it proved absolutely valueless. As the house had, during this very time, fought for and obtained the cherished privilege of exemption from episcopal jurisdiction, an appeal had ultimately to be made to the papal legate, and in the end the abbot was deposed.

The case is of course exceptional, both in the depths to which the abbot descended and in the fact that the exemption of the house from visitation played a part in allowing him to go so far. But it gives a clear idea of the absolute power, irrespective of Rule, custom or opinion, which an abbot could exercise over the funds of his monastery. Upon the business qualities and the business morality of the head of a religious house, there depended the temporal well-being of the community. These forces overwhelmed practically every other influence save those of nature or of social change. A capable and business-like abbot could generally overrule incompetent or peculative obedientiaries; but no amount of shrewdness, economy, or devotion on the part of the convent's officials could afford protection against the abbot's corruptibility, extravagance, or lack of business qualifications.

Many attempts, it is true, were made to ensure that the house should have full cognizance of the main financial transactions carried out in its name and some control over them. The raising

[1] W. D. Macray, *Chronicon Abbatiæ de Evesham*.

of loans, in particular, was one of the points upon which the co-operation of the Chapter was most firmly enjoined. The Benedictine Provincial Chapter held at Bermondsey in 1249[1], repeating a provision of Gregory IX, laid down a rule that if any "prelate" raised a loan in the name of a monastery without the consent of its Chapter, the house should be under no obligation, unless it could be proved by trustworthy men that the loan has been turned to the manifest good of the house. Gregory IX, in his reform of the Cluniac Statutes[2], also insisted on the necessity of absolute publicity in the raising of loans: the counsel of the brethren was to be taken, and "witnesses were to be added" so that the terms of the loan might be perfectly clear. Benedict XII, in his reforms of the Benedictine and Augustinian Orders[3], early in the fourteenth century, again found it necessary to insist that loans were to be raised only with the consent of the Chapter, to whom the reason for the loan as well as its terms must be clearly explained. Unless these rules were observed, the loan was null and void, while the offender was forbidden to enter the church until all injury to the monastery had been remedied: if this was not done within six months, he was to be suspended from his spiritual functions and the collation of benefices. Provisions were made as to the necessity for the consent of the house in any alienation of its property, whether perpetual or temporary, the sale of woods, the conversion of copyhold land into freehold, or similar business, in the Benedictine Provincial Chapters of 1225[4] and 1249[5], in the reformed Benedictine Constitutions of Gregory IX (1238), in the confirmation of them by Innocent IV (1253)[6], and in Benedict XII's various reforms mentioned above. In this respect, indeed, the English temporal courts came to the aid of the monasteries. An action was granted for the recovery of lands alienated without the consent of the convent, although, consistent in its refusal to recognise any legal representative of the convent other than the abbot, the English law granted the action only to one of the abbots who succeeded the delinquent,

---

[1] Matthew Paris, *Chronica Majora*, Additamenta, p. 175 *et seq.*
[2] Leo Marsicanus, *Chronicon Casinense*, p. 836 *et seq.*
[3] Wilkins, *Concilia*, II, p. 585 *et seq.*
[4] Dugdale, *Monasticon*, I, p. xlvi *et seq.*
[5] Matthew Paris, *Chronica Majora*, Additamehta, p. 175 *et seq.*
[6] *Ibid.* p. 235 *et seq.*

and, until 1267, only to his immediate successor[1]. The same end
was aimed at in the numerous ordinances[2] as to the custody of
the convent seal, which had to be affixed to all documents bind-
ing on the house, and which was usually ordered to be kept under
at least three locks, one in the hands of the abbot, the second in
those of one of the obedientiaries and the third in those of one
of the monks. Here, too, the State interfered, though with what
effect is doubtful. The Statute of Carlisle (1306) ordered that in
Cistercian, Premonstratensian and other houses whose seal was
wont to be in the hands of the abbot and not of the convent, the
monastery was to have a seal of its own to be kept, under the
private seal of the abbot, in custody of the abbot and four discreet monks, so that the abbot by himself could conclude no
contract[3]. Parliament, no doubt, in this case desired not so much
to protect the monasteries, as to prevent the enrichment of the
King's enemies by payments made by English houses to their
foreign superiors.

Moreover, persistent attempts were made to secure for the
convent a knowledge of the exact state of its own affairs. It was
repeatedly ordered—decrees to this effect will be found in all
the documents mentioned above, as well as in the earlier Articles
of the Council of Oxford (1222)[4], the Constitutions of the Legate
Ottobon (1268)[5] and those of the Benedictine Chapter of 1422[6]—
that the obedientiaries were to present accounts to the head of
the house, usually in the presence of some of the elder brethren
of the house, and that the abbot also was to lay before the house

[1] Pollock and Maitland, *History of English Law*, i, p. 505. Professor
Maitland points out, however, that English law, in the time of John of Ayton
(writing between 1333 and 1348), failed to enforce the protections offered to
the convent by canon law. When an abbot borrowed money and gave a bond
under the abbey seal for its repayment, "the canonist, before deciding that
the abbey was bound, would be inclined to discuss the manner in which the
borrowed money was expended. But the law of the realm...says John, will
hold the abbey bound, even though the money were thrown into the sea."
English Historical Review, 1896, p. 657.
[2] This rule seems generally the result of episcopal visitation: it appears,
however, in the decrees of the Benedictine Provincial Chapter of 1444, cap. ii.
(Reynerus, Appendix, p. 113 *et seq.*).
[3] *Rot. Parl.* i, p. 217a *et seq.* The same thing had been advised by the
Parliament of Westminster (33 Edward I), but the law had not been promulgated.
[4] Wilkins, *Concilia*, i, p. 191 *et seq.*
[5] *Ibid.* ii, p. 1 *et seq.*   [6] *Ibid.* iii, p. 413 *et seq.*

or some of its elders a full account of his administration and the condition of the monastery's finances. But for the observance of all these things, it will be observed, the real check upon the abbot was simply the visitor. The co-operation of the Chapter, despite the stress laid upon it in the monastic legislation of the thirteenth and fourteenth centuries, remained exactly what the abbot chose to make it. Apart from the very slight help given by the temporal courts—a help which might not become available for years, and which even then could only be claimed by the offender's successor and not the convent—the only way in which the monastery could thwart an abbot who ignored the Chapter, or took possession of the common seal, or refused to give account of his administration, was by an appeal to the bishop or the visitor of the Order. Independent action on the part of the monks was looked on askance, as contrary to the monastic virtue of obedience. How little weight the rights of the Chapter had behind them may be seen in one most significant case. The legislation of Benedict XII for the Augustinian Canons in 1339, be it remembered, had included provisions that loans were to be raised only with the consent of the Chapter, that the Chapter must be consulted in any case where land was leased or farmed out for any length of time, that at the annual Chapter the abbot, like all other officials, was to give account in writing of his administration, the debts which he had incurred, the names of the creditors, the reasons for the obligation and the interest (if any) which was being paid on the debt. Provision was made, it is true, that if the abbot thought it dangerous to reveal in open Chapter the amount of a surplus, he might entrust the secret to four canons, two chosen by the Chapter, two by himself, who were sworn not to reveal the secret except in the case of his death, or for some other valid reason. But of debt, at any rate, the monastery was to be kept informed. None the less, about 1400, the canons of Oseney Abbey "cunningly and without the knowledge of the bishop" extorted from Abbot John an oath to reveal to the elder and wiser canons the names of all the creditors of the monastery, and the sums due to them; never to burden the monastery with debt without the counsel and consent of these same canons; to reveal within a month the common goods of the monastery pledged by him in its name, in whose hands they were and what were the obligations; to appoint the four "officiarii" of the monastery with the counsel and consent of the wiser of the canons, and not to hinder the said "officiarii" in the exercise of their office. By virtue of this oath, the "officiarii" said that the abbot had no right, even for the relief of his monastery, to receive loans of money, or to support or remunerate friend or benefactor, or to remove the "officiarii" from their administration. The abbot appealed to John, Bishop of Lincoln, who ordained that, notwithstanding his oath, the abbot might, as often as necessary for the advantage of the monastery, receive loans, remunerate the labours of his friends on its behalf, remove the "officiarii" and other ministers as often as necessary, and substitute others according to the ancient observances of the monastery. In 1400, the Bishop's decision was confirmed by Boniface IX, who pronounced the abbot to have been in no wise bound to observe the oath, and restored him to the state in which he was before he took it. It is hard to see what the effect of this last proviso would be, but the story leaves little doubt as to the weakness of the Chapter, and the slight regard shown even in the highest places for its rights[1].

The Chapter by itself, then, was practically helpless. So far as the monastery was concerned, the main checks upon the abbot were his own moral sense, and the possibility of revolt within his monastery and a consequent scandal. The power in which the authorities of the later Middle Ages put their main trust for the control of the abbot was that of the visitor. Dilapidation of the monastery's property was one of the things for which an abbot could be deposed, and the episcopal visitations, or those of the visitors of the great Orders, gave an opportunity of criticism. Thus in Gregory IX's reform of the Benedictine Constitutions (1238), it is provided that if any head of a house is a dilapidator, the visitors of the Provincial Chapter are to make report to the diocesan, and the offender is to be removed from his post without disturbance, and an administrator put in until the next abbot is elected[2]. More frequently exercised was the power, also entrusted to the bishop, of associating with the abbot one or more of his monks, or possibly a secular ecclesiastic,

---

[1] *Calendar of Papal Letters*, v, p. 329.
[2] Matthew Paris, *Chronica Majora*, III, p. 503.

without whom no action was to be taken by the abbot; or even of withdrawing the temporal affairs altogether from the abbot's hands, and forbidding him to interfere at all with business matters.

All through this latter period we find the burden laid upon the bishop growing heavier: it was the bishop who had to intervene to depose an abbot guilty of dilapidation or suspend him from his temporal functions: it was the bishop who had to criticise the business management of the monastery, forbidding the abbot to increase or decrease the numbers of his abbey, or farm out its lands, or charge it with pensions or corrodies without the diocesan's leave. From the bishop, or the visitor of the Order, the only effective check could come; and it may be doubted whether this was very effective. The multiplication of duties in the hands of the visitor must to some extent have defeated its own object, both by increasing his burden, and by quickening that jealousy of interference on the part of the secular clergy which made the monasteries prize so dearly the privilege of exemption from episcopal authority. The Calendar of Papal Letters shows that numerous successful attempts were made towards the close of the fourteenth century to shake off the bishop's veto upon the grant of leases. Between 1397 and 1400 indults were granted, which allowed the monastery to lease any of its possessions, or even in some cases to sell them, without the ordinary's licence, to St Mary's, York, to Eynsham, Burscough (for one church only), Butdelle, Elnstowe, Welbeck, Newburgh, and the Order of Sempringham. And for the rest, there is not wanting evidence that the monastic virtue of obedience, and the monastic *esprit de corps* were responsible for an unwillingness to make complaint even in extreme cases of mismanagement. It is to be seen in the struggle already mentioned of the Evesham monks against Abbot Roger Norreys. The outrages of the abbot were temporarily hushed up in order to obtain exemption from the authority of the bishop, and it was only in the very last extremity that the help of the legate was invoked, so that the legate actually charged the monks with collusion with the abbot in his scandalous misdeeds[1]. We find in the episcopal registers warnings to the abbot not to punish any monk for the disclosures

[1] W. D. Macray, *Chronicon Abbatiæ de Evesham*, p. 234.

made in the visitation: cases leak out in which the convent has
been put on oath to tell the same tale: in Benedict XII's reforms
there is even a decree that a monk laying a charge against his
superior is to be punished if he fails to prove it. All these things
tended to diminish the importance of a supervision which,
whether exercised by the bishop or by the visitor of one of the
Orders, at best was intermittent and cursory. Where the abbot
and his monks got at loggerheads there was some likelihood of
the bishop's interference being effective: but in cases where the
quarrel was slight, or where a course of quiet and mutual extravagance was being pursued, the danger of a conspiracy of
silence must have been a real one. In one case at least, the visitor
found out the difficulty. The visitor of the Cluniac houses in
1279 found Wenlock Priory in a thoroughly bad financial condition through the prior's mismanagement. His remarks are
almost despairing[1].

Moreover when the Lord Abbot [of Cluny] was in England, the
Prior affirmed that the debt of his convent amounted to 2200 marks,
although he had then been in office for six years; but when I was in
Berdmondsey he told me the debt was only 800 marks. Coming here,
as I have, during his absence abroad (for he is out of the country),
I have not been able to ascertain the exact truth, either from the
brethren of the house, or from those whom the convent's debt of
500 marks chiefly concerns, and I have quite come to the conclusion
that it is almost impossible to elicit the truth from English monks.

With all its drawbacks, the system of visitation put some check
upon the abbot's autocratic authority over the finances of his
house, and it is the more important as being the only one which
had any real weight behind it. It remains true, none the less,
that it was upon the abbot's business morality, and his business
capacity, that the prosperity of the house ultimately depended.
All this, it must be observed, does not necessarily imply a wholesale condemnation of the monastic system: it may be doubted
whether, as things went then, a better could have been devised.
It had its good side as well as its bad. A blind inertia on the
part of the monks, a selfish conservatism, a pride which was
jealous of interference even in cases of manifest incompetence,
were as great dangers to the well-being of a monastery as

---

[1] Sir G. F. Duckett, *Visitations of the English Cluniac Foundations*, p. 29.

malversation or incapacity on the part of an abbot. If it was by reason of the autocratic power of the abbot that such men as Roger Norreys could go far to ruin their houses, equally it was by reason of the same power that Abbot Samson could end the extravagance of the obedientiaries at Bury St Edmund's, and put a stop to the carousings and feastings which injured alike the morals and the finances of the monastery. The abbot's control, if it had all the vices of a despotism, had also its virtues. But that this power was absolute, for good or evil, is a thing which it is necessary to recognise and to bear constantly in mind.

One more point remains to be considered before leaving the consideration of this system upon which the business of the mediaeval monastery was worked. Dean Kitchin's claim that the religious houses "showed the pattern of an organisation for the conduct of life and business which could hardly have been found elsewhere in mediaeval times" is beyond question true for the earlier part of the Middle Ages. But the case is far from being clear for the later centuries. There is no question here of mismanagement, or disregard of the rules of the establishment: the point at issue is one simply of organisation. It is possible to compare the system of management adopted in the monasteries with that of the household of one of the great noblemen of the early sixteenth century, Henry Percy, fifth Earl of Northumberland: and the comparison is not over-favourable to the religious houses. It suggests that the old predominance had been lost, and that, granting an equality of good intentions, the nobleman's household was managed upon distinctly better business lines, was both easier of supervision and less wasteful of energy.

One of the most striking things about the account-rolls of the great monasteries is the extreme difficulty of generalisation which in many directions shows itself: and this difficulty is of a nature which must have been contemporary. If we wish to discover the amount spent in pittances in any one year, it is in vain to trust to the pittancer's account: even in monasteries where such a special official existed, not only did the pittancer's roll contain much that had nothing to do with pittances, but pittances were to be found, in all probability, scattered about through all the other obedientiaries' accounts. If we want to find the amount spent on clothing, the chamberlain's account alone will not give it us, for the obedientiaries very often clothed themselves and their assistants out of the funds of their own office. It is not usual to find in any one account the amount given to such monks as were studying at the university, or the gifts in food, wine or money which were distributed among the monks, or the amount which the abbot received in one shape or another out of the funds of the monastery. Neither, it may be, was the payment of taxation made from one account; each obedientiary may be found responsible for the taxation of his separate revenues[1]. One illustration of an obedientiary's roll of late date will show the confusion of items which make their appearance. The main duties of the Custos Operum at Winchester centred round the upkeep of the fabric, but he was actually busied with much else. In 1532–3, out of his income of £113. 2s. 6½d., £44. 13s. 6½d. was spent upon building-work; but then there follows a list of "expenses within the convent" amounting to £5. 2s. 11d., and including such items as follows: "Wine for the Prior 5 times, 6s. 8d.," "Wine for the subprior when on the Table of the Mass 1s. 4d.," "Payments to the brethren on the Table of the Mass 13s.," "Wine to the Hosteller, Cellarer and Infirmarer for their feasts 2s. 8d.," "Beer for the Boy Bishop 2d.," "Courtesy to the Prior for knives 13s. 4d.," and so on. There follows a series of "Emptiones Robarum"— payments for cloth for the warden's two garciones and the wages of the man in charge of the conduit; then come the expenses of the marshal's house, and the costs of the office, which include £5. 1s. 7d. spent at the feast of St Katherine: next "foreign payments and expenses," chiefly rents for small pieces of land, but including 10s. for two Oxford scholars: and, finally, £4. 1s. 3½d. paid as the second fifth of a spiritual subsidy. In this way the £44 odd actually spent upon the fabric was swelled to £82. 5s. 1d.

So deeply rooted in the monastic mind was this tendency to treat each obedience as a separate corporation, and to load it with a number of little payments made chiefly to those within

---

[1] At St Albans, however, in the time of Thomas Walsingham, these payments from the obedientiaries for taxation and the maintenance of scholars were made to the treasurer, and would therefore appear together in his account. (J. Amundesham, *Annales S. Albani* (R.S.), ii, p. 207.) But for such actual account rolls as have been printed the statements in the text appear to be correct.

the monastery, that it is to be seen even in cases where a fund was set aside to be applied to some absolutely definite and limited purpose. No better example of this could be given than one which has been pointed out to me in the history of Westminster Abbey[1]. As a consequence of the disastrous fire of 1298 which destroyed the larger part of the building, in 1335 a special fund for building purposes was formed under the charge of a new official, the warden of the new work (*custos novi operis*), whose post was known as the "office of the new work." One of the main pieces of work which this office had to fulfil was the building of the present nave of the church, which was begun in 1376. The nave was not finished until 1528, for interruptions were not infrequent. The result was that this new obedience became an old-established one, and was treated as were the other offices. Accordingly, by the first quarter of the fifteenth century, it was called upon regularly to make payments for various purposes in no way connected with the buildings. Thus we find the custos paying pensions to aged monks, to the succentor (3*s*. 4*d*. a year), and to others: and giving presents to monks when they first celebrate mass or preside in the refectory, to the prior (3*s*. 4*d*. a year from 1461–2 onwards), and sometimes to the abbot. Thus, in 1452–3, "paid for ii grene trees dat'dño abbati ii*s*. viii*d*., also ii dossein sokers i*s*., and iii wodecokkes i*s*." If there was a balance in hand at the annual audit, grants were made in relief of other offices. Thus, contributions were made towards the salaries of the paid singers—"pro cantat' secular'." The debts of past officers might also be paid from the fund. In 1423–4 the auditors allowed 36*s*. 5*d*. to the warden "for his labour," and this became an annual allowance, which, after some variation, was fixed at £2, "pro suo bono et assiduo labore." After 1457 there was also a regular allowance, generally 8*s*. 4*d*., "for a recreation for the abbot (or prior) and auditors at the time of the audit."

All this, it is true, was not usually done in any haphazard way; the custumals of these great monasteries are elaborate in their directions as to the pittances and payments due from the various offices. None the less, it must have detracted largely from the

---

[1] R. B. Rackham, *The Nave of Westminster*, p. 19.

value of the system of book-keeping. The difficulties which to-day the fragmentary state of the accounts makes insuperable, must have been a great obstacle in the path of an abbot seeking for ways in which waste might be checked and economies effected; while as a further augmentation of the difficulty there must be added, if the suggested interpretation of the functions of the bursar be accepted, the lack of any one channel through which passed all the payments and receipts of the house. The overlapping of duties, the muddling together in one account of all sorts of disconnected items, the lack of any one account which would show roughly at any period of the year the gross receipts and expenditure of the whole establishment must have made it a task of singular difficulty for the most willing of abbots to keep track of the business affairs of the house. To the visitor, called on at a moment's notice to see how things were going, anything beyond a general suggestion that stricter economy should be observed must have been almost impossible.

These difficulties were really felt. The interest shown by the visitors in the establishment of bursaries, especially in those few cases where they insisted that the obedientiaries' revenues should also pass through the bursar's hands, was doubtless prompted by the defects of this system of book-keeping. But apart from such attempts to arrange for one central business office, which, as we have shown reason to believe, were not general, the difficulties of obtaining a clear insight into the management of affairs gave rise to other attempts at reform.

Stephen Langton, in the Council of Oxford (1222), ordered that all obedientiaries, as well as the greater prelates (the abbots and priors), should present their accounts four times a year, or twice at least. The higher number seems to have been regarded as over-strict[1]; and the measure probably was not observed, for we find later reformers returning to the charge, with measures, however, less stringent.

The two Innovations or Reformations of the Status of the Black Order [by Gregory IX in 1238 and by Innocent IV in 1253] addressed to the Abbots and Priors in London—a recent writer has pointed out[2]

[1] The reforms of Benedict XII for the Cistercians in 1338, as cited by the Chapter of 1402, also provide for the presentation of accounts four times a year. (Martène-Durand, *Thesaurus*, IV, 1539.)
[2] F. R. Chapman, *Sacrist Rolls of Ely*.

—were motived to a great extent by the consideration that the financial condition of the monasteries was being jeopardised, partly by the practice of borrowing money, but more especially by the faulty system of accounts.

In particular they included attempts to secure the presentation of accounts more frequently. Gregory IX ordered that the obedientiaries were to present accounts, before their superior and some of the older monks, three times a year at least, and that the abbot, or prior not having an abbot over him, should give before the convent or a deputation, a full account of the state of the house, once a year at least. Innocent IV also ordered the obedientiaries' accounts to be presented three times a year, but the abbot was to give account of the state of the house twice a year, on the 1st October, when the year's harvests were in, and on the 1st April. But Matthew Paris records that St Albans protested that once a year, about Michaelmas, was found to be enough for the presentation of accounts[1]: and as by far the greater part of the obedientiaries' rolls which we possess are for the whole year[2], it is exceedingly doubtful whether the reforms of Gregory and Innocent were carried into effect. The obedientiaries and others in charge of the funds of the monasteries seem as a general rule to have been left practically unsupervised from one year's end to another; the annual auditing of accounts was apparently the only check upon them, and, as we have seen, the difficulty of pointing to the ways in which economy might be effected must even then have been very great.

It cannot be claimed, therefore, that this organisation was other than loose, abounding in overlapping offices, and lacking a clear and easily comprehensible system of accounts. In all these points, it would appear, the monastic arrangements were outdone by those of the Earl of Northumberland[3]. Let us take the duties of "my Lordes Coufferer," who also is named "the Generall Receyvour of all my Lands in the North Parties."

[1] *Chronica Majora*, Additamenta, p. 247.
[2] The cellarer and kitchener kept weekly accounts, it would seem: for St Swithun's, Winchester, the kitchener's weekly accounts remain, while at Worcester the cellarer refers to his journal for the details of each week's expenditure. But there is no evidence of any auditing of accounts save once a year, and even this was frequently neglected.
[3] *Northumberland Household Book*, edited by Thomas Percy. The references to the cofferer's duties will be found on pp. 85, 282, 394, 397, 398.

He that shal be apointed Coufferer...to stand charged with all my Lords Receites for the year. The said Coufferer where any particuler Receyvour comes in with any money to any other manour of personne to deliver Money to his handes for my Lordes use. The said Coufferer shall have Leasour at all such tymes to receyve the said Money And to make up his Acquitance And to entier the Receiptie into his Booke And to bring it to my Lorde to signe or he deliver his Acquitance to him or theim that bringis the said Money. Item that the Coufferer shall every Satterday cast up his owne Booke of Receiptie of Money from Michaelmas to that Day and his Delivery together And to bring my Lorde in a Bill what Money remaynes in handes.

What these said "deliveries" were appears from further regulations. From the cofferer the clerk of the "Forin Expenses" received the cash which he administered, and with him he made up his reckonings every Saturday. To the cofferer warrants were issued seven times a year stating the sum which he was to pay to himself, the chief clerke of the kitchen and the Yeoman usher of the chamber "standing charged with my Hous this Yeir." From the coffers were paid the fees and wages which were paid in money, and every week the cofferer had to present an account of his expenses for the week. Here, then, was an account which would show at a glance something like the gross money receipts of the house, and the way in which they were apportioned out for the needs of the household. The rest of the system of supervision is equally careful and elaborate. The clerks of the brevements in the countinghouse "have an Ee and on syght dayly to every Officer in theire Offices." They pass the breves whereby these officers are authorised to receive food and drink for various purposes, they enter in the journal book "all gross Empcions when they are bought: but before such purchase is made my Lord is to be consulted, or his council." The brevements of the "Expens of the Hous" are taken twice a day "becaus the Officers shall not forget for long bering of it in their minds." Monthly the clerks of the brevements see the reckoning between the tanner, the glover, the chandler and the slaughterman who supplies them: they see the breving "of all suche Floure as is Delivert oute of the Bakhous to the Kechynge": they cast up the "Catour Parcellis" to know whether they exceed or fall below the sums assigned to them; they make up "the Pies of all th' expenduntours"; they take the "Remains" and a bill is brought to my Lord to see: they make a bill of the "Deficients of each Office...what Deficient he fallethe in the Mounethe.... With the price and sum" which is also presented to my Lord at the month's end; so also they present a monthly account of the "Clere Expenses of my Lord's Hous." Quarterly accounts also are presented, as also at the half-year and year, showing what are the sums owing in various directions, the sum which still remains of the yearly assignments, the stores in hand, and the balance which thus remains to be paid off.

All this, it will be observed, presents, on the surface, a much more business-like and strict appearance than does the monastic system. The strictness of supervision, the control of the counting-house over all expenditure of money or goods, the frequent accounts, all suggest that the monasteries had been outgone by the great noble. The whole tone of the Northumberland Household Book shows a very strict system of economy; the earl's mind was not above descending to the minute particulars of his household's work. No herbs, he orders, are to be purchased, for they may be obtained from his own gardens; no mustard is to be bought ready-made, but all is to be made within the house. There is even a minute calculation of the relative expenses of several ways of supplying the household with beer. If brewed at home it costs $\frac{3}{4}d.$ a gallon: if brewed at Wresill and carried to Topcliffe it costs $1d.$ a gallon. But if Wresill malt is carried to Topcliffe and brewed, beer is only a little over $\frac{1}{2}d.$ a gallon, or if malt is bought at Topcliffe and brewed there it costs nearly $\frac{7}{8}d.$: while beer bought ready brewed at Ripon costs $2d.$ a gallon. Whenever visitors are with the earl, he is to be presented with a list, that he may be kept acquainted with the extra expense involved thereby: he insists upon full and continual information upon every point. The whole account shows a greater interest, a less intermittent overseeing, on the part of the earl than can be traced anywhere in the monastic records. But the system of working seems of itself to be better. The task of conducting this great household can have been no less difficult than that of managing a religious community; the external matters which claimed the earl's attention must have been as multifarious and important as those which fell to the lot of any great abbot. Both methods of government, it may be said, were despotisms;

but the machinery whereby the secular despot was kept informed seems, to my mind, incontestably superior to that upon which his spiritual peer was dependent[1].

[1] The advantage of the Northumberland Household system was doubtless not so great over that of such a house as Eynsham where the cellarer's account covered practically all expenditure and receipts, or over the system prescribed by Peckham for Reading and Glastonbury. But, speaking generally, the statements made seem to be amply justified.

CHAPTER III

THE MONASTIC REVENUES

IT is unfortunate that at no point in the period under consideration is there any general survey of the possessions of
the English monasteries such as is provided for the period of
the Dissolution by the *Valor Ecclesiasticus* on which Professor
Savine has based his elaborate study of the economic condition
of the religious houses in the first half of the sixteenth century.
The valuation of the possessions of the French Benedictine
houses ordered by Benedict XII and taken in 1338, the results
of which have recently been published in the case of three
monasteries, seems to have had no English parallel[1]. One document alone is available which at first sight seems to give an
account at least of the sum total of the monastic revenues, if
not of the details. This is the Taxation of Pope Nicholas—a
valuation resulting from a crusading vow taken by Edward I in
1288, in consideration of which Nicholas IV granted him a tenth
of the revenues of the Church for six years, according to a
"verus valor." The document is important, if only because it
formed the basis on which the possessions held by the clergy in
1291 were taxed until the time of the Reformation. At first sight
it seems to offer a complete statement of the revenues of such
monasteries as were within its scope. The bull giving instructions as to the valuation seems extensive enough; practically all
ecclesiastical property comes under it, except the revenues of
such "nuns and other regulars" as had to beg their sustenance,
the Hospitallers and the Templars. Some few exceptions would
affect the monasteries, notably those of pittance-money, legacies
especially granted to purchase rents, as well as alms and oblations,

---

[1] It seems very likely that the order was given for such a valuation, but
that the time was unpropitious and the royal veto prevented the execution
of the command. Such at least was the case in the Augustinian Order. The
Rev. H. E. Salter informs me that Wood MS. 2.21, fol. 23 (Bodleian Library)
contains a royal prohibition dated the 8th March, 14 Edward III, addressed
to the Abbot of Thornton and the Prior of Kirkham forbidding them to make
such a valuation of the Augustinian houses of England as Pope Benedict had
ordered (*ibid.* fol. 173), on the ground that he will not have the secrets of his
kingdom revealed.

salaries paid to judges and officials in the manorial courts, and the expenses on the land in ploughing, reaping, and harvesting the crops[1]. These terms point to the conclusion that the taxation ought to be a sufficiently near approximation to the net ecclesiastical income. Miss Rose Graham[2], however, has shown that despite the term "verus valor" this was not the case, and that "it is clearly misleading to represent the assessment of the temporalities of a religious house as its income, either gross or net from that source." She shows that the ecclesiastical revenues "do not correspond even approximately to the assessment," that the receipts in 1293 from a number of churches appropriated to the monastery of Durham "were much higher than the assessment although the receipts represented a net income, and no provision for a vicar or parochial chaplain had to be deducted from them," and that in a number of other cases the actual value of appropriated churches to the monastery holding them was considerably greater than the assessment: that (in the printed text at all events) many appropriations are not specified: that the considerable revenues derived by many houses from the sale of wool are not assessed in the taxation, and that "the text of the taxation affords no safe clue to the division of property between the abbot, convent and obedientiars of the Benedictine houses." Her conclusion as to the method of valuation adopted is that in the case of benefices, manors and granges, alike, the "verus valor," like the "valet" of Domesday, was based on the rental at which the property could be farmed out. The following additional facts confirm Miss Graham's conclusions as to the worthlessness of the Taxation as a record of actual income. The total value of the possessions of Tickford Priory in Bucks., according to the Taxation, was £39. 16s. 7¾d., or £28. 5s. spiritualities plus £11. 11s. 7¾d. temporalities. But on the one hand, Dugdale gives an extent of "the manor of Tickford" (which, however, includes other manors) taken in 1294 when the house, as an alien priory, was taken into the hands of the King. In this, the appropriated church of Aston, which accounts for most of the spiritualities in the taxation, makes no appear-

---

[1] Rymer, *Foedera* (ed. 1705), II, p. 475: Bartholomew Cotton, pp. 191-8.
[2] *English Historical Review*, 1908, pp. 434-54.

ance whatever. On the other hand, tithes to the extent of £78. 18s. are recorded which are ignored by the Taxation, and the total income is £141. 15s. 2¾d.—a striking difference from the "verus valor" of the papal valuation. Again, it is quite impossible that the Taxation can be correct in the case of Careswell in Devon. It represents the total income of the house at £6. 2s. 8d. But from the reports of the Cluniac visitors of 1279[1] we learn that the prior of this house, besides supporting four monks, had in three years paid off a debt of £40: a feat beyond the ablest financier's skill with only £6 at command. The taxation, then, gives no trustworthy basis for a calculation of the monastic revenues, and for this purpose must be set aside[2]. It is therefore impossible here to make any general statement as to the amount of the income enjoyed by the English religious houses in England, or to enter into generalisations such as Professor Savine gives, as to the proportions in which it was derived from various sources. All that this chapter can do is to call attention to the diversity of these sources, the number of ways in which the ascetic renunciation of the world was inevitably broken down by the possessions which the world's favour heaped upon those who had turned their backs upon it, and the manner in which the monks were brought on many sides into direct contact with the world without. Even here it will be impossible to touch upon more than a few points; the accounts reveal such a variety of ways in which income arose as is almost beyond description. This chapter then merely purports to give some idea of the general types of possessions from which the wealth of the religious houses was drawn: questions as to the methods by which that wealth was acquired or expanded will be better reserved for consideration in connection with the general questions of the capability of the monastic management, and the extent of monastic debt.

The first distinction which must be noticed is the familiar

---

[1] Duckett, *Visitations of the English Cluniac Foundations*, p. 26.

[2] Professor Tout, moreover, has pointed out that a comparison of the "nova taxatio" necessitated in 1318 by the ravages of the Scottish war, as printed for the Diocese of Carlisle, with the same document as given in the Register of Bishop John de Halton "convinces one of the unwisdom of taking the printed figures as authoritative." *Register of John de Halton, Bishop of Carlisle* (Canterbury and York Society), Introduction, p. vii.

one between spiritualities and temporalities. The spiritual income was that drawn from the tithes granted to the monastery, from the appropriated churches, the oblations at shrines and on the altar of the monastic church itself. Revenue of every other kind comes under the heading of temporalities. It will be well to deal with the two classes separately, beginning with the spiritualities.

The most interesting and important components of this class are the tithes and the income derived from churches. The offerings at shrines were very often appreciable, although apt to vary: thus, as Canon Fowler points out, the feretrar's rolls at Durham show us the waning popularity of a local saint, John Warton, the offerings to whom declined from £5. 14s. 9½d. in 1456 to 16s. 6½d. in 1461 and from 1513 to 1534 varied only between 8d. and 15d. The value of these offerings goes far to explain the eagerness shown to acquire relics, the elaborate care taken of them, and the appearance of the distinctly mercenary considerations which show themselves in such an account as that of the wonder-working crucifix at Meaux, carved from the nude model, of which the chronicler relates that despite the number of pilgrims, the gains were not sufficient to cover the expense to which the monastery was put. But these offerings formed an element in the monastic budget which varied greatly. Some monasteries had well-known relics and were popular places of pilgrimage; others had few or no such attractions; and even in houses with celebrated saints or shrines the relative importance of the offerings ranged between extreme limits. The feretrar's rolls at Durham with its great shrine of St Cuthbert show an average income which drops from about £39 in the later fourteenth century to about £26 in the later fifteenth. The importance of this must have been little to a monastery where the bursar's roll alone for 1370–1 shows an income of £1736. 14s. 7⅜d., or, including the arrears, £2652. 13s. 8⅜d., and in 1435 of £3071. 9s. 10½d., while other obedientiaries had considerable, although smaller, endowments. On the other hand, these offerings must have been of the utmost importance to such a house as the Norman Abbey of Mont-Saint-Michel, where in 1338 out of a total income, including the obedientiaries' endowments, of £6789. 16s. tournois, no less than £1100 tournois were given as offerings by pilgrims[1]. At Canterbury the international fame of the shrine of St Thomas made the offerings of pilgrims an element of the greatest value in the monastery's finances. In 1220 the translation of the relics from the crypt to the new shrine, which drew together many royal and noble pilgrims and hosts of lesser rank, almost doubled the income which passed through the treasurers' hands. For the next six years the average income remained almost at this new level, and the improvement remained permanent, if not constant. Only once or twice in nearly 200 years did the income of the treasurers fall as low as before the translation[2].

The offerings of the pious were precarious and variable. But tithe or the income from churches was an important item in every monastic budget. Bishop Frere[3] has pointed out that the appearance of the spiritualities as separate items in the charters of the benefactors to English monasteries dates only from the time of the Confessor, and was then due to Continental influence: that while previous to this date "the gift of a vill may include the church, in the foundations of the last thirty years of the eleventh century the church was becoming a separate or separable property." The same writer has explained what was meant by "church" and "tithe" and what was the effect produced when these sources of wealth were handed over to the monasteries. In the case of tithe, "it is necessary to banish from the latter term the thought of a payment due to an incumbent of a parish; and to recover for it the wider meaning, viz. that proportion of a man's incomings which he was bound to set aside for religious and charitable objects." Tithe, therefore, was not due altogether to the Church, and it did not cover the whole of a man's payments for ecclesiastical and charitable purposes.

For (1) tithe was held to be due partly to the Church, partly to the bishop, and partly to the poor; and at various times, various divisions of tithe among these and other objects were prescribed. Also (2) the landowner had other dues to pay which varied with place and

---

[1] L. Delisle, *La Fortune de l'Ordre de St-Benoît*, p. 18.

[2] J. B. Sheppard, *Literae Cantuarienses* (R.S.), II, p. xlvi *et seq*. The receipts of the treasurers in 1219 amounted to £1527, and in 1220 to £2707.

[3] *Fasciculus J. W. Clark dicatus*. The following two pages summarise Bishop Frere's conclusions.

time—such as a Rome-scot or Peter's Pence, which went to Rome; a church-scot, which was probably, in some cases at any rate, one of the contributions due to the bishop; or local dues that went to the priest, either in payment for services done, such as fees for burial, or for his general support, like Easter dues.

The result of this was that the Church had an income attached to it apart from such proportion of the tithes as local custom allotted to it: but tithe as such was not of necessity appropriated to the maintenance of the incumbent. Hence it follows, Bishop Frere points out, that the transference of tithe to the monasteries was an obvious way of applying the portion of income allotted to charitable purposes.

It was natural for the tithe-holder to allocate what was in his hands to the religious orders who undertook voluntary poverty. He did so to a very large extent in this [the eleventh] and the following centuries: and in thus allocating such "tithe" he was not, as is often supposed, taking away the pay of the parish priest to give it to the monks or canons, but he was giving the portion of the poor to those who had come to poverty voluntarily under a vow rather than to those who came to it involuntarily.

The case was different, Bishop Frere goes on to show, when not the "tithe" but the "church" was handed over to a monastery. Then the payments due to the parish priest actually fell into the hands of the monks, and the monastery thereby became responsible for the maintenance of the church and its services. The regular canons were at liberty to serve the church themselves, and in many cases did so: and the same system, although discountenanced, was adopted in some cases by the monks of other Orders. But from the beginning (as when a church was given to a nunnery) there must have been cases of "appropriation" in which the evils showed themselves which became so pronounced at a later date; in which "the priest and church were sweated for the benefit of the middleman in the shape of the corporation." It is necessary to distinguish carefully this appropriation of churches from another right which the monasteries frequently enjoyed, that of presentation to a benefice. In the latter case, the advowson alone was the property of the monks; in the former, the whole endowment of the benefice, whether in land, tithe or such other sources of revenue as oblations, church-scot or Easter offerings, became the actual property of the monastery, which thus became bound to provide for the religious needs of the parish by instituting as vicar either one of their own monks or a secular priest.

The possession of an advowson, it is hardly needful to remark, ought not of itself to have implied any direct pecuniary advantage to those in whose hands lay the right of presentation. Nevertheless a traffic in patronage showed itself in which various monasteries were implicated. In 1285 Archbishop Peckham found it necessary to speak his mind to the Abbot of Cluny about the management of the Priory of Lewes and the men who ought to be put at its head[1]. One special need, he said, was that they should have a zeal for men's souls, and should

take care to present to the cure of souls men who by example and word may show themselves shepherds, not robbers. We have passed the flower of youth, and already are attaining to old age, and on careful retrospection, we can hardly remember that, to the present day, we ever saw a man presented by the Prior and College of Lewes to the cure of souls in the sincerity which is needful[1].

To take another case, much later, the frequent shiftings of the holders of the livings belonging to the great Abbey of St Albans in the time of Abbots Albon and Wallingford (1465–88), have, as the editor of the Register of these abbots pointed out, anything but a satisfactory look[2]. An example or two will suffice. Six vicars of Abbot's Langley resigned in nineteen years: there were eight presentations to the rectory of Brantfelde, three, however, caused by death, in twenty-three years. At Idelestre, apparently, nine rectors were presented in sixteen years, and to the vicarage of Shephall, near Stevenage, there were five presentations in six years. In the cases both of Lewes and of St Albans it is just possible that no considerations in any form were received; but that the appointments were uninfluenced by worldly considerations of some kind it is difficult to believe.

It is interesting to notice, also, that the possession of an advowson was very frequently a step towards complete appropriation—possibly with one or two intervening stages. One of these stages seems to have been the institution of a pension, or

---

[1] C. T. Martin, *Registrum Epistolarum Fratris Johannis Peckham* (R.S.), III, p. 902 *et seq.*
[2] *Registrum Abbatiae Johannis Whethamstede* (R.S.), II, p. xxxii.

annual payment. A pension, it is noticeable, might also be due from the vicar of an appropriated church. Thus there is a document of the Priory of St Neot recording the confirmation, by John, Bishop of Norwich, of the grant of the church of Bevelingham with all its appurtenances, given by Walter Fitzrobert, and a pension of 20s. from the same church for ever: also the church of Birtona Binnedic and a pension of 40s. from it[1]. A pension of this type was probably the result of a composition made with the vicar over some of the possessions of the church left in his hands. But the pension as a rule seems to be due from a rector, and represents a step towards appropriation. Thus in 1327 the rector of Eyton was under an obligation to pay to the nuns of Pollesworth two-thirds of the income of the church by way of a pension[2]. In 1227 we have a case in which the final step is taken: in that year an indult of Gregory IX allowed the Abbot and Convent of Bardney to appropriate the churches of Hale and Hekynton, which were of their patronage and from which they received pensions[3].

The second possible stage was a temporary appropriation of the revenues of the church for a limited period only. Thus, in 1219, Innocent III granted to the monks of Glastonbury an indult to retain for their own use during six years for hospitality and alms all the churches of their advowson falling void, on condition that they appointed fresh vicars: the reason being the loss they had sustained by the composition between them and the Bishop of Bath on the dissolution of the union between the two houses[4]. When the church of Glastonbury was destroyed by fire, the monastery obtained, in 1255, a similar papal licence to transfer to the building fund the proceeds of the benefices of its patronage for one year after their voidance[5]. Instances of this kind, however, seem rare: no other examples are to be found in the *Calendar of Papal Letters*, and it is possible that these two are quite exceptional. As a general rule, the appropriations seem to have been made at one blow, and not by slow stages.

The practice whereby one of the members of the monastery was placed in charge of an appropriated church, it is possible,

---

[1] Dugdale, *Monasticon*, III, p. 476.
[2] *Calendar of Papal Letters*, II, p. 271.   [3] *Ibid.* I, p. 119.
[4] *Ibid.* I, p. 67.   [5] *Ibid.* I, p. 324.

was originally contemplated by those bestowing these churches, and may originally have been of benefit, especially in the case of houses of regular canons. It is worthy of note, however, that even regular canons by no means served in person all the churches appropriated to them, but as early as the beginning of the twelfth century were appointing secular vicars[1]. In other Orders, work of this kind seems to have been discouraged from a very early date, possibly as tending to break down the strictness of monastic seclusion, in accordance with the same spirit which prompted the Lateran Council of 1179 to prohibit the placing of one monk by himself in charge of a parish. But in the late fourteenth century, when the practice was revived, probably on account of the advanced incomes demanded by secular priests after the Black Death, the interference of Parliament was based upon other grounds which show that the system was held to work badly as regards the interests of the parishioners.

The *Calendar of Papal Letters* shows that, side by side with many new appropriations at the close of the fourteenth century which involved the establishment of a vicarate, other arrangements were made which permitted the religious to serve the church themselves, or to revert to the long-condemned system of instituting a secular priest removable at pleasure. In some of these cases churches were appropriated which had not been touched before; in others the monastery was allowed to suppress an established vicarate and transfer the vicar's stipend to its own funds. Thus, in 1397, Thornton Abbey, an Augustinian house, was allowed to suppress the anciently endowed perpetual vicarate of the parish church of Thornton appropriated to it, and to serve it by one of the canons or a fit secular priest[2]. This was a house of regular canons and the church must have been hard by: other cases are more remarkable. In the same year, for example, the Cluniac monks of Prittlewell[3] were allowed to appropriate the parish churches of "Ertwode and Northscobi," and to serve them in person: in the same year also the Cistercian Abbey of Pipewell was allowed to take the same course[4]. It is

---

[1] Merton Priory, founded in 1171, had six churches served by vicars, by 1198 at latest. A. Heales, *Records of Merton Priory*, pp. 39–40.
[2] *Calendar of Papal Letters*, v, p. 74.
[3] *Ibid.* v, p. 76.   [4] *Ibid.* v, p. 77.

impossible not to connect these and similar cases with the steps taken by the Parliament of 1403, which attempted to check the practice by ordering that in every appropriated church a perpetual secular vicar should be appointed, and that no monk should be made vicar in any churches so appropriated or to be appropriated[1]. No penalty was attached to a breach of the Act, and it remained a dead-letter. One reason for the objection to having a religious as vicar was perhaps, as Dr Whitaker states[2], that the monk instituted, being still bound by his vow of poverty, could not even accept the salary (often meagre enough) assigned as the vicar's portion, and that therefore the parish suffered from a diminution of the alms distributed there. But other reasons appear in a further attempt on the part of Parliament to end the system. In the Parliament of 1432[3] a petition was presented which, if it may be believed, shows that the monasteries failed to fulfil the work in the parishes which they had taken upon themselves. "Old men and women," it was said, "have died without confession or any of the sacraments of the Church," and "children have died unbaptized" because vicarages were left void for several years for the sake of gain. The remedy proposed was that every monastery leaving a church without a secular vicar for six months should lose the appropriation and retain only the advowson or right of presentation. The royal assent, however, was refused.

The difficulties involved in appropriation were great, and its disadvantages were recognised from an early date. Difficulties were found both in insisting that a vicar should actually be maintained and that his stipend should be adequate. Church legislation concerns itself with these points in a way which shows how stubbornly abuses persisted. The first steps taken were in the direction of the establishment of episcopal control. The appropriated churches, to all appearance, were originally bestowed simply by the patron of the living; but as appropriations became more and more common, councils both national and oecumenical took the matter up. As early as 1102, the Council of London[4] decreed that the sanction of the bishop was necessary for an appropriation to take effect, and that the monastery was not to

---

[1] *Rot. Parl.* 4 Henry IV.   [2] *History of Whalley*, I, p. 208.
[3] *Rot. Parl.* 10 Henry VI.   [4] Wilkins, *Concilia*, I, p. 383.

impoverish the priest serving there by taking too large a share of the profits of the church. The Lateran Council of 1179 also ordained that the bishop's consent must be obtained, but went still further in the regularisation of the system by ordering the bishops to appoint fixed stipends for the vicars, who were, moreover, to be perpetual and not removable at the will of the monastery[1]. The result of this decree is seen in the activities of such men as Hugh de Wells, Bishop of Lincoln, who, between 1209 and 1235, instituted no less than 174 vicarages in his diocese, only 200 in all being recorded some forty years later in the Taxation of Pope Nicholas[2]. The average income of the vicar in this diocese was fixed at about one-third of the total income of the church, and usually consisted of the small tithes (those on other produce than corn) and the offerings on the altar of the church, together with a house: and this seems to have been the most common division of the profits.

This step in advance was by no means conclusive: difficulties persisted more or less. The Council of Oxford (1222)[3] attempted to deal with the actual amount of the vicar's stipend. It insisted that a perpetual vicar should have revenues allotted to him which could be put at farm for at least five marks, except in those parts of Wales where on account of the poverty of the churches the vicar was content with less; and it further added that the diocesan was to decide whether the vicar was to bear the ordinary burdens of the church, viz. the bishop's visitation fees, the archdeacon's promotion, the synodals and so on. The decree is interesting as affording an example of the favourite mediaeval method of valuation—the rent which a fermarius would pay; but it is important also as requiring a definite settlement of the respective obligations of the vicar and the appropriators, and, still more, as fixing for the first time the vicar's stipend at a minimum, irrespective of the value of the church.

In 1261 there was issued to the Bishops of Worcester, Lincoln, Salisbury, Coventry and Llandaff, a papal mandate[4] which must be added to this lengthening list of steps directed against what has been represented as merely an academic grievance. It makes

[1] Labbe, *Sacrosancta Concilia*, x, 1514.
[2] So the *Victoria County History of Lincoln*, Vol. ii.
[3] Wilkins, *Concilia*, i, p. 587.
[4] *Calendar of Papal Letters*, i, p. 375.

mention of reports as to the cupidity of the religious in getting churches appropriated, to the extinction in such churches of divine worship, the loss of episcopal rights and the closing of the doors of promotion against poor and proficient clerics. The religious in some cases boast that they have bought such churches. The Pope has instructed the said bishops to make inquiry, which has resulted in the confession of simony. To remedy this, he has ordered an examination to be made into the motives for such appropriations, whether they were obtained under pretext of poverty; and also an inquiry as to what benefices have been annexed to the use of the bishops or secular chapters, whether sufficient vicarages have been instituted, and how many of the appropriated churches are served by the monks themselves. The division of the proceeds of churches distant four or five miles from the monasteries to which they are appropriated is to be regulated, an eighth or a tenth part being set aside for poor parishioners—a provision which lends its support to the complaint that hospitality or alms was diminished by appropriation.

Seven years later the legate Ottobon, in his constitutions promulgated in the Council of London (1268), said his say against the evils of the system[1]. He insisted that vicars must be resident. He emphasised the doctrine of the Canon Law, that appropriations were not to be made unless the appropriator was manifestly pressed by poverty, or unless other legitimate causes existed, so that the appropriation might be considered consonant with piety. He asserted that some, in their greed to obtain the whole revenue of an appropriated church, left it void of a vicar, or that, if a vicar was instituted, so small a portion was allowed him that it was not enough to support him and bear the burdens due to archdeacons and others; so that "quod in elemosynam est provisum, in sitim avaritiae confluat et transeat in rapinam." He therefore ordered that all monks, exempt from episcopal authority or not exempt, Cistercians as well as others, who had churches where there was no vicar, must present one within six months. Yet another ordinance dealing with the amount of the vicarate is to be found passed in a synod for the Diocese of Exeter held by Bishop Peter Quivil, in 1287[2]. This orders that in the case of churches of a true value of 40 marks, the vicar's

---

[1] Wilkins, *Concilia*, II, p. 1 *et seq.*   [2] *Ibid.* II, p. 147.

portion is to be five marks (a sufficiently low proportion) and that as the value of the church rises, the vicar's stipend is to increase proportionately.

Even while Parliament was restricting the salaries which might be claimed by secular priests[1], scarce after the Black Death and therefore raising their demands, it found it necessary, also, to step in to prevent undue diminution of the vicarates by the monasteries, and a withdrawal of the charities connected with the church. The Parliament of 15 Richard II provided that, because of the damages and hindrances to which the parishioners were subjected through these appropriations, in every licence thenceforward made in the Chancery for an appropriation a clause was to be inserted to the effect that the diocesan should ordain a convenient sum to be paid to the poor, and that the vicarate should be well and sufficiently endowed. This provision was confirmed by the Parliament of 1403 in the statute already mentioned. Yet, despite all these provisions, complaints continued of the ill consequences of appropriations. Thus, in 1391, the Priory of Lewes obtained an appropriation of four churches and a chapel; by 1426 the parishioners were complaining that since the appropriation took effect, the church buildings had fallen into ruin, divine service and parochial administrations had been neglected, and the hospitality shown to the poor by the former rectors had been withdrawn[2].

So far only those consequences have been taken into consideration which arose from the starving of the vicars. Some appreciation of what else the system, even if decently worked, often meant to the parishioners, will best be gained by an examination of the customary arrangements at Pershore, as shown in a document of 1288, the record of an inquiry into the privileges of the house after its charters had been destroyed by a fire[3]. From this it appears that the bodies of all the deceased for a large distance round Pershore, in the parishes whose churches

---

[1] 36 Edw. III, 1. c. 8, ordered that no parish priest or yearly priest should take over six marks a year: 2 Henry V fixed the payments at seven marks for a yearly chaplain, and eight or possibly nine marks by leave of the ordinary, for a parish vicar.

[2] *Calendar of Papal Letters*, VII, pp. 445-6.

[3] Dugdale, *Monasticon*, II, p. 419.

were appropriated and thus degraded to the rank of chapels to the monastic church, had to be brought, together with the "principale legatum" or best belonging of the dead person (in theory a payment for arrears of tithe), to the convent church. There the mortuary was valued by the sacristan and the chaplain of the appropriated church, half its value going to the one, and half to the other. The body then was carried to the chapel or appropriated church, where Mass was said for the soul of the departed, the oblations going to the chaplain: after which the body was buried either in the churchyard of Pershore or the cemetery of Parva Cumbrinton according to the dwelling-place of the deceased.

The galling nature of such restrictions as these upon the right of burial, and similar limitations as to baptism and the rest of the sacraments, arising from the close subjection of appropriated churches to the monastery when it was near at hand, is evidenced by the fact that instances actually occur of riots aiming at their removal. At Sherborne the "monks and the tounes menne felle at variaunce bycause the tounes men tooke privilege to use the sacrament of baptisme in the chapelle of Allhalows": riots ensued, and a priest of Allhalows shot an arrow with fire into the thatch upon part of the conventual church, setting it on fire and doing much damage[1]. The monasteries, there seems but little doubt, were stringent in exacting the rights which thus fell to them. Two striking examples occur in the history of King's Lynn[2]. Here the authority of the mother-church, St Margaret's, was strictly maintained by the Prior of Lynn. To this was subjected the Chapel of St Nicholas. Originally granted to the monastery of Norwich but apparently partly independent, it was restored at some date before 1200 to St Margaret's of Lynn, and to that church were granted all its oblations and obventions. The people chafed at this subjection, and about the end of 1378 incited their chaplain, John Peye, to obtain secretly from Urban VI a bull authorising the celebration of the sacraments of baptism and marriage, and the churching of women. These rights were strongly opposed as needless and prejudicial to the mother-church, and 76 burgesses were found

[1] Dugdale, *Monasticon*, I, p. 335.
[2] Both narrated at length in Beloe, *Our Borough, Our Churches*.

who declared that they did not require and freely renounced the privileges thus obtained. None the less, the chaplain stood his ground, and the bishop had to intervene to decide the dispute, referring it for decision to the Prior of Pentney. The prior decided downright against the privileges obtained, as the chapel was only three furlongs (*stadia*) from St Margaret's, and there was no difficulty or scandal or danger in going to the parish church. In 1432, some forty-five years after this attempt at securing the right of these sacraments, a second attempt was made, this time by petition to the prior, and backed by the "Mayor, Aldermen, Burgesses and Community." The request was fruitless, and no font appeared in St Nicholas for two centuries.

The other interference of this kind, less remarkable in itself, which took place at King's Lynn, had occurred in 1234. The Hospital of St John the Baptist had attached to it a chapel for the use of the master and brethren of the confraternity, and, it appears, the chaplain of the hospital began to say Mass there and to administer the sacraments to the neighbouring parishioners. The Prior of Lynn promptly intervened to check this encroachment upon the privileges of St Margaret's. The dispute was referred for decision to the Priors of Bury St Edmund's and Thetford and the Sacrist of Bury. Their decision was totally adverse to the hospital. The chaplain was to celebrate Mass only once a day and then in a low voice, and no one else was to celebrate save the Prior of Lynn or his deputy. All oblations of whatever kind were to be restored to the Church of St Margaret, the brothers and sisters dying in the hospital were to buried in St Margaret's, the chaplain was not to hear confessions or grant absolution to penitents, and the Prior of Lynn was to visit the hospital once a year.

One more instance may be quoted of this enforcement of rights, interesting as giving an insight into the burial dues in at least one district. In 1396 the monastery of Abingdon obtained a papal interference in their defence. They presented a petition setting forth that of ancient custom, on the death of the parishioners of the parish church, called a chapel of St Helen, incorporated to them, and on the burial of these parishioners in the cemetery of the monastic church, they had the right of taking and exacting legacies and bequests made to them (on account of burial), and for each body a candle and a farthing, with all oblations and other emoluments arising from obits and anniversaries. The perpetual vicar and the parishioners tried to get a burial-ground consecrated near the parish church, and to take the said legacies and oblations. A long struggle ensued, both parties appealing to the Pope. Meanwhile 60 persons were buried in the new cemetery. The Papal Chaplain, to whom the appeal was committed, annulled the consecration, ordered the exhumation of the bodies buried, and sentenced the vicar to make restitution and, with the parishioners, to pay the costs. Two further appeals failed, save that for some reason not given two bodies were allowed to remain in the new cemetery: and, in the end, the vicar and the parishioners were to pay costs of 60 and 40 gold florins respectively. The florin being in 1333 reckoned at 3s. 2d., the monastery's costs thus came to £15. 16s. 8d., or something like £235 in pre-war money, while as the vicar and parishioners would also have to pay their own expenses, their struggle for emancipation must have been a costly one[1].

One of the most difficult questions connected with these burial-dues is that of the extent to which mortuaries were taken, and how far they went to the monastery in the case of churches in monastic hands. The system varied from district to district, being of customary origin. The *Calendar of Papal Letters* contains a document which goes to prove that in some districts the right to mortuary was pushed even to extortion. In 1248 a mandate was issued to the Archdeacon of Canterbury[2] to decide the cause set forth by Peter of Savoy for himself and his archdeaconry of Richmond, "in regard to certain prelates, rectors, vicars and perpetual chaplains who on the decease of their men take not only, as is customary in England, one of the best of their cattle, but also the next best, and sometimes a ninth, a sixth, or in a certain case a third of their personal property." Kennett, in his *Parochial Antiquities*[3], says that in the case of appropriations it was common for the religious to reserve for themselves the live heriot, or mortuary, and to allow the inanimate

---

[1] *Calendar of Papal Letters*, v, p. 5.   [2] *Ibid.* I, p. 252.
[3] II, Glossary, *s.v.* Herietum, Legatum.

heriot to the vicar: he cites in support of his statement the endowment of the vicarage of Oakle by the Priory of St Frideswide. As a further instance of the practice of exacting two mortuaries, he quotes the case of all churches appropriated to the Abbey of Oseney, in which the perpetual vicars by endowment were to have every second mortuary if to the value of 6*d*., and one-half of it beyond that value. A similar practice prevailed at Burcester. On the other hand, the account-rolls of Durham, by far the most complete set of monastic accounts yet issued, show singularly scanty traces of the reception of mortuaries by the monastery, although the appropriated churches were not a few. The almoner's roll of 1374 records the receipt of 20*s*., the mortuary of Robert de Graystans dying in the infirmary. In 1515–16 the same office received 20*d*. for a tunic, the mortuary of a stranger on the holding of Robert Johnson in the parish of the Blessed Mary Magdalene, together with 1*d*. as an oblation at his burial, and in 1518–19 the almoner records the receipt of a gown, the mortuary of William Borell, hermit of St Mary Magdalene, also with 1*d*. as oblation on burial. In 1378–9 the bursar gave 12*d*. to two men for driving bulls, cows and horses, "de mortuar' parochie de Norham." To the same account, in 1400–1, came 106*s*. 8*d*., the price of the arms and saddle of Lord Thomas Gray, the almost incredible sum of £26. 13*s*. 4*d*. for his horse, and 40*s*. for the helmet and corselet of William Urde; in all cases as mortuaries. One other unimportant case completes the list of mortuaries in a series of accounts ranging from 1278 to 1536. It is possible, however, that the abbreviation of many of the accounts for purposes of publication has excluded other mentions of dues of this kind. In 1383, at least, they were considered worth the expense of a law-suit, for the hostillar spent £7. 10*s*. 9*d*. "in causa tangente mortuaria viva contra Johannem Legg et communitatem parochie ecclesie sancti Oswaldi."[1]

The apportionment of the shares of the vicar and rectors in the burdens which the church had to bear, synodals, procurations, building expenses and so on was left, as has been seen, to

---

[1] The probability seems to be that the mortuaries were as a rule left to the vicar as part of his portion: such at least was the case in most of the taxations of vicarages recorded in the Exeter Registers.

the bishop who allowed the appropriation. It is necessary to observe, however, that so far as the maintenance of the fabric was concerned the parishioners bore a large part of the cost, from which duty appropriations afforded no relief. The synodal statute (1250) of Walter Gray[1], Archbishop of York, regulating these matters was followed by the Southern Province under Winchelsea, and was accepted by the Papal Curia as "the laudable custom of the realm of England" when enforcing it in 1397 in the case of St Olave's without the Walls, a York church appropriated to St Mary's Abbey[2]. By this statute, the parishioners were bound to provide all vestments and vessels, to light the church, to keep in repair the books, the nave and the bell-tower both inside and out, the glass windows, the close of the cemetery and other such things. The rector or vicar was bound to keep the chancel in repair, its roof, windows and ornaments included. In very many cases, however, the vicar or the convent was bound to provide and repair the books and vessels, as is shown both by the parochial visitation records and the institution of vicarates. But in some of the chapels dependent upon an appropriated church, the parishioners' share of the expenses was very much more. Thus, in 1333, when the Bishop of Lichfield visited the Chapel of Chirche, dependent upon the appropriated church of Whalley, the chancel was found so badly roofed that when it rained Mass could not be celebrated; moreover, there was no cleric attached to the chapel. An inquiry showed, however, that the burden of repairing the chancel here fell from time immemorial upon the parishioners, and that it was the duty of the parishioners also to provide a cleric. If any contribution towards meeting this latter expense was due, it was due not from the appropriating convent but from the vicar of the appropriated mother-church[3]. Nor can it be claimed that the monasteries were particularly zealous in performing the duties which were actually allotted to them. Parochial visitations show a record of ruinous buildings, tattered books and damaged vessels sufficiently discreditable to warrant the assertion that no benefit in the direction of improved maintenance accrued as the result of appropriations.

[1] Wilkins, *Concilia*, III, p. 676.   [2] *Calendar of Papal Letters*, v, p. 8.
[3] W. A. Hutton, *Coucher Book of Whalley Abbey*, I, p. 237.

On the whole, the system of appropriation seems but bad at the best and intolerable at the worst: it was very certainly an actually recognised evil, and no mere invention of modern times. The plea has been put forward as at least a palliation of the degree of responsibility which the monasteries must bear on this account, that the bishops were equally ready to admit appropriations by colleges and hospitals[1]. If the implication is intended that the spoils were shared in something like equal proportions between the monasteries and such institutions, it must be denied. Apart from the fact that the first appropriators, and that on a large scale, were the religious houses, an inspection of the documents shows that, to a very late date in the Middle Ages, the lion's share was still in their hands. In fact, if any body of men can be bracketed with the monasteries as profiting by appropriation, it is the bishops themselves and the cathedral chapters. Large numbers of churches were actually taken over by these bodies. In other appropriations, they were compensated for the consequent loss of fees by clauses requiring the annual payment of a pension either to the bishop or the cathedral chapter. Thus in the diocese of Exeter, the "taxations" of vicarages in the time of Bishop Stapeldon (1307–26) show that pensions were due to the dean and chapter from two out of the 14 churches which there appear as newly appropriated to the religious: or to take another diocese (Lichfield, under Bishop Norbury, 1322–58)[2] two such cases are noticed out of 15 "ordinationes" of vicarages.

With regard to the relative proportions of monastic and other appropriations a few figures may be given. The Register of William Gray, Bishop of Ely (1454–86)[3], contains a list of livings and patrons which (the vicarages being counted as representing appropriations) may be taken as indicative of the state of things late in the Middle Ages. As the diocese contained a University it would probably be expected that the churches appropriated to colleges of the University would here be well up to the average. On the other hand, the cathedral church being monastic, the number of appropriations to religious houses

---

[1] Cardinal Gasquet, *English Monasticism*. It is not clear whether the reference is to collegiate churches, or the colleges of the Universities.

[2] *Salt Collections*, vol. I.

[3] Summary published in the *Ely Diocesan Remembrancer*.

would most probably appear as larger than in a diocese with a secular chapter. The list mentions 157 livings in all: of these 75 are rectories. Of the remaining 82 appropriated churches, 21 were in non-monastic hands, eight of which belonged to colleges of Cambridge or Oxford, and two to hospitals; 61 appropriated churches belonged to religious houses, including 14 held by the Prior and Convent of Ely. In this diocese, then, three-quarters of the appropriations had been made to religious houses. This may be contrasted with the diocese of Exeter, where the cathedral chapter was not conventual. The Registers in this case give lists of institutions which afford a possibility of seeing something like the number of appropriations, and the persons to whom they were appropriated. The list in the Register of Bishop Stapeldon (1307–26) mentions 454 livings, of which 331 are rectories. The proportion of appropriations is therefore much less than was the case with Ely. Of the 123 vicarages, in 31 cases the patrons are not mentioned: of the remaining 92, 58 were in monastic hands, and 34 in non-monastic, hospitals accounting for two only, and the Dean and Chapter of Exeter for no fewer than 26. Nearly two-thirds, that is to say, of the appropriations which can be accounted for were monastic, and practically the whole of the rest belonged to the dean and chapter. A similar list from Bishop Stafford's Register (1395–1419) gives a somewhat different result for the same diocese. Of 423 livings mentioned, 152 are vicarages. In 17 cases the patrons are not mentioned: in 74 cases monasteries presented; in 61, non-monastic patrons. Of these latter appropriations, 25 belonged to the dean and chapter, and four only to hospitals. This shows a proportion of a little over half belonging to the monasteries in cases where the patrons can be named. The apparent decline is however very probably due to the fact that the alien priories were at this time in the King's hands, and he was presenting to their livings. If the eight royal presentations found in the list are taken as arising from this cause (as was certainly the case with three of them, although the fact is not mentioned in the records of institution), the monastic share in the appropriations rises again to three-fifths and the dean and chapter once more account for most of the rest. The records of the papal confirmation of appropriations given in the *Calendar of Papal*

Letters tell the same tale. In the 37 years between 1305 and 1342 there are 68 appropriations to monasteries recorded, and 23 others, of which latter hospitals were responsible for four, colleges for four, bishops for 13 and non-monastic cathedral chapters for two. If we take the 42 years between 1362–1404 very much the same results appear[1]. Between 1362 and 1404, 44 churches were appropriated or perpetual vicarates suppressed in favour of religious houses (in a few cases in Scotland), and 14 others only were given to other persons or institutions; of these five went to University colleges, one to a hospital, four to bishops, two to cathedral chapters, one to a collegiate church and one to the Dean of Chester. On the whole the responsibility for appropriation seems mainly to rest with the religious houses, and secondarily with the bishops and cathedral chapters, rather than with colleges and hospitals. The *Calendar of Papal Petitions* from 1342 to 1378 shows much the same result: 43 petitions for appropriations were presented on behalf of monasteries, and 18 for others, of which colleges account for four and hospitals for two, the rest coming from chantries, cathedral chapters and bishops. It should be remembered however in dealing with this question of appropriation that non-residence would have much the same effect, and was very prevalent throughout the later Middle Ages.

It is when we leave this question of the spiritualities and turn to that of the temporalities that the great lack of evidence on which to base statistics is most obvious and regrettable. The Taxation of Pope Nicholas being unavoidably set aside, no basis is left for a general calculation such as is essential for comparison with the work of Professor Savine. The fragmentary nature of such few series of monastic accounts as have yet been published, as well as the abbreviated form in which many are, doubtless unavoidably, presented, makes them of very little value for such work. All that can here be done is to call attention to the remarkable diversity of appearance which these accounts present. It is not too much to say that every form of temporal income

---

[1] I do not here include the appropriated churches transferred during this period to William of Wykeham's new foundation at Winchester, for none of the appropriations recorded in the Calendar were new, all having heretofore belonged to alien priories. The endowment of Winchester therefore involved no fresh inroad upon the parish church funds.

will be found represented in the charters or the account-rolls of these monasteries. They were great landowners of course, keeping part of their estates in demesne, though, as has already been observed, this diminished during the fifteenth century until by the time of the Dissolution, according to Professor Savine's calculations, the income from the land in demesne was only about one-thirteenth of that arising from the estates leased out or held by tenants. This system of maintaining home farms, it must be noticed, leads to a further difficulty in the interpretation of accounts: for much of the produce of these manors was consumed in the monastery, and not infrequently records as to its amount are lacking. For the rest, their position as lords of the manor brought in feudal dues of every kind which were clearly collected with the usual insistence upon full rights. The monasteries, it is noticeable, were often troubled with a diminution of their villein services by the fact that free men were often allowed to hold land under servile conditions together with their free holdings and then claimed that all their land was freehold: and prohibitions of this practice often occur. There was income from pool, and wood, and pasture: as usual, the manorial mills proved a constant source of revenue, as did also the feudal courts whose profits were taken by those who held them. There were revenues arising from the relations of the monks with the towns which often rose up beneath their shelter. There were quarries and mines; Bolton Priory, for instance, in 1301 was paying for the working of a lead-mine, and the Durham account-rolls contain much interesting information on coal-mining from the fourteenth century onwards. There were regal privileges granted which brought in profits: thus two instances at least of the privilege of coining occur, one at Bury St Edmund's, one at Reading granted by the founder Henry I, withdrawn by Edward II (1315), but restored by Edward III (1338). Fairs and markets, with their attendant tolls and opportunities for disposal of the goods of the monasteries, are also prominent.

The connection of the monasteries, especially of the Cistercian houses, but of others also, in no small measure, with the growing English wool trade, must also be borne in mind. An example or two will show its importance to individual houses. A compotus roll of Bolton Priory for 1298–9[1], apparently giving the whole annual receipts of the year, shows that of the £860 of income which passed through the hands of the monastery in actual cash[2], the sale of wool, both tithe-wool and that from the monastery's own sheep, brought in no less that £289: and since in the £860 a loan of £359 is included, it would appear that over half the actual cash income of the house for this year was realised by the sale of wool. A general practice prevailed, however, of selling the wool for several years in advance for a lump sum down, and it is possible that this payment at Bolton represents some such transaction. Certainly the proportion seems unduly large; in 1324–5 it was much less. Out of an income amounting (if the items of the account are correct) to £599, but calculated (according to the editor of the account) by the monks to come to £444 odd, only £121 arose from the sale of wool[3]. In other instances the proportion is still smaller. At Meaux, a Cistercian house[4], Abbot Thomas Burton in 1393–4 reckoned that out of an income of £529 (to which, however, a later account of 1396 shows that for the corn and other profits of the land and granges in the monastery's own hands £150 must be added, bringing the total to £679) only some £46 was derived from the sale of wool and hides combined, and the calculation of 1396 puts the figure still lower, £30 out of a total of £614. But at Meaux, in the middle of the thirteenth century, the cloth needed by the monastery was provided by weaving up the convent's wool on the spot[5], and the system possibly still continued at the close of the century. A compotus of Sallay for 1381[6], however, gives a still smaller proportion, only £16 out of a total of £348 being due to the sale of wool.

All these sources of revenue deserve—and require—a much closer investigation than it has been possible to give. Light may be thrown by such examination on many interesting points of economic history: the development and course of town life, the management of estates, the growth of the practice of commuta-

---

[1] Whitaker, *History of Craven*, pp. 448–50. I have some suspicion that this is a bursar's roll, in which case the income may not be complete.
[2] Much of the produce, it must be remembered, was used within the house.
[3] Burton, *Monasticon Eboracense.*
[4] Sir E. A. Bond, *Chronica Monasterii de Melsa*, III, p. lx.
[5] *Ibid.* II, p. xiv.   [6] Whitaker, *History of Craven*, p. 63.

tion of tenant-services, the history of prices—all could be illustrated by an elaborate examination of these and other monastic account-rolls, manorial or general. But only the very broadest generalisation is possible here. One salient feature, however, forces itself upon the attention, in the management both of the temporalities and the spiritualities. Everywhere as the period progresses, we see a withdrawal of the monasteries from an active share in the management of the sources of their income. The practice of farming everything out grows more and more common. In the case of the estates, this doubtless reflects a change which was common, and over which the monks had little or no control. Economically, no doubt, after the great disasters of the fourteenth century had made labour dear and scarce, it was more profitable to let out estates on lease than to endeavour to carry on the old system. But in every direction the same thing went on: tithes were farmed out, mills were farmed out, every source of income was transferred to the hands of some outsider and the monks simply subsided into the position of men receiving rents. The process must have been disastrous to the influence of the monasteries upon society, and even from the narrower point of view of their mere popularity it must have been injurious. The close contact between the monks and the world in general, which had given monasticism its chance of doing something for the regeneration of the world which it had renounced, was ceasing to exist; life was more and more confined to the precincts of the monastery, narrowing the sympathies and dulling the intellect in a long round of routine from which the old element of manual labour had died out. Everything must have tended to the stagnation which is the bane of all secluded life unanimated by devotion to some overpowering ideal. So long as the monks managed their own estates, there was almost forced upon them some realisation of the possibilities of service in the ordinary duties of life. But with the restriction of the main interests of the monks within the bounds of their own dwellings once more, at a time when the original ascetic enthusiasm had been lost, the ties whereby direct good could come from them to the world lost their strength, and the monastic horizon was narrowed in a way which obviously proved injurious to the whole tone of their lives.

CHAPTER IV

ASPECTS OF MONASTIC EXPENDITURE

As in the last chapter it was impossible to do more than hint at the remarkable number of sources from which the monastic revenues were derived, so in this it will be impossible to go fully into the question of how they were spent. The accounts show such minuteness that much must be neglected and only a few salient features dwelt on at any length. The bewildering profusion of the details of everyday expenditure presented would be of the utmost value for a history of prices, but must here be left out of account. There are records of money spent in almost every conceivable variety of way; payments for pittances (or extra dishes at dinner) to the house, presents of wine to the abbot or the priests on the list of celebrants, presents of knives to boys in the monastic schools, and payments for beer for the boy-bishop on Innocents' Day. There are payments to workmen of every kind, hedgers and ditchers, woodcutters and carpenters, slaters and tilers, quarrymen and stonecutters and miners. There are kitcheners' weekly accounts, with the details of every day's meals; repairs to this building or to that, where account is given of every lath and tile and nail, the workman's wages and the price of his food; expenses in the church, in the monastery, on the manors; records of the stores laid in at the great fairs, of the journeys made by sundry monks to do the business of the house; entries made which show the system of treating the diseases of sheep and horses, and the medicines used within the infirmary; the spices of which such large quantities were consumed, the dress of the monks, the payments to the clerks who wrote the accounts, the provision of wine made by the obedientiary when the day came for auditing his accounts. These quaint and curious entries bring home more vividly than any chronicle the way of life of these monks. But consideration must here be restricted to a few of the most interesting causes of expense to the monasteries; and some of these fortunately present themselves sufficiently clearly to be fittingly treated without loading the page with the mass of detail which forms the main staple of the monastic accounts.

Five subjects which thus disentangle themselves are considered. The first of these—the material standard of the life of the religious and the evidence which it gives as to the maintenance of the ascetic ideals which formed the foundation of the monastic rule—is sufficiently important to be treated by itself, and will therefore be reserved for a subsequent chapter. This leaves the following four points for examination here: the expenses of episcopal or other visitation, the general relations of the monasteries with the Universities, monastic hospitality and monastic almsgiving. The first of these subjects is interesting as throwing light upon the conditions under which these visitations were made upon which so much depended; the second as illustrating the expenses of University life in the Middle Ages, and the attempts to secure for the monks a percentage at least of men versed in the best knowledge of their time; while the two remaining points touch in the most obvious and direct way upon the main subject of this essay—a consideration of the general financial workings of the monastic system from the twelfth to the sixteenth century, and of its bearing upon the problems of the Reformation.

First, then, for the cost of the official visitors to the house visited. The importance of these visitations is sufficiently obvious. They gave practically the only effective opportunity for outside criticism of the state of monastic life, and in the administration of the monastic finances. It was by the interposition of the visitors alone that a chance was given of checking persistent waste on the part of the house as a whole, or, in particular, by the abbot or prior, who, as we have seen, was able for the most part to work his will irrespective of the opinion of his monks so long as he did not goad them to open rebellion. Various persons were charged with this duty of supervision. In general it fell to the lot of the bishop: in the case of the Orders exempt from episcopal authority, notably the Cluniac and Cistercian Orders, visitors were appointed for the various provinces by the General Chapter of the Order. The Benedictines, after the Lateran Council of 1215, were subject to a double system of visitation: for by that council the Benedictine houses were organised in a congregation, divided into provinces, and it was ordained that the Provincial Chapters should appoint visitors in the Pope's name. These visitors were, however, responsible in the main only for reports to the diocesan[1], who was to carry out the necessary reformation. Some of these Benedictine houses had obtained, however, the eagerly sought privilege of exemption from episcopal authority, and were subject only to the Pope himself.

One of the great defects of the system was that it proved extremely expensive. The bishops, more especially, were great men, and like all mediaeval great men, travelled in state with a large retinue: and the mere burden of entertaining the visitor and his household, quite apart from any payments due to him as fees, was considerable, while, when the fees were included, the amount became almost an intolerable exaction. The bishop, in fact, found it a convenient way of avoiding spending his own income, and so a not despicable source of profit. The bishops, as will be seen later, were not alone in this respect: the visitors appointed by the various exempt Orders were liable to the same accusation. The accounts not infrequently show what a large slice of the year's revenue went in the expenses of a visitation. An example or two may be given by way of illustration.

The Augustinian Priory of Bolton seems at the close of the thirteenth century to have had a normal income of some £500, and was not managing to make both ends meet; the expenditure in 1304, for instance, exceeded the revenue by no less than £306. 19s. From 1316 to 1319 it was suffering from the inroads of the Scots during the disastrous years after Bannockburn. It was harried, apparently, in 1316, and again in 1318; while in 1319 the community was dispersed by a fresh inroad, and during 1320 the house was heavily burdened by the repairs thus made necessary. None the less in 1321 Archbishop Melton arrived with his household on a visitation. The expenses of his entertainment amounted to practically £24, together with fifteen quarters of oats (then at about 2s. a quarter) used as food for his horses and dogs. Some £25. 10s., then, or roughly a twentieth

---

[1] Or, in some cases, to the Provincial Chapter. It is not clear whether these visitors had the right to demand the production of accounts, as the bishops had.

of the house's income, even in this time of difficulty, went in the expenses of the visitation[1].

With this may be compared a visitation of a later date held at the Benedictine house of Eynsham in 1406. Here we get fuller details. The bishop personally received £36. 13s. 4d. which included £26. 13s. 4d. "pro una dimissione habenda et pro indempnitate ecclesiarum de Stoke et Combe," his suffragan got £3. 6s. 8d. for consecrating three altars in the church of the monastery, and other officials received further payments. Then purchases of provisions had to be made at Oxford for the occasion, and there were further the expenses of the cellarer's journey thither for the purpose and the cost of carriage. Nor was this all: for presents had to be given to the bishop's servants; and some £6 was divided between his cook, his nine squires, his thirteen valetti, his three grooms, his kitchen-varlet, his two kitchen-pages and his messenger. In all, the expenses involved in this visit came to a few shillings over £63. The sum represents roughly one-twentieth of the income given in the cellarer's account of 1390: and, as previously pointed out, the other obedientiaries could have had little more.

The case shows how little success attended the persistent attempts made throughout the Middle Ages to restrict the fees which the visitors might take. The earliest steps were directed towards reducing the number of attendants with whom the visitor appeared. Thus a decree of the Lateran Council of 1179, which mentions only the case of parishes, but in all probability applied to the visitation of monasteries also, allowed archbishops from 40 to 50 horses; bishops, from 20 to 30; cardinals, 25; archdeacons, five or seven; and deans under the bishops, two. They were not to demand sumptuous banquets and not to take procurations unless a visitation was made. About a century later, the Second Council of Lyons (1274) under Gregory X struck at the whole system of visitation fees, by forbidding the visitors to demand any money at all, or even to receive it if it was offered[2]. This position, however, was found untenable: Boniface VIII modified its severity as leading to inconvenience,

---

[1] Whitaker, *History of Craven*, p. 467. See, however, p. 93 above, footnote 1.

[2] W. W. Capes, *Registrum Ricardi de Swinfield*, p. 348.

by ordaining that money might be taken "pro sumptibus modicis faciendis in viatico" from such rectors or persons (I take it that here also the stipulation would apply to the monasteries) as were willing to make a payment, but only one procuration might be taken on one day whether one place only was visited or not. Benedict XII, himself a monk and well acquainted both with the failings and the difficulties of the monastic life, took the whole question of visitation fees in hand. In 1335 he laid down a most elaborate scale on which these charges were to be taken[1], graduated according to the country in question, to the dignity of the visitor (archbishop, bishop, archdeacon or archpresbyter), and to the size of the religious house visited, and with yet further variations if the visitation were made by deputy. The figures are given in "silver (shillings) of Tours," the exchange value of this "turonensis" being authoritatively fixed in England between 1343 and 1423 at one-eightieth of the pound sterling[2]. On this scale of reckoning an English bishop was entitled, as one day's procuration from a cathedral church visited in person, to £2. 15s. sterling, in victuals or, if the persons visited were willing, in cash: from a monastery with over 12 inmates to £2. 5s.; and from those with under 12 to £1. 17s. 6d. The house of Eynsham had in 1406 over 12 members: the bishop therefore personally received in cash over 11 days' maximum visitation fees, while he and his household together received the equivalent of a little over 28 days' standard procuration.

A comparison between Benedict's scale of visitation fees and those taken some 80 years previously in Normandy by Odo Rigaldi, Archbishop of Rouen, one of the most celebrated and upright of mediaeval prelates, gives interesting results. The size of the procuration taken by Odo bears no relation to the size

---

[1] Wilkins, *Concilia*, II, p. 578: in a fuller form in Labbe, *Sacrosancta Concilia*, X, 1794.

[2] Reynerus, p. 194. It is possible that a somewhat higher rate of exchange should be taken. Benedict values the "turonensis" at 12 to the florin of Florence. The florin according to the *Gesta Abbatum S. Albani* was in 1302 ¼ mark sterling: the *Calendar of Papal Letters* (II, p. 514) shows that in 1333 it was reckoned at 3s. 2d., which is near enough to the same sum. This makes the pound sterling equal to 72 livres tournois: a calculation agreeing with an independent one of 1331 given by Thorold Rogers (*History of Agriculture and Prices*, II, p. 631).

of the house visited. When in 1256, for example, he visited the priory of Vauville which contained four monks his procuration was £4. 19s. 5d. tournois, whereas in the same year at Sartilly, a house of two monks only, his fee was £7. 4s. 1d., and at Cherbourg, where there were 26 monks, he took only £7. 1s. 1d. His average procuration from 20 houses of all sizes in 1263 was £7. 17s. tournois. Benedict's scale for France, established in 1335, was graduated according to the size of the house, an archbishop being entitled to a maximum of £15 tournois from a cathedral church, £12. 10s. from a monastery with over 12 members and £10 from one with under 12. The average official procuration is therefore £12. 10s.: a fact which reflects very creditably upon the Franciscan archbishop's moderation.

A good deal of evidence exists to show that the visitors appointed by the various Orders were also liable to the objection that they were over-expensive. For the Cluniacs, Gregory IX found it necessary to include in his revision of their rule an order that the visitors were to take nothing from the persons or places visited except their necessary expenses in victuals, "sed, excutientes ab omni muneri manus suas, cum paucis incedant." Nicholas IV restricted the daily expenses of the Cluniac visitors to £9 of Tours, or £2. 10s. sterling of that date[1]. Similar difficulties were experienced with the Benedictine visitors appointed in accordance with the organisation of 1215. The Provincial Chapter held at Northampton (1225)[2] forbade the visitors to have over 12 attendants. That held at Bermondsey (1249)[3] ordered them to beware lest by reason of them the monasteries should be burdened with superfluous expenses. Benedict XII, in his revision of the Benedictine Statutes, ordered that the visitors' stay in any one monastery should not exceed two days unless for some clear advantage to the house: that they were not to be burdensome or to require sumptuous banquets: and that they were to take no money or reward, under penalty of a twofold repayment.

The burden laid upon the monasteries by the visitor's expenses is curiously illustrated by the prominence of the prospect of

[1] Leo Marsicanus, *Chronicon Casinense*, p. 638.
[2] Dugdale, *Monasticon*, I, p. xlvi.
[3] Matthew Paris, *Chronica Majora*, Additamenta, p. 175.

relief in the minds of such as attempted to obtain the much-sought privilege of exemption from the episcopal jurisdiction. Nothing could be more striking than the arguments whereby Thomas Marleberge, the leader of the opposition against the scandalous Roger Norreys at Evesham, and a man of the highest character and capacity, resisted the proposals whereby some wished to conquer Norreys by submitting to the Bishop of Worcester's claims to hold visitations. There was little pretence that the bishop could not help them. Marleberge, in fact, accepted him throughout as an honourable and upright man, though, in general, he thought that an abbot could easily use a bishop as a tool against his monks. The main force of his argument rested upon the pecuniary burden implied in submitting to visitation. There was, no doubt, something of the jealousy of regular and secular in it—a feeling that for any of the non-professed clergy to share at all in the endowments of the religious was detestable: but the mere financial aspect of the case was evidently uppermost in his mind.

They knew not (says he) the episcopal burdens, to wit, that not only once in the year but as often as there is need according to the canons, the bishop will visit the monasteries subjected to him, and ever procuration goes with visitation. Not only the bishops, but even their archdeacons, officials and ministers are admitted to the great grievance of the monasteries, and their horses are put to lodge until they are bettered by their stay there: and even the rents of monasteries are wont to be given to the clerks of the bishops and archdeacons, with other intolerable presents, all of which we have borne at one time, and our neighbours yet more heavily. They understood not that the bishops are wont to be corrupted most easily by the abbots to oppress the monks, which we even now have experienced[1].

So Thomas Marleberge wrote early in the thirteenth century; and, in view of such facts as those which have been cited for Eynsham, it is difficult to see that matters had improved by the fifteenth century.

There is, moreover, one question of considerable importance suggested by these procurations. How far was the effectiveness of these visitations diminished by the prevalence of a practice whereby the bishop made profit out of the monasteries? The

---

[1] W. D. Macray, *Chronicon Abbatiæ de Evesham*, p. 138.

question is a difficult one to answer, for much would naturally depend upon the bishop in question. Nevertheless Grosseteste's words, when preaching in 1250 before the Pope and cardinals, support the belief that strictness and close inspection were diminished by the opportunity of making money.

Unless the Holy See provides a remedy (he says) my successors will exact and extort new and unwonted procurations....Cupidity will induce them to this unless they are men altogether spiritual; and they will be able to live altogether of their procurations, and lay by the whole episcopal revenues in the treasury. If anyone answer that without a procuration they will be slothful in the office of visitation, I reply that those who visit for greed of procurations will either omit the duties of visitation and be zealous only to receive the procurations, or they will become farmers of sins[1].

He is speaking indeed of procurations arising from parochial visitations, and in fact sets aside the monastic procurations as "familiar, and by long custom proven and bearable": none the less, the temptation must have been operative in both cases. Exactly the same influence must have been at work in the minds of those visiting the monasteries.

If, as I have tried to show, the monasteries which so eagerly sought exemption from the authority of the bishops were chiefly actuated by a desire to escape these exactions, it is to be feared that the Pope's little finger was thicker than the bishop's loins. The case of St Albans is illuminating. The Lateran Council, under Innocent III, decreed that the newly-elect abbots of houses exempt from episcopal authority should receive confirmation from the Pope himself. St Albans was one of these houses. Abbot John Maryns (1302-8) went in person to Rome for confirmation, and the record of the expenses, not of his journey, but of his confirmation, has been preserved[2]. Including a sum of 2258 marks, which went to the Pope and cardinals for visitations, the abbot elect had to spend in the Roman court £1707. 6s. 8d. which, at a moderate estimate, represents in purchasing power about £31,000 of our pre-war money. The next abbot, Hugh de Evresdone (1308–26), according to Walsingham, had to spend over £1000 in getting his election confirmed, exclusive of the sum paid to the Pope and cardinals as first-fruits. The sum total of his successor's expenses in going

[1] Wharton, *Anglia Sacra*, II, pp. 347-8. [2] *Gesta Abbatum* (R.S.), II, p. 107.

to Avignon was £953. 10s. 11d.: no mention is made of the first-fruits. After the house had thus suffered for a century, a bull, apparently obtained from Honorius III, was confirmed by Boniface IX in 1395[1], permitting the abbey to obtain, for any candidate they chose to elect, the papal benediction at the hands of any of the English bishops, in consideration of an annual payment of £14 to the Pope. Thus for St Albans, at least, the exaction was diminished and spread over a period of years. In the letter of Richard II to Boniface asking for the confirmation of this privilege, it is not a little interesting to see St Albans, one of the richest of the English religious houses, described not merely as "situate in the uttermost parts of the earth," which as regards the distance from Rome may pass, but also as "in comparison with other monasteries of the realm over-slenderly endowed" and as being situate in "a barren place."

There was nothing abnormal in these sums which St Albans had to pay. Evesham seems to have escaped lightly, for Richard's letter speaks of the privilege which he sought for St Albans as having been granted to Evesham by Innocent III and confirmed by Urban V. But the rest must have suffered heavily. The first abbot-elect to go from England in accordance with the decree of the Council was Simon de Luton, Abbot of Bury St Edmund's (1257–79): and he paid to Alexander IV, for his confirmation and the right to give an episcopal blessing, £2000[2]. In 1302 Thomas de Totynton, elected abbot of the same house in January of that year, obtained a papal faculty to raise a loan of £833. 13s. 4d. to meet his expenses at Rome[3]. In 1361 the newly elect abbot was still bound to go to the Pope for confirmation[4]: and it was not until 1398 that, on the petition of Richard II, the monastery was allowed to compound for an annual sum of 20 marks[5]. The fortune of Westminster seems to have been even worse. In 1259 Richard, Abbot of Westminster, obtained a papal faculty to contract a loan of 1000 marks to meet expenses incurred at Rome "in expediting the affairs of the monastery"[6]: which business is defined clearly by the fact that Richard was

---

[1] *Calendar of Papal Letters*, IV, p. 293.
[2] Dugdale, *Monasticon*, III, p. 106.
[3] *Calendar of Papal Letters*, I, p. 602.
[4] Dugdale, *Monasticon*, III, p. 110.
[5] *Calendar of Papal Letters*, V, p. 152.   [6] *Ibid.* I, p. 362.

elected in that same year and went to Rome for confirmation[1]. In 1262, another loan of £400 was raised towards meeting the expenses of the confirmation of Abbot Philip: this time an agent only had been sent[2]. In 1320 Abbot William was relieved from excommunication incurred by delay in paying 8000 florins (some £1334) owing to the Papal Camera and the College of Cardinals. Richard, his predecessor, who had contracted the debt, had paid off about £917 of it[3]. In all probability this also was a debt incurred for confirmation. In 1345 Simon, Abbot of Westminster, was allowed to contract a loan of 2000 florins (or about £270, the florin's exchange value in 1344 being only 2s. 9d.) to meet his expenses at the Apostolic See[4]. It was not until 1478–9 that, after urgent letters from Edward IV, Westminster was allowed to purchase freedom from this burden at a price of 100 florins a year. Roger, Abbot of Glastonbury in 1259, had to raise a loan of £1021. 6s. 8d. for this same reason[5]: William, Abbot of St Augustine's, Canterbury, in 1343, one of £136. 10s.[6] In 1399, Waltham Abbey also bought freedom for 100 florins a year[7]. It will be observed that these loans are by no means a criterion of the actual amount expended. They represent, no doubt, only that proportion which had to be raised by borrowing. But even if we take them as fully representative of the cost of confirmation, the average for the 11 cases given above is a little over £958, which, as most of the figures fall within the fourteenth century may be taken as representing in terms of pre-war money about £16800. It is necessary to bear these demands and other similar exactions in mind, in a consideration of the difficulty found by houses exempt from episcopal authority in making both ends meet.

Frequent entries in the monastic accounts record payments to a scholar, that is, a member of the monastery in residence at one of the Universities. It is thus possible in this way to get an interesting glimpse of the cost of residence in the Middle Ages, and to obtain a little light upon the efforts made to keep up the standard of monastic education. The monks were never so

---

[1] Dugdale, *Monasticon*, I, p. 273.
[2] *Calendar of Papal Letters*, I, p. 376.
[3] *Ibid.* II, p. 209.
[4] *Ibid.* III, p. 176.
[5] *Ibid.* I, p. 365.
[6] *Ibid.* III, p. 4.
[7] *Ibid.* v, p. 267.

closely associated with University life as were the mendicant orders: still something was done in this direction, and the practice of sending one at least of the brethren to study at Oxford or Cambridge was very common.

The earliest piece of information as to the cost of University life is given by Abbot Samson's remark, recorded by Jocelin of Brakelond, that if he could have had five or six marks of income wherewith he could have been supported in the schools, he would never have been monk or abbot. We may take it, then, that it was possible at the beginning of the thirteenth century to be in residence on about £4 a year—say, roughly, £80 of pre-war money. By the middle of the next century, Benedict XII, energetic in this as in all his monastic reforms, had organised and regularised the practice of sending these scholars, by a series of most interesting articles in his additions to the Benedictine, Augustinian and Cistercian statutes. Each house of the two first Orders, he decreed, was to send to the University one monk for every full twenty of its inmates, houses with under eight members being exempt. Each Cistercian house of 40 members was to maintain two, those between 18 and 30, one only[1]. A scale of stipends to be paid was also laid down, the sums being stated in livres tournois. Reduced to English money, the livre tournois being in 1250 one-fourth of the pound sterling, the scale runs as follows: A Master in Theology was to receive £15 yearly, a Bachelor or Scholar in Theology, £10. A Doctor of Canon Law was to have £12. 10s., a Bachelor or Scholar of Canon Law £8. 15s. Regulations were also laid down as to how the scholars were to spend their money: £5 a year was to be for daily expenses, £2. 10s. for clothing and shoes: the rest was to cover the expenses of books, illness or other inevitable charges. Abbot Samson must have been very moderate in his wish for some £80 modern, or else the expenses of those sent to "scoleye" had risen by 1337: the lowest scholarship was equivalent to about £150 of pre-war money.

Benedict seems to have had his eye on the great university of Paris in laying down this tariff, and the accounts of various

---

[1] So stated by the General Chapter of 1405: Martène-Durand, *Thesaurus*, IV, 1544. It is difficult to see why the smaller proportion for the Cistercians was established.

monasteries seem to show that English scholars did not receive quite the full sums stipulated. Thus Brother James Kepas of the Cistercian Abbey of Sallay, Scholar, received in 1381 £5. 13s. 4d.[1] Two students from Abingdon in 1383–4 were paid £5. 11s. 4d. each by the treasurer, but they also received other sums from the chamberlain, the cellarer, and the refectorer, as well as "the wonted oblations" which cannot now be traced[2]. St Peter's, Gloucester, in 1391, petitioned for an appropriation on the ground that the house had to maintain three or four students at a cost of £10 each[3]. Brother Peter Erdynton of Eynsham, student at Oxford, was receiving in 1406 £6. 10s. a year[4]. Probably we shall not be far off the mark in saying that a monk's expenses at the Universities towards the close of the fourteenth century was nearly covered by about £7, or £115 pre-war. A Benedictine Chapter (apparently of 1351) ordered, however, that the standard set by Benedict XII should be maintained, as it was necessary on account of the excessive dearness of victuals and other necessaries, "quae modernis temporibus plus solito inolevit."[5] The great difficulty here, as on other points, lies in the curtness of the entries in the accounts: the Durham rolls, for example, continually record payments to the scholars at Oxford, or, in one instance, at Stamford (1351), but never mention the number of scholars maintained. It is, however, possible to give one last estimate of the cost of University life at the beginning of the sixteenth century. In 1504 Westminster was maintaining three monks only at the Universities; the King stepped in to order the appointment of three more to study Divinity, to be called the King's Scholars, their stipend being £10 each: a sum which may roughly be taken as equivalent to £120 as money went before 1914[6]. This allowance may have been royally generous. When Bishop Nicke visited Westacre Priory in 1514[7], Brother Robert Bekham deposed that, studying at Cambridge he should have received eight marks a year for his food and clothing, but had only got 40s.

---

[1] Whitaker, *History of Craven*, compotus of Sallay for this year.
[2] R. E. G. Kirk, *Accounts of Obedientiaries of Abingdon*, p. 44.
[3] *Calendar of Papal Letters*, IV, p. 406.
[4] H. E. Salter, *Eynsham Cartulary*, II, p. lxxx.
[5] *Gesta Abbatum*, II, p. 462.
[6] A. F. Leach, *Educational Charters*, p. 437.
[7] A. Jessopp, *Norwich Visitations* (C.S.), p. 105.

A guardian, accounting for his ward's property in 1374, reckoned that in the course of 13 years' study at Oxford £5. 4s. had been spent yearly on board, and £2 on clothing. Teaching for 10 of the 13 years accounted for £1. 6s. 8d. a year, but sundry expenses, which were reckoned at £1 a year, included "a master for the said Thomas" as well as his riding expenses. The total for the 13 years works out at approximately £9. 4s. 6d. a year[1]. The monk's stipend, however, would seem not to have been liable to claims which bore upon Thomas. Travelling expenses, it had been ordered, were to be provided in addition to the cost of living. The monasteries would seem also to have provided lodging free, hiring rooms at Oxford usually in the "Monastic College," later known as Gloucester College, as did Christ Church, Canterbury, before Islip's foundation of Canterbury College.

This attempt to establish a general connection between the convents and the Universities, which dates only from the later thirteenth century, clearly represents an endeavour to keep the religious houses in touch with the latest developments of mediaeval thought and learning. Equally clearly, it did not meet with the full success which it deserved. It is evident that the number of scholars was not maintained as it should have been, even among the Benedictines. The Provincial Chapter of Northampton, held in 1343, had to deal with no fewer than 15 houses, including some of the most important, such as Battle, Burton, Winchester and Evesham, for not maintaining scholars, although in two cases the failure was ascribed to the illness of the scholar appointed. A later Chapter in 1346 had to add to the penalties which Benedict had ordained for failure, a fine of £10 for the use of the Congregation. A century later, the Provincial Chapter of Northampton (1444) was still complaining of the paucity of students arising from the negligence of the prelates[2], and ordering, as a fine for every term in which the proper number of students was not maintained, a third of the yearly payments laid down by Benedict XII. None the less, in 1452, on the accession of John Whethamstede for the second time to the Abbacy of

[1] G. G. Coulton, *Social Life in Britain*, p. 95, from Riley's *Memorials of London*.
[2] For the records of these Chapters see Reynerus, *Apostolatus Benedictinorum*, Appendix.

St Albans, it appears that for some years this great abbey had hardly been keeping one monk in continual residence, and at the moment there was not even one. Whethamstede is said to have reformed this and other faults complained of by the monks: but the facts do not inspire much confidence in the efficacy of the penalties laid down by the Provincial Chapter[1]. In 1492, Bishop James Goldwell was informed that his Cathedral Priory at Norwich was not sending anyone to study at Oxford, "to the great scandal and damage of the monastery," and gave instructions that two of the confraternity, apt for study, were to be sent to Gloucester College.

The Cistercian authorities also found difficulty in enforcing the work of education. Mr A. G. Little[2] has called attention to the fact that the first monastic "studium" (or college for monastic students only) established in England was Rewley Abbey, built for the Cistercians by Edmund of Cornwall in the years immediately following 1280. By order of the General Chapter in 1292 the Abbots of Waverley and Quarr were authorised to force the abbots of the Order in the province of Canterbury, who had proved unwilling to send their scholars to this studium, to maintain there one monk from every house of over 20, with an exhibition of £3 as the General Chapter had ordered. The sum, it may be noted, is smaller even than that mentioned by Abbot Samson some 80 years before, probably because house-room would be provided free at Rewley. But the document shows the unpopularity of this college among the abbots of the Order, and their inertia in the end overcame the efforts of the authorities. Despite the reforms of Benedict XII and the raising of a levy of £127. 6s. 8d. on its behalf by the Chapter General of England and Wales in 1400, Rewley sank into the position of an ordinary Cistercian monastery, and the Cistercian students were left

[1] Whethamstede carried out his reforms by suppressing the cell of Beaulieu. The net income of the cell, estimated at £18, was declared insufficient for the maintenance of two monks there. The suppression was allowed on condition that an anniversary was celebrated yearly for Lord Grey of Ruthin, who also received £1 a year. Each student of the house at Oxford received 13s. 4d. from the master of the works to pray for the soul of the founder of Beaulieu and of Whethamstede's father, mother and uncle. (Dugdale, Monasticon, II, p. 274 et seq.)

[2] English Historical Review, VIII, p. 33 et seq. On this article, and a subsequent note by R. C. Fowler (XXIII, pp. 84–5) the following paragraph is based.

without a college of their own until the foundation of St Bernard's in 1437. The difficulty of keeping the Cistercian houses to the observance of Benedict's ordinances seemed to have been general: in 1405 the Chapter General of the Order complained that these rules had been neglected by many abbots, and attention is called to the penalties, that appointed by the Pope being suspension "a divinis," that by the Order, excommunication[1].

In spite of all failures, it is to the credit of those in authority that this attempt to promote the higher education of the monks was made. Men of learning stood rather aloof from the monasteries, if we may judge by the inducements which had to be held out to them. The Benedictine Provincial Chapters tried to encourage their entry both by lending a helping hand in the way of fees, and by relaxing the claims of the monastic life upon their time. Thus the Chapter of Northampton (1343) imposed a tax of $\frac{1}{2}d$. in the pound upon the houses belonging to the Congregation for the purpose of sending messengers to Rome to secure if possible the appropriation of churches, "principaliter pro scholarium pensione," and then for other business of the Chapter—to wit, conducting a suit against the Prior of Christ Church, Canterbury, and others who would not attend the Chapter: the inevitable raid upon parochial endowments being employed even for the conduct of a law-suit. The fund to be applied to education, it seems probable, would be used as contributions to the expenses of degree-taking: such, at any rate, was the practice as revealed by the Provincial Chapter of Northampton in 1444. This, besides ordering that the Chair of Theology in the "Monastic College" at Oxford was always to be occupied by a monk, a D.D., who was to have £10 "de communi collecta," ordained that an Inceptor in Theology, if there were only one, should receive £20 from the same fund, or if two £10 each: while an Inceptor in Common Law was to receive £13. 6s. 8d., or if there should be two, £6. 13s. 4d. The same Chapter shows the difficulty of inducing learned men to join the religious. Lest "lettered men and others 'constituti in dignitatibus'" should draw back from entering the Order "propter metum suum reddendi servitium," if any Masters of

---

[1] Martène-Durand, *Thesaurus*, IV, p. 1544.

Arts or other persons of good capacity for study, "aut alias in dignitate constituti" should wish to enter religion, when they had repeated the nocturnal service, they might (if their superiors thought fit) receive a dispensation for the rest[1].

In view of such facts as these, it becomes easy to understand the difficulty which forced Benedict XII, when ordering the appointment in each monastery of a master to teach the monks grammar, logic and philosophy, to make provision for cases where no inmate of the house could be found fit to undertake the duties, or which led to the remark of Henry VII on increasing the number of scholars of Westminster,

The Kyng hath by long experience perceyued and often seen that for lakke of grounded lerned men in the lawes of God, vertue emonges religious men is little used, Religion is greatly confounded, and few or noo able persones found in dyvers houses of Religion, lakking lerned men to be the heddes of the same house[2].

It is time to examine the work of the monks in the direction of hospitality and almsgiving. The service thus rendered by the religious houses has been made one of the main bases of the defence of their social utility. It has been pointed out with perfect truth that the destruction of the monasteries threw upon the world many who had hitherto found support from their endowments, and that those who received the lands once owned by the monks did not acknowledge that special duty of almsgiving which was recognised by the monasteries. It has been argued that the large increase of pauperism which made necessary the Tudor Poor Laws was, if not altogether the result of, yet to some extent fostered by, the Dissolution. All this must be acknowledged freely and ungrudgingly; and to criticise the work of the monks in this direction without appearing churlish or

---

[1] Reynerus, Appendix, p. 113 et seq. caps. x, xiii.

[2] A. F. Leach, *Educational Charters*, p. 437. In 1423, Bishop Flemyng, after a visitation of St Frideswide's, Oxford, ordered the statutes of the General Chapters of the Benedictine Congregation, the statutes of Otho and Ottobon, and his own injunctions, to be read aloud in the Chapter twice a quarter; this publication was to be made "in the mother tongue, that none of the same canons may be able at all to plead ignorance." So also Bishop Gray's injunctions of 1432 for Kyme Priory were to be read in the mother tongue eight times a year. Uncertainty as to the meaning of the Latin may, of course, have been confined to the younger members of the house. A. Hamilton Thompson, *Visitations of Religious Houses*, I, pp. 68, 81.

biassed is difficult. It seems invidious to admit all this, and yet to point out that, after all, very little was done and that, as many would think to-day, what was done was dearly purchased at the expense of the absorption of wealth by the religious themselves. Yet the facts seem to bear out that conclusion to the full. An inspection of the records of monastic charity from the fourteenth century onwards is disappointing, whatever may be said of such almsgiving as that of the Cistercians in their early enthusiasm. A brief examination of a few figures for these centuries will show how little monastic almsgiving meant.

A few words must first be spoken on the point of hospitality: for that, it will be claimed, is a form of charity which cannot be expressed in figures. It was undoubtedly one of those things in which monastic generosity was especially open to abuse, more especially by the rich and powerful. The great lord with his train would appear demanding hospitality, and would even take it by force. To such a pitch did this go that, in the first Statute of Westminster, provision was made against it. None was to come and eat or lodge in any house of religion other than his own foundation, at the cost of the house, except by special invitation, and none, even at his own cost, was to enter and lodge in a monastery against the wish of the inmates. No suit was to lie for the refusal of hospitality. The statute explained that this was neither intended to deprive the needy of the grace of hospitality, nor to open the way for a burdening of the houses by their patrons through frequent visitations. An example of this last evil is to be found in 1279 at Thetford Priory, where the Cluniac visitors found the house much crippled by the residence of its patron, the Earl Marshall's brother, who was costing the house more than the whole number of monks put together[1]. It is quite clear, however, that the remedy afforded was insufficient. Late in the fifteenth century, for instance, an entry complaining of the abuse of hospitality occurs in the Chronicle of Evesham. "Magnates convolarunt adeo frequenter ad monasterium ut non sufficerent redditus." The house was burdened in consequence with a debt of 1000 marks[2].

---

[1] Duckett, *Visitations of the English Cluniac Foundations*, p. 34.
[2] *Chronicon Abbatiæ de Evesham*; the complaint is made during the abbacy of Richard Hawksberry, 1467–77.

But at the same time, in the fourteenth and fifteenth centuries, the same tendency which showed itself in the monks'
management of their estates, showed itself in their hospitality.
They began to pass the burden on to others, to save themselves
the trouble of receiving and looking after guests. Canon Capes[1]
points out the decline at St Albans, at Abingdon, at Glastonbury,
Burcester, and probably at Gloucester, in all cases before the
first quarter of the fifteenth century was over. It was marked by
the erection of inns to take the place of the monastery's hostelry
—in some cases by the actual conversion of the hostelry into
an inn. Hospitality to the great doubtless continued, but there
is enough evidence to show that for the poorer traveller little
was being done in the end, and that the monks in this direction
also were centring their interests more and more on their own
ease and welfare, and less and less on any services which they
might do to their neighbours.

The examination of a few cases illustrative of the extent and
nature of monastic almsgiving will show much the same thing
in this direction. First may be taken the case of Bolton Priory
early in the fourteenth century. Burton[2] gives a compotus for
the year 1324–5. It is hardly satisfactory in one way, inasmuch
as its receipts add up to a total of nearly £600, whereas (if Burton's
copy is accurate) the monks brought it to a total of £444 only.
But it is valuable in another way because it draws a distinction
between the "dona et exennia" of the house and its alms, which
does not often occur. The exact significance of the "gifts and
presents" is shown by an entry in a similar account of the same
house for 1298–9[3], in which it is explained that they were "made
to magnates for the advantage of the house." The list of these
presents in 1324–5 begins with one to the archbishop and goes
down to sundry "tips" to messengers and servants of various
great men, its total being £13. 6s. 5d. The alms given in cash
amount to £2. 5s. 4d. To this must be added a small proportion
of the produce received by the monastery from its farms, and
in all probability the fragments from the monk's table: but this

---

[1] *History of the English Church in the Fourteenth and Fifteenth Centuries*,
p. 287.
[2] *Monasticon Eboracense*, pp. 121, 126. I have some doubts whether the
whole expenditure of the house is included.
[3] Whitaker, *History of Craven*, p. 453.

proportion works out at even less than that of the actual cash. From $\frac{1}{250}$th to $\frac{1}{170}$th, then, of the revenue of this house was roughly the proportion given this year in alms. If the alms and presents be added together, the percentage is about $2\frac{1}{2}$ or $3\frac{1}{2}$, according to the total chosen for the account. It may be urged that the house had suffered heavily from the Scots a few years before. But, if the items of the account are correct, the canons were handling a revenue not much, if at all, less than that enjoyed before the Scottish devastations. If this is not accepted, the need for alms must have been all the more intense owing to the destruction wrought. If we take the same house in 1298–9, the proportion of alms, gifts, and presents taken together, compared with the total cash expenses of the year is only about 2 per cent., although allowance must be made for the proportion given to the poor of the produce used in kind, which here seems to be a little more than in 1324. The total expenditure of grain of all kinds was 1842 qrs. 7 bushels: the alms recorded (if a corrody of 4 qrs. $2\frac{1}{2}$ bushels of wheat is included) comes to 36 qrs. $4\frac{1}{2}$ bushels, or roughly 2 per cent.

In this case we have been dealing with an account which purports to be a balance-sheet for the whole year: on turning to the more elaborate obedientiary rolls we are met by the difficulty that a full set for any one year practically never exists, and as nearly all the obedientiaries gave small sums in alms, this makes an estimation of the proportion of alms to income very difficult. Mr G. G. Coulton, by taking the last example of every official's roll in the Durham account book, which represents at some stage or other most of the offices of the monastery, calculates that about 4 per cent. covers the amount given away. But it should not be assumed that all this was given to the "deserving poor." It covers all kinds of gifts—presents to "histriones" (i.e. minstrels) and "cantors" at the prior's merry-makings, "tips" to messengers and servants bringing presents, gifts to all sorts of great men for protection, to the archbishop, his huntsman, his fool, and so on. Even the almoner's accounts—those of the monastic official especially charged with this duty of looking after the poor—are disappointing. In 1339–40, the almoner received in cash from various sources a few shillings over £70, and the expenditure was £44 and a few shillings. Of this, the poor actually received only £15. 10s., the rest going in servants' wages, payments to priests, building expenses, and so on. The expenses were necessary, no doubt, in part: but they seem to bulk far too large. In 1340–1, £54. 12s. 1¼d. was spent, the poor receiving £14. 10s. 6d. So the accounts of this great monastery continue.

Other accounts show nothing much better. The Finchale rolls show that in 1346–7 the prior's gifts, presents and alms, which apparently comprise the whole amount of cash gifts for the year, came to roughly 4 per cent. of the whole cash income, while the grain given away was only about 2 per cent. of that used in the house. In 1347–8, the amount of cash given away, as nearly as it can be calculated, was £3. 9s. 3d. out of a total income of £237. 8s. 2d., or roughly 1·25 per cent.: the grain given away is only 1 quarter 3 bushels, as compared with 253 quarters 5 bushels used in the house. In 1348–9, the plague year, condonations of rents for the first time make their appearance: but even these only raise the cash gifts to a little under 2 per cent. of the total income, which seems to have remained practically unaffected[1]. If we go on for a century much the same thing appears. In 1409–10, out of an actual cash income (excluding debts still owing to the monastery and loans raised in that year) of £187. 15s. 1d., only £2. 10s. 3d. is given away, or roughly 1·3 per cent.: no account is given of the income in kind. The next year the proportion sinks to under 1 per cent. In 1442–3, only 11s. 5d. is recorded as given away out of an income of £177. 14s. 6½d. These proportions are so pitifully small, and compare so unfavourably with other monastic accounts, that it is tempting to suppose either that some class, say of almoner's accounts, must have been lost altogether, or that some such arrangement prevailed as that instituted at Evesham in 1206 whereby one-tenth of the bread baked in the monastery was to go in alms. Although there is no trace of such a system having ever prevailed at Finchale, it may be noticed that a calculation on this basis from the earlier accounts, wherein the amount of corn used in the house is given, brings the alms up to about 5 per cent. of the total income.

---

[1] The allowance claimed in 1354 for bad debts of this year was only a little over £24. Others may have been condoned before.

In the case of St Swithun's, Winchester, it will be best to let the editor of the Compotus Rolls speak[1].

It will be seen from a careful inspection of these rolls that in actual charity the office did very little indeed, and not much even in doles of bread; there is not a trace of the visitation of the sick on which Archbishop Lanfranc lays so much stress. As we have said, the charity of the monastery showed itself in supporting the Sustern spital, in keeping open house for pilgrims and other visitors, in distributing bread half a dozen times in the year, in providing mats for the monks' feet in church and refectory, and elsewhere, and in distributing the Almoner's old clothes to the poor once a year, instead of giving them back as the other brethren did to the chamberlain. But there is very little of what we deem charitable work performed by the Almoner himself or his servants; one finds none of that giving to wayfarers passing through the country which forms so marked an element in the accounts of the Dean and Chapter in the seventeenth century: even Lanfranc's Decrees gave no sanction to indiscriminate alms-giving. And when the mishap at Hinton [a fire] straitened the means of the Almoner, the poor dependents were the first to suffer—one can always retrench comfortably by cutting down one's alms.

This picture, which the accounts fully bear out, is not very pleasant.

It must be remembered, moreover, that the monasteries were frequently merely the administrators of funds left by others. The lands bequeathed to them were often held on condition that a certain proportion of the proceeds went to the poor. These statutory alms, as they may be called, at the time of the drawing up of the Valor Ecclesiasticus in the sixteenth century, were exempted from the payment of the tenth to the King and were therefore recorded in order to get the net value of the possessions to be taxed. Professor Savine calculates that these fixed alms, in giving which the monasteries were often merely fulfilling the necessary conditions for holding their lands, amounted on the average to a little less than 3 per cent. of the annual income[2].

[1] The accounts both here and at Abingdon are so fragmentary—the almoner's rolls at Abingdon, for example, are lacking entirely—that it is impossible to make any calculation as to percentages. The bursar's account at Whalley (printed by Whitaker, *History of Whalley*, I) shows that in 1477 the alms and gifts were a little under 4 per cent. of the amount handled by that official, and in 1527 about 2¼ per cent. It is just possible, as pointed out in Chapter II, that Whitaker is right in taking the bursar's roll as containing the whole income and expenditure of the house.

[2] A. N. Savine, *The English Monasteries on the Eve of the Dissolution*, p. 265.

If we state the average gifts of the monasteries during the centuries under consideration as high as 5 per cent., and remember that this included much that we should not now consider as alms, the subtraction of these fixed payments leaves but little for the spontaneous charity of the monasteries. How difficult it was to maintain even such a natural form of almsgiving as the distribution of the remnants from the monk's table, can be seen by anyone caring to inspect the series of decrees of the Benedictine Chapters, and Papal Constitutions so often mentioned in these pages, and comparing them with such a document as the Visitations of Odo Rigaldi.

It may be thought that in fixing the proportion of alms to income at about 5 per cent., some possible channel of charity has been overlooked, which would leave no trace in the account-rolls. But the conclusion receives a most valuable confirmation from the evidence as to the French Benedictine houses whose income and expenditure was calculated by order of Benedict XII in 1338[1]. Saint Ouen de Rouen, a house of 62 monks with a total income of £11,647. 10s. 4d. tournois, returned the alms given as follows: alms of the abbot when outside the house £90, net alms of the almonry £360. 18s. This gives a percentage of roughly 3·7; this, it should be remembered, does not include the expense of the guests, or the distribution of scraps from the table. Mont-Saint-Michel, with 40 monks and an income of £6379. 9s. 9d., reckoned as alms an "erogatio" of pork on Lundi Gras to a crowd of poor from all parts, and the almoner's revenues. An indefinite part of the latter, however, went to maintain poor clerks at the University—very possibly the convent's own students—and part in working expenses. But the monastery claimed that hospitality was heavy, owing to the situation of the monastery: and if this is allowed as a counterpoise, the alms may be taken at the figures given by the monastery, and reckoned at about 5·7 per cent.

On the whole, if we bear in mind the presents to great men for the good of the house, the payment of mummers and singers, the presents to men bringing venison and so on, there will seem to be much in the bitter words of the sufficiently pessimistic "Poem on the Evil Times" of Edward II, which

[1] L. Delisle, *La Fortune de l'Ordre de St-Benoît*.

applies not only to monastic hospitality but to almsgiving as well.

> For if there come to an abeye to pore men or thre,
> And aske of hem helpe *par seinte charité*,
> Unnethe wol any don his ernde other zong or old,
> But late him coure ther al day, in hunger and in cold,
> > and sterve.
> Loke what love ther is to God whom theih seien that hii serve!
>
> But there come another and bring a litel lettre
> In a box upon his hepe, he shal spede the bettre;
> And if he be wid eny man that may don the abot harm
> He shall be lad into the halle, and ben imad full warm
> > aboute the mawe.
> And Godes man stant ther oute; sory is that lawe.[1]

The sketch, with its assumption that it is always "Godes man" who stands without, may well be overdrawn: yet it seems far from unrecognisable.

Enough has been said, at all events, to show that it is easily possible to over-estimate the amount of the alms distributed by the monasteries. It should be remembered also that much of the distribution was quite indiscriminate. Even though we make every allowance for other methods of charity—the maintenance of almshouses or hospitals endowed from the possessions of the monastery, and the occasional charitable granting of corrodies taking the chief place among them—the result of an examination of this side of monastic life during these later centuries is disillusioning. It may well be doubted whether any increase of pauperism which followed on the Dissolution was not due more to the sudden dispersal of the large companies of servants than to the withdrawal of the monastic alms. What was given was doubtless of inestimable value to the recipients; the mere fact that the monastic ideal did inculcate the duty of care for the poor had counted for much, and still doubtless counted for much. But the meagreness of the gifts of the monks during this time, the absence of any systematic distribution among the really needy, the haphazard way in which many of the gifts of the religious were obviously scattered, and the lack of living personal interest in the poor which lies at the root of all

---

[1] T. Wright, *Political Songs* (Camden Society), p. 329.

indiscriminate charity, cannot be ignored. It is probably the side of their life which attracts the most sympathy from the modern mind. But equally it is the side on which the difference between theory and practice is the most keenly appreciated. To come fresh from the theory of monastic almsgiving, as laid down in the custumals, to an inspection of these accounts is to take an unequal view of things. Ideals are never attained. But the charity of the monks as revealed in their accounts gives a very different idea of things from that in which some would have us believe.

CHAPTER V

MONASTIC DEBT

THE general state of monastic finances at the time of the Dissolution is one of the main subjects treated by Professor Savine in his study of the Valor Ecclesiasticus. It has been asserted that throughout the fourteenth and fifteenth centuries the religious houses were plunging deeper and deeper into debt; that their affairs drew nearer and nearer to a crisis until, by the sixteenth century, practical bankruptcy was threatening many foundations. Professor Savine has shown that this was not the case. He proves that in only a very few instances was a house burdened with a debt exceeding a year's income, and that in most cases the monastery's debt was well within the limits of that mark. This is not a state which can be called bankruptcy. Nevertheless, the continual indebtedness of the religious houses, and their consequent difficulties, are facts which strike one forcibly.

The lack of continuous records in the case of the majority of houses, and the consequent fact that only here and there can we trace the varying fortunes of any one house through anything like its whole life, together with the lack of any general statement of the income of the monasteries in the Middle Ages make it difficult to give any general assertion as to the period when debt was deepest and most common. The disease seems to have broken out at nearly every date in some house or other. One fact, however, seems plain. The financial difficulties of the religious houses were frequent and serious throughout the thirteenth century. They seem, if anything, to have grown more serious as the century progressed. No universal statement, of course, can be made. The greatest difficulties at Evesham and Bury St Edmund's would seem to have occurred at the close of the twelfth century. Fountains, at the time, was in a flourishing condition. On the other hand, Bolton and Fountains were in low water at the close of the thirteenth century, but the abbots of Evesham by that time were adding greatly to the revenues of their house. Throughout the later years of the thirteenth century, however, and the early years of the fourteenth century, the accumulated evidence of financial difficulties is such as to throw very grave doubt upon any theory which represents the English monasteries as continuously flourishing and prosperous until they were overwhelmed by the chaos of the Black Death.

Taking the years from 1290 to 1330 as an example, the following list, though not exhaustive, will serve to illustrate the situation.

Bolton, as has been mentioned[1], was failing year after year to make both ends meet. Fountains was taken into the King's hands in 1291, and a secular administrator was appointed to help it out of its difficulties. Lewes, which as late as 1262 was free from debt, by 1279 was in such a state that, according to the Cluniac visitors, it would be very difficult to relieve its liabilities at all, and at least twenty years would be needful to free it from debt. As a matter of fact, it seems not to have got clear till 1414. Most of the Cluniac houses were in a bad state financially at the end of the century, notably Bermondsey and Wenlock. In 1279, 11 Cluniac houses, with a total population of 342, were in debt to the extent of £7836, or about £22. 18s. per head[2]. St Albans began to get into serious difficulties apparently for the first time during the abbacy of John Maryns (1302–8). Meaux, after recovering from its early difficulties, caused first by an attempt to maintain too large a number of monks for its originally scanty endowments, and then by the quarrel between John and the Cistercians, was deep in debt again by 1280, and after a slow recovery up to the time of the Black Death, remained more or less burdened (though never to such an extent as in 1280) up till the end of the fourteenth century when the Chronicle closes. St Albans in 1328 was petitioning for appropriations on the score of a debt of 5000 marks and a diminution of its income owing to the Scottish wars[3]. Bardney, in Lincolnshire, was in so bad a condition in 1308 that Edward II asked the Pope to intervene and prevent its ruin[4].

[1] See p. 97, above.
[2] See Appendix A, The Cluniac Houses.
[3] *Calendar of Papal Letters*, II, p. 270.
[4] Rymer, *Foedera*, III, p. 72.

Peterborough was in dire straits in 1273 owing to the civil wars[1]. The Gilbertine houses, as Miss Rose Graham has shown[2], reached their greatest prosperity during the reign of Edward I, but suffered heavily from debt under Edward II. The anarchy of the time, famine, murrain and heavy expenses incurred in building and the purchase of lands played their part in the change. Sempringham, Chicksand, Malton, Watton, St Andrew's outside York, St Catherine's outside Lincoln, Fordham, Cattley and Shouldham were all in debt. "On August 14, 1335, William Prior of Malton, and the Convent, owed Thomas de Holm of Beverley 127 sacks and 4 stones of wool of the price of 1393 marks and ten pence, besides £446. 10s."

For the West of England, the register of the energetic John de Grandisson illustrates the position in the diocese of Exeter during the twenty years immediately preceding the Black Death. The financial situation was obviously none too easy. Mismanagement and debt were common. At Forde Abbey in 1329, some "dilapidation" of the monastery's property had obviously been going on. Barnstaple Priory, a cell of St Martin's, Paris, was suffering from the frequent appointment and recall of the priors. In 1332 Grandisson sequestrated the income and goods of the house, as the prior was an absentee in Paris. In 1335 he warned the Abbot of St Martin's that if changes were made too often the house would be ruined. The income was already hardly enough for the prior and monks. The prior's predecessor, whom the bishop had appointed with many misgivings[3], had done irreparable harm.

At Modbury Priory, a cell of St Pierre-sur-Dive, in 1329 the mother-house was keeping three monks, though it was only founded for two. Hospitality could not be maintained under these conditions, and the bishop sent one of the inmates back to Normandy. The Priory of St Michael's Mount, a cell of Mont-Saint-Michel, was visited in 1336 on account of charges of waste brought against the prior. The income of the house was stated at £100, together with the oblations in the church[4], and

---

[1] See p. 128, below. *Chronicon Petroburgense* (C.S.), pp. x, xi.
[2] Rose Graham, *S. Gilbert of Sempringham and the Gilbertines*, pp. 136–47.
[3] And a claim for a pension for one of his servants.
[4] The mother-house stated it in 1338 at £106. 13s. 4d. L. Delisle, *La Fortune de l'Ordre de St-Benoît*, p. 33.

the debts only at £5. But the prior, who for a month or more had been left alone in the house[1], had farmed out land at a low price to the grave damage of the house, had lent corn and other goods worth £12 to persons from whom he dared not reclaim the money, and had allowed one of his kinsmen to waste the convent property. At Bodmin Priory, in 1328, an administrator was set by the side of the prior until the bishop could visit the house. The visitation showed that the goods of the monastery were being dissipated by the carelessness and "insolencies" of the bailiffs and servants. The Rector of Wythiel and one of the canons were associated with the prior in the management of the house; and in the following year, the prior was warned to leave the whole administration in his coadjutor's hands, as there had been a great improvement. In 1338–9 leave was given to sell a "livery or corrody" to repair the chapter-house and dormitory, which, partly through age and partly through gales, were in ruins. The prior was allowed to resume control of the business affairs of the house. In 1343 his bad management, with that of some of the canons, had again produced a collapse. The bishop satisfied himself with injunctions which, if carried out, curbed the prior's extravagance, deposed the cellarer, handed over the administration of the property to two canons, ordered the dismissal of 13 menservants by name, as well as all other such private servants of the canons as were not exempted by the new administration, and stopped the sub-prior's excessive meals. But in 1346 the bishop heard that Bodmin was still badly governed, and in 1347 he pronounced it in great debt, "through carelessness," forbade the canons to wear "unseemly" clothing, to keep dogs or grooms, or to play dice or chess, and bade them dismiss six useless servants and reform in other ways. At Tywardreath Priory, a cell of St Sergius near Anjou, an inquiry held before 1328 gave grounds for suspecting waste, and the prior was deprived of the management of its affairs. In 1328–9 he was allowed to resume control, with the assistance of a knight, a secular priest and a monk; but arrangements were made to reduce the monks' living allowance, and to get rid of servants, horses and hounds. In 1330 further reports of waste demanded inquiry and the Prior of Minster was appointed as coadjutor to

---

[1] Three other monks should have been there with him. *Ibid.* p. 33.

the prior. In 1333 the priory fell vacant; the bishop wrote to the mother-house pointing out that seven monks could no longer be maintained there—indeed, hardly one—without begging. He advised the recall of three of the inmates, and meanwhile cut the monks' living allowance down by nearly half. In 1338 Grandisson allowed the inmates to live at any church or chapel appropriated to the house, at a distance from the sea, on account of the risk from pirates and other foes. But it seems doubtful whether the move was made, for in 1338–9 the monks were allowed to have a house within the precincts where they might eat flesh-meat with their guests, the guest hall having fallen down altogether.

A commission was appointed to visit Launceston Priory in 1336–7 because Grandisson had been informed that the prior was an absentee, living with seculars and totally dissipating the goods of the monastery. In 1341–2 the bishop ordered the alms which the prior had withdrawn to be restored, and arrangements to be made to restrict the daily almsgiving to old men and "some poor boys fit to learn grammar," excluding women and the able-bodied. The damaged books and the torn and dirty vestments in the church were to be replaced, the usual lights were to be maintained, and the sacristan was ordered to keep proper accounts. The canons were to abstain from "unbecoming drinkings" at home or outside, to get rid of the hunting-dogs and hawks, and to dismiss the burdensome household of servants, especially those attached to single canons. In 1344 the bishop adjudged the prior to be a dilapidator, weak, in ill-health, and imprudent, and appointed a coadjutor to manage the business of the convent. In 1346 the prior was made to resign.

Meanwhile a great struggle between the bishop and Tavistock Abbey had been proceeding. In 1328 Grandisson was warning the abbot not to admit more monks before a visitation; he had heard that the community was not far from the completest desolation. A heated protest led the bishop to decide on a friendly visit, instead of a visitation; but he followed this up by instructions for the return of books, silver vessels, and other goods alleged to have been purloined by the monks when the abbey had last been vacant. In 1330 a commission was appointed to inquire into the statements that the church and buildings were threatening ruin, that some of the monks were wandering abroad, and that the goods of the house were daily being dissipated. Two years later the whole convent was excommunicated; and in the next year the abbot was deposed, on the score of "dilapidations" carried so far that some of the monks had to beg for food, and on other grounds. A new abbot was elected, and the excommunication withdrawn. In 1338 inquiries were again necessary, and the bishop found that the obedientiaries held their revenues in farm. The abbot was deprived of the administration altogether, until the house was in a better state. Some £1300 was owing, and other burdens were weighing the house down. The bishop's arrangements for reform do not seem to have been very effective. In 1345 a visitation, which left many charges open for further inquiry, showed that the abbot was wearing a dress like a secular priest, with "buttoned sleeves" and "unseemly" shoes; three of the monks were copying him; the abbot, the prior, the abbot's friends and Brother Thomas Coffyn were keeping hunting-dogs; and nearly all the monks complained that three of the lay officials, one being the abbot's chamberlain, received large sums for which they never accounted. In 1348, according to the bishop, the abbot was still "dilapidating" for his own pleasures, pledging, selling or giving away the monastery's property. He had got hold of the convent seal which had been put under the charge of some of the monks. The property of the house was thereupon sequestrated, and all business dealings with the abbot were forbidden. It remains to add that in 1349 the abbey was allowed to appropriate the parish church of Whitchurch, partly on the plea of the pestilence, and partly because of the ravages of pirates in the Scilly Isles, where much of the convent's property lay.

To complete this sufficiently dismal picture, the bishop in 1338–9 warned Earl Warenne that St James' Priory, Exeter, which claimed as a Cluniac house to be exempt from visitation, was so injured by the prior's follies and alienations that hardly one monk could be maintained. The prior was deprived of control. In 1339 administrators had to be appointed at Hartland Abbey in consequence of the abbot's illness. The bishop found Plympton Priory much burdened with debt "owing to bad management," and hearing in 1331 that things were worse than ever he appointed a commission to investigate. In 1338 the priory was allowed to appropriate a church; and the poverty of the house was then ascribed to its proximity to Plymouth and the burden of hospitality which this involved, as well as to oppressions and exactions incurred without fault of the monks. Arrangements had to be made at Frithelstock Priory in 1340 to prevent the alienation of property without consent of the bishop and the house, and to cut down the convent's expenses to pay its debts. The nunnery at Cornworthy was allowed to let a lady lodge there "at her own expense" at the end of 1333, and Canonsleigh Abbey was allowed to sell a corrody in 1334–5, steps which usually pointed to some financial embarrassment. No stress perhaps should be laid on appropriations to Buckland Abbey and Lilleshull Abbey, though the plea, as usual, was poverty.

The position here was to some extent exceptional. The proportion of alien houses visited was apparently large, and the houses, in many cases, belonged to that class of smaller monasteries whose shortcomings gave colour, at a later date, to the demand for the dissolution, in the first place, of convents with less than the dozen inhabitants recognised by monastic legislators as necessary for a well-ordered house. Grandisson, moreover, was an energetic administrator, likely to discover or lay stress on difficulties which other visitors would pass over with little notice. But the registers of his predecessors show a state of affairs not very much different, and other episcopal registers of the thirteenth and early fourteenth centuries show that financial troubles were frequent[1].

Continental evidence, so far as I have inspected it, is to much the same effect. Prof. Pirenne, writing of the French houses, indeed, points to the earlier thirteenth century as the period when financial difficulties were most frequent and serious. But the register of Odo Rigaldi shows that, in Normandy at least,

[1] The theory, tempting at first sight, that the "common form" of episcopal injunctions represents the issue, by way of warning, of general instructions, with possibly little relation to the immediate state of the house, becomes untenable on close inspection of the evidence. Prohibitions of the alienation of property, or "delapidations," though couched in general terms, must be accepted as evidence of financial difficulties, though their nature and extent are frequently left vague.

the third quarter of the century was not one of general prosperity.

In the diocese of Rouen itself, a calculation for the years 1256–
58 shows that 42 monasteries with a total population of 618
members were on the average in debt to the extent of about
25 per cent. of their income, or roughly a debt of £14 tournois
(about £70 sterling before 1914) per head of their population.
In the other dioceses of the archbishopric, at the same time, 33
houses owed roughly 30 per cent. of their annual income, also
representing a debt per head of some £70 sterling before the
war[1].

In England the effect of the diversion of popular favour to the
friars, which Prof. Pirenne suggests as one of the main causes
of difficulty abroad, can hardly have been serious for some years
after the middle of the thirteenth century. For the rest, the
main external causes in England may well have been those put
forward by Prof. Pirenne, namely, the "renaissance of com-
merce and industry," and the "enormous drop in the value
of money which characterises the twelfth and thirteenth centuries." But the effect of the first may well have been felt
later in agricultural England, with its exports limited to raw
materials, its foreign trade in other hands and its towns still
concerned mainly with local markets.

The fall in the purchasing power of money, however, continued all through the centuries under consideration, until at
last, from the early fifteenth to the middle of the sixteenth
century, it reached a period of comparative stability. The result
must have been a growing economic pressure on those who with
a fixed income were steadily confronted with rising prices. The
monks, with their income derived in the main from land, were
in this unfortunate position; and the inelasticity of their revenues,
after the rush of endowments frequently lavished on them in
early days, must have become more and more of a difficulty.
The reduction of the monastic population which, as we have
seen, may be generally suspected before the great drop in the
fourteenth century, may be attributed in part to this diminution
of the purchasing power of income. It was the simplest way
of coping with the difficulty.

[1] See further Appendix B, The Province of Rouen.

Other external forces were at work. The effect of troublous times, and the accompanying exactions, must be taken into account. The time when Henry III and the Pope in union were drawing on the funds of the English Church was one when the monasteries, in particular, suffered severely, and the difficulties of many houses in the later thirteenth century were doubtless directly connected with the exactions then instituted. The "crusading tithes" of 1254, 1274 and 1291 which went to the King were each accompanied by a special assessment of ecclesiastical revenues. The "verus valor" disclosed by these assessments rose higher on each occasion. However inaccurate the Taxation of Pope Nicholas, it was justly considered the most oppressively stringent assessment which had yet been made. The crusading tenth of 1305, payable for two years to the King, was accompanied by the imposition on the English Church for the first time of the payment of annates. The monasteries suffered side by side with the secular clergy.

We have seen also that the episcopal visitations might prove oppressive and that the rights claimed by the papacy over the exempt monasteries led to the abstraction of large sums. It may be merely a coincidence, but it is noticeable that the period when St Albans seems first to have got into low water was that also when the Pope was helping himself to the enormous confirmation fees already noticed. The convent, however, when appealing to the papacy, judiciously put down its difficulties in the main to a decrease of its income through the Scottish wars. The extravagance of Abbot Hugh de Eversdone was also a contributory cause. The monasteries, it must also be remembered, found themselves very frequently called upon throughout the Middle Ages to provide loans for the King, often upon very imperfect security: a burden so oppressive as to make it worth while in some cases for the monastery to go to the expense of a papal bull forbidding the incurrence of all such debts. Thus in 1258 when Henry III was trying to raise a loan, the Abbot of St Albans produced a papal provision, prohibiting any such thing; the Abbot of Reading apparently did the same thing; the Abbot of Waltham cited the decretals as forbidding such loans and followed this up by obtaining a document similar to that possessed by St Albans. But the papacy proved a weak prop, for eventually the Bishop of Hereford with the Pope's sanction devised a scheme which evaded the opposition of the monasteries[1].

The political disorganisation during the later fourteenth century and the Wars of the Roses in the fifteenth must inevitably have been productive of much distress and difficulty[2]. But local disasters, affecting only particular houses, figure almost as prominently. Meaux, for instance, found its lands perpetually diminished by the inroads of the Humber; and this went on to such an extent that in 1401 an inquisition held as to the liability of the house to taxation disclosed the fact that from possessions valued in the Taxation of Pope Nicholas in 1291 at £253. 10s. a year, only £6. 7s. came in, by reason of the floods[3]. Other revenues to a considerable extent had since been added, but the loss involved must have been severely felt. Waverley, during the thirteenth century, suffered from three disastrous floods. Fires were very frequent indeed. The Northern houses, more especially during the earlier fourteenth century, were constantly liable to the danger of an inroad by the Scots. It has already been noted how Bolton Priory suffered: Fountains also came well within the raiding area. The Letters from the Northern Registers, in the Rolls Series, let us see something of the difficulties of this period. The nunneries of Molseby and Rosedale had to disperse in 1322, owing to the ruin brought upon the house by the Scots. Eggleston Abbey in 1328 was in such a state, for the same reason, that it obtained an entire remission from taxation. But most houses in the North must have suffered in this way. The general difficulties of the alien priories have been already mentioned: they were ground between the upper and nether millstones of exploitation on the part of the mother-houses abroad, and the royal demands in time of war.

But when every allowance for such causes as these has been made, there still remains evidence that mismanagement of the revenues of the monastic houses was answerable for much of this debt. The abbots or priors, with their autocratic power over the spending of the monastic income, were frequently responsible

---

[1] *Gesta Abbatum*, I, p. 373; the bull for Waltham, dated 1262, is in Rymer, *Foedera*, I, p. 612.

[2] The abbot of Peterborough, about 1265, had to pay one side or the other over £4300 in two years.

[3] *Chronica Monasterii de Melsa*, III, p. 284.

for the debts in which their houses were involved. It was not always wilful or even conscious mismanagement which lay at the root of the evil. Often sheer lack of business qualifications did the mischief. Naturally enough, it is not very often that we get in the larger houses such bad cases of misappropriation as that, already mentioned, of Roger Norreys of Evesham. Yet the business morality of the abbots and priors might often have been much higher than it actually was.

Nepotism was one of the ways in which the property of the monasteries was dissipated. Those in authority failed to shake off the ties of kindred, and there were pickings to be had in many ways. It will be remembered how, as Abbot Samson returned towards Bury St Edmund's after the confirmation of his election by the King,

> a multitude of new relations came about him offering to serve him, but he answered all of them that he was content with the servants of the prior, nor could he retain others until he had obtained the assent of the convent.

Not all, however, had the rectitude of Samson. A remarkable statement is made by Matthew Paris about the abbots of St Albans. Writing in the twentieth year of the 23rd abbot, John de Hertford (1235–60), he says:

> This same Abbot John (which can truly be written of none, or few of his predecessors) never dissipated the possessions or goods of his church on account of carnal affection or friendship for his parents, kinsfolk, or acquaintances: I speak from the time of his creation to the twentieth year of his prelacy. In this year, to wit, this page was written by Brother Matthew Paris, who presumes not to make assertions about the future.

The reform of the Benedictine Statutes by Benedict XII in 1337, so often cited already, discloses some of the ways in which this dispersion of goods went on. One of the chapters, headed "Of feigned and deceitful contracts," explains that it sometimes happened that abbots, priors and other administrators entered into feigned contracts, acknowledging by public documents that they had received, as a loan or otherwise, money or goods for the use of their convent from their father, mother, nephew or some other relative, or from a friend, servant or merchant. The monastery was thus made responsible for the repayment of a sum which it had never received. The punishment provided by Benedict for such offences was excommunication until restitution had been made as far as possible. Other instances besides those at St Albans might be cited. Thus in 1324 Simon, Abbot of Croyland, was forced to resign because he loved his kinsmen in the flesh over much, and scorned his spiritual relatives[1]. At Eynsham, to give one more example, in 1520 the abbot's sister was maintained in the house and was a burden to it: it was believed by the monks that she and other relatives of the abbot received £140 a year out of the revenues of the monastery[2]. The same abbot was maintaining a scholar at Oxford who received all the revenues of the monastery in the city and gave no account of his disposal of them.

The heads of houses were often not alone in their waste of the funds. It will be remembered how, at Bury St Edmunds, Abbot Samson had to intervene to put an end to the "excess of feasting in the prior's house by the assent of the prior and cellarer, and superfluous expenses in the guest-house by the carelessness of the hospitaller," which were reducing the house to poverty. At St Albans, again, on the death of Abbot John de Stoke, there was a scandal concerning a sum of 1000 marks which the abbot had said he had in his purse; no details are given, but peculation had been going on and some of the spoils were recovered[3]. At Meaux, to give one more example, the worst which has come under my notice, the Chronicle records that under the lax rule of William of Wendover, elected abbot in 1399, a man more skilled in matters of the cloister than in temporal affairs, the monastic officials became mere proprietaries, seeking only profit for themselves. The bursar, Robert Lekynfeld, who had charge of the house during the vacancy of the abbacy, destroyed all his accounts to conceal his embezzlements, and with his spoils went to the Court of Rome and purchased the bishopric of Killaloe in Ireland. Not daring to go to his see, he became suffragan of the diocese of Coventry and Lichfield and held the post till his death[4].

But to multiply such instances as these, and to dwell on them

[1] Dugdale, *Monasticon*, II, p. 104.
[2] H. E. Salter, *Eynsham Cartulary*, I, Appendix, visitation of 1520.
[3] Dugdale, *Monasticon*, II, p. 176.
[4] *Chronica Monasterii de Melsa*, III, p. 278.

overmuch, would give a wrong impression. The period we are considering is long, and the scandals of this kind which have come beneath my notice seem after all comparatively few[1]. Dr Jessopp's statement[2] that really bad abbots or priors were the exception and not the rule, seems abundantly justified. What was far more frequent was a lack of business capacity, a general wastefulness, extravagance, and neglect of the ordinary rules of prudence. The difficulty clearly was to get a really effective despot—a man who, like Abbot Samson, could manage the business affairs of the house without losing sight of its spiritual condition, and keep to the general ascetic lines of monastic life without letting material affairs slide. The best monk was not the best abbot; it may be said that to put a man noted for monastic piety in charge of a house was to court disaster. Abbot Hugh, Samson's predecessor at Bury St Edmund's, is an example. So too is the Abbot of Meaux lately mentioned, William of Wendover. Yet a third is to be found in Abbot John of St Albans (1195–1214), who involved his house in much difficulty and ridicule by embarking on elaborate building schemes which were beyond his capacity to manage[3]. The difficulty was ever present: the competent business manager was liable to become secularised and care little for the inner life of the monastery; the saintly monk often took too little thought for the things of this world, and business discipline was relaxed. And what was true of the abbot was true also of the obedientiaries. The fact seems fairly obvious that the monastic life was not likely to develope a type of man noticeable for business capacity. This shows itself in many ways. The preference displayed by Abbot Samson for secular clerks as men of business, so exasperating to his monks, finds throughout the whole period a reflection in the way in which, time after time, the bishops, when called on to intervene in the interests of economy, thought it necessary to set a secular by the side of the religious entrusted with the management of the property of the house in question. The same practice may also be observed in the cases where the King took in hand the

---

[1] "Anyhow, as things went in those days, the King was often ably and sometimes honestly served. In the atmosphere of slackness and peculation which prevailed in the middle ages, we can expect no more than this." T. F. Tout, *The English Civil Service in the Fourteenth Century*, p. 16.

[2] *The Coming of the Friars*, p. 160.   [3] *Gesta Abbatum*, I, p. 218.

task of reorganising the affairs of some monastery plunged in difficulties. The monks' lack of business capacity is occasionally recognised in express terms. When William Gray, Bishop of Ely, in 1458 transferred the mastership of St John's Hospital, Ely, to his domestic chaplain Robert Normann, he thought fit to explain that he trusted to his sagacity and probity to redeem the previous maladministration whereby "regular" and "religious" persons had reduced it to the utmost want and misery, from which no "religious" persons could be found capable of relieving it[1].

It may be suspected that the monks as a rule felt the details of business beneath their attention. It is very noticeable that from about the middle of the fourteenth century the accounts were kept by clerks, who received payments for their services, instead of by the monks. In the later fifteenth century, the difficulty of finding suitable officials, combined, perhaps, with the divided responsibilities and overlapping functions of the obedientiaries, seems to have led to an attempt at evasion by the accumulation of offices in the hands of one man, sometimes the abbot, sometimes one of the monks. Thus at Westminster Abbot John Esteney, the first abbot to hold an office in the monastery, was at one and the same time sacrist, warden of the new work and cellarer[2]. At St Albans, in 1452, there was one officer known as the "Official General," who was cellarer, sub-cellarer, bursar, forester, and chamberlain at once[3]. At Norwich, in 1492, Bishop James Goldwell found Dan Dennis acting as communar, almoner, infirmarer, pittancer, and master of Norman's Hospital. At St Faith's Priory, where there were nine monks, all the offices were held by the prior[4].

Neglect of the most ordinary business precautions shows itself. Innocent IV found it necessary to order in his reform of the Benedictine Statutes (1253) that all the rents of an abbey,

as well of the head as of the members should be set down in writing; and the incomings which were not fixed should be faithfully estimated;

[1] Gray's register is summarised in the *Ely Diocesan Remembrancer*.
[2] Rackham, *Nave of Westminster*, p. 35.
[3] *Registrum Johannis Whethamstede*, I, p. 102.
[4] A. Jessopp, *Visitations of the Diocese of Norwich*, pp. 3, 19. Other examples occur in the Lincoln visitations edited by Mr A. Hamilton Thompson.

and a copy of the book was to be kept by the abbot and a second by the convent.

That such a thing should have to be commanded by papal authority is remarkable. It was one of the first acts of Abbot Samson to draw up such a book, and to consult it frequently, "as the mirror wherein was reflected his own probity"; and it would be thought that such an elementary necessity for good business management would never be neglected. Yet the episcopal visitations show that the warning was far from unnecessary. Odo Rigaldi had to order it to be done even at the great house of Bec. The constant difficulty found in ensuring that the house should be kept fully informed of the state of its affairs has already been illustrated in the chapter on the Monastic Organisation, by reference to the frequent ordinances touching on the presentation of accounts. The constant repetition of these decrees will to most minds imply a failure to get them observed; and this impression is fully borne out by the episcopal visitations, in which, it may be safely said, the most frequent of all orders is that the obedientiaries, and the abbot in particular, must observe the rule as to giving account of their administration.

Then, too, amazing laxity showed itself at times over the raising of loans. The obedientiaries were sometimes found with seals of their own, and borrowed money for the use of their office without the knowledge of the abbot or of the convent. The case of Bury St Edmund's will at once come to mind. Under Abbot Hugh, every official had a seal of his own, and bound himself at his own pleasure to Jews as well as to Christians. Abbot Samson collected no fewer than 33 of these seals, and forbade any official to incur a debt of over £1 without consent of the prior and convent. Thomas de la Mare, in his Constitutions of 1351 for St Albans and its dependent cells, forbade any obedientiary of the abbey to raise a loan of over £5 without the abbot's special leave; the sub-obedientiaries were not to borrow a sum exceeding £1[1]. In the cells, no obedientiary was to borrow more than 30s. without leave of the prior.

One fact by itself shows that the indebtedness of the monasteries was frequently due to mismanagement and waste; namely,

---

[1] *Gesta Abbatum*, II, Appendix, p. 442.

the ease with which a competent abbot could drag a house out
of apparently hopeless debt even in the face of the inertia of
his monks. Where there existed such powers of recovery as
were often shown, laxity and waste, it would seem, must have
been going on for the house ever to have got in so bad a financial
state. Once again the best-known example is that of Bury St
Edmund's under Abbot Samson, who in his first year of office
made arrangements for the discharge of the debts of the house,
and within twelve years had paid off the whole, amounting to
£3052. 13s. 4d., irrespective of the interest, which could never
be ascertained. The case does not stand by itself. We may compare, for instance, Pontefract, where, according to the Cluniac
visitors of 1279, the prior then in office had in twelve years
reduced a debt of over 3200 marks to less than 350, and had
also added to the revenues of the house. At Lewes, again, in
1414 the debt of the house was 3200 marks, yet the next prior
freed the convent from debt entirely[1]. It may be urged that
these two examples are hardly parallel, inasmuch as both were
alien priories, and liable as such, from time to time, to exactions,
beyond their own control, but occasional and therefore leaving
greater room for recuperation. But a case exactly analogous to
that of Bury St Edmund's is found in the recovery of Evesham
after the destruction brought upon it by Roger Norreys. The
work was mainly done by Thomas Marleberge, who as dean,
sacristan, and prior under Roger's successor Randulph was
clearly the soul of the administration, and who from 1230 to
1242 was himself abbot. He found the abbey burdened with a
debt of £370, with nothing in hand but a stock of corn and hay,
and with its plough-teams lacking a third of their proper numbers. Yet in the first year of his abbacy he paid off nearly £112
of the debt, bought 100 acres of land, brought up the plough-
teams to full strength, had episcopal effigies made for the tombs
of his predecessors, prepared his own sarcophagus, and managed
all this without a fresh loan. Abbot Henry, his next successor
but one (1256–82), though burdened at his accession by a debt
of 1400 marks, paid it all off, "living honorably without a loan,"
and added to the revenues of the house.

At Belvoir, again, a cell of St Albans, William de Heron,

---

[1] *Victoria County History of Sussex*, II, p. 68.

prior from about 1340 to 1361, in that short space of time paid off a debt of £733. 6s. 8d., built two chapels, planted 1000 trees about the monastery, and gave to the monks 100 marks[1]. Even more remarkable is the recovery of Kirkstall between 1284 and 1301[2]. In the former year its stock consisted of 16 draught-oxen, 84 cows, 16 yearlings and bullocks, and 21 asses. It had no sheep at all, and was in debt to the extent of £5248. 15s. 7d. and 59 sacks of wool. In 1301 this gigantic debt had been reduced to £160, and the stock increased to 216 draught-oxen, 160 cows, 152 yearlings, 90 calves and 4000 sheep and lambs. As a final example of this possibility of recuperation, there may be noticed what was expected from the monks of Bath by Bishop King in 1500, when he set to work to reorganise the monastery[3]. The document is rather difficult to interpret in places, but its purport is much as follows. The prior is allowed 80 marks a year. The bishop estimates that the monks could be better kept than is ordered by the bare letter of the Rule for £80, or £5 each. The accounts which they have presented to him show that they have actually had £160 or more—£10 a head: he cuts this down to the first figure named. He also reduces their estimate of £50 for building expenses on the manors to £40, and halves their estimate of £20 for servants' wages. In all, the prior and 16 monks are to be allowed £183. 6s. 8d.: the total income of the house being £480. 16s. 6½d.; this leaves a balance of £307. 9s. 10¼d., which is to be applied to rebuilding the church. The bishop may have been rather optimistic; but the mere fact that he should think it possible to save over three-fifths of the income each year shows how easily debt might have been avoided.

To these evidences of the presence of maladministration and extravagance, the more remarkable as drawn haphazard from all centuries of the Middle Ages, there may be added the over-frequent occurrence of cases in which the visitors deprived the abbot of his administration or even deposed him altogether, cases, it would seem, the more frequent the more the energy of the visitors in question. We have already seen that in 13 houses visited by Bishop Grandisson fairly continuously between 1328 and 1348 there were seven cases in which the management

---

[1] Dugdale, *Monasticon*, II, p. 285 *et seq.*   [2] *Ibid.* V, p. 529.
[3] *Ibid.* II, p. 270.

was so bad that either the business of the house was transferred to coadjutors, or the head of the house was made to resign. Enough, however, has been said upon this point to make it clear that, beside the causes of debt beyond the control of the monks, for which all due allowance must be made, there was also present extravagance, maladministration, even in some cases downright embezzlement, together with an inertia and indifference which refused to take advantage of the unusual recuperative power which lay ready for application. As regards the directions in which extravagance was actually shown, discussion may better be reserved for the chapter upon the material comfort of monastic life. Meanwhile it is interesting to notice the means used for clearing off liabilities, and for bringing about general improvements in the state of the house.

We may divide these methods into two classes, taking our basis of division from the general purpose for which they were used. The first class comprised those schemes which aimed at a merely temporary increase of revenue of the house employing them, the second those aiming at a permanent increase in the monastic revenue. In the first class we may place all those schemes which aimed at a mere anticipation of income, and which therefore might be of advantage, but were often of very doubtful value. The class includes the raising of loans, the sale of produce in advance, the granting of long leases of monastic property, and the sale of corrodies. A word or two must be said on each of these methods.

The raising of loans may be dismissed very briefly. Little new light is to be thrown upon the matter from the monastic accounts. The chief money-lenders of the Middle Ages in England were the Jews, succeeded after their expulsion by the great Italian merchants. Interest, condemned by mediaeval opinion and banned by the Church, had to be paid nevertheless, and at usurious rates. Occasionally a loan might be had without the necessity for paying interest on the money, but as a general thing it was dangerous to raise a loan, and the effects were unsatisfactory. Yet it was frequently found necessary to have recourse to this expedient. The need for ready money may have been as much responsible as debt.

More interesting was the practice of selling produce in advance for cash down. This was especially done in the case of wool. It practically amounted to the raising of a loan paid off in kind instead of in money. The practice of entering into such contracts with the Italian merchants, in whose hands the mediaeval wool trade largely lay, seems to have been perfectly regular[1]. The contracts usually stipulated for the delivery of wool at a certain place and on certain dates in return for a payment in ready cash, and a provision was included whereby failure on the part of the convent to fulfil its obligations involved a fine to the merchants to make up for their expenses in paying a second visit to the stipulated place where the wool was to be delivered. It is interesting to notice how nearly this system approaches to one of the mediaeval relaxations of the laws against usury, whereby an agreement for repayment at an impossible date was made and the borrower had to pay the lender for the damage and trouble involved by the failure to make repayment at the set season. The system of selling produce in advance, legitimate enough in itself if the cash obtained were distributed over the number of years for which the wool was sold, was in fact used as a means of raising a loan by anticipating revenue. It was therefore readily abused, and might leave a heavier burden of debt to those who came after. Thus Robert, eleventh Abbot of Meaux, who resigned in 1280, sold to the merchants of Lucca for 1200 marks in advance 120 sacks of wool at one time, of which hardly any were delivered during his life. His successor, Richard, had recourse to the same expedient. So, too, during the terrible period of difficulty after the Black Death, when practically every possible way was tried to raise money, Abbot William sold corn for 20 years in advance, and also 200 sacks of wool to be delivered within 10 years, under a double penalty in case of failure[2]. One more example may be given because it shows a clear case of mismanagement. One of the mistakes of the Prior of Lewes, who in 1279 had plunged his house into debt, was entering into one of these contracts for the delivery of wool. The monastery found itself unable to meet the demand, and the transaction ended badly[3].

[1] A good example of such a contract will be found in Wallram's *Memorials of Fountains*, I, p. 117.
[2] *Chronica Monasterii de Melsa*, II, pp. 156, 175, III, p. 85.
[3] Duckett, *Visitations of English Cluniac Foundations*, p. 36.

The granting out of the lands of the monastery on a long lease at a small rent, accompanied of course by the payment of a large fine on entry, was another of these ways of anticipating income, and was, like all such ways, liable to prove disastrous if badly managed. The type of these agreements may be seen in a document of Pershore (34 Edward III)[1], in which the monastery grants "omnia tenementa sua tam in redditibus quam in dominicis in Stokewell infra manerium suum de Couleye" for ten years, saving to the abbot wards, reliefs, escheats, heriots, suits in court, attachments and amercements: the annual rent being an arrow. No mention is here made of the fine on entry, but it is morally certain that it was made. Instances could easily be multiplied of this practice and its attendant dangers, but one or two examples must suffice. To take the case of Meaux once more, during the troublous period after the Black Death, the sixteenth abbot, William, raised £113. 13s. 4d. by this method, one item being the lease of a messuage for 100 years in consideration of 50 marks down. His successor, John (1353–6), who played a large part in getting him dismissed for bad management, proved even less successful. One of his transactions was to lease rents amounting to £11 a year, for a period of 20 years at least, or for the life of the lessee, should he survive that period, for £11 down. The times were terribly hard, but the business methods were not of the best. In some cases not even the excuse of necessity could be pleaded. Hugh de Eversdone (Abbot of St Albans 1308–26), who is said to have been the first abbot to introduce this system at that place, was accused of doing it simply for the easier maintenance of his own splendour and pomp[2]. Occasionally a stroke of luck would befall a monastery in connection with such transactions. Thus Bermondsey at the close of the thirteenth century had leased four of its manors to Adam de Straton, clerk to the Exchequer, who is very prominent in the reports of the Cluniac visitors as engaging in many such transactions. But in 1290 Adam de Straton was convicted of felony[3]; and Edward I restored the manors of Bermondsey, which thus fell into his hands.

---

[1] Dugdale, *Monasticon*, II, p. 422.   [2] *Ibid.* II, p. 196.
[3] *Ibid.* V, p. 98. He was one of the judges removed by Edward I in his great clearance on returning from abroad. Stubbs, *Constitutional History*, II, p. 125.

Lastly there comes the corrody. The nature of this expedient has already been described. It was an agreement entered into by the monastery for one cause or another to provide a person with food, clothing, money and usually lodging. It was distinguished apparently from the pension by the fact that the latter was more generally a grant of money, and did not involve personal residence of the recipient in the monastery. But it does not seem possible to draw a hard and fast line: the corrody seems to melt imperceptibly into the pension, and cases are to be found in which the grant is described both as corrody and as pension. One of the stages of transition may be seen in one of the earliest known examples of the corrody, those in the Burton Surveys. Here the recipient of the corrody was given power to transfer the enjoyment of it to another if he were absent for a considerable time from the monastery[1]. Two kinds of corrody are often distinguished—the "monk's corrody" in which the recipient was granted the same maintenance as one of the "religious," and the "servant's corrody" in which the corrodier received the same grant of food, clothing or money as one of the monastic servants. But there were often other grants of particular amounts of food, etc., which do not come under either of these heads.

The Rev. W. Hunt has registered a protest, not perhaps unnecessary[2], against the treatment of the corrody as merely an ingenious and extravagant device for raising money in advance. It is true, as he states, that even where money was raised by the sale of these corrodies, the bargain need not always have been unprofitable. It is also true that it had other uses besides that of raising money. At least four may be distinguished. First, it was a kind of compulsory charity, or recognition of gratitude due to "founders of fortuns," to quote Mr Pumblechook. In the case of monasteries of royal foundation, except where the house was held in frankalmoign, the King had the right to demand a corrody for one of his servants[3]: and even where this obligation was not due, the royal influence was frequently strong enough to ensure the grant, coupled perhaps with an acknowledgement

[1] Cited by J. H. Round, *English Historical Review*, 1905 (April), p. 288.
[2] *Two Cartularies of Bath*, Preface.
[3] So Rastell, *Les Termes de la Ley*, s.v. Corrody.

on the King's part that the concession was of favour and not of right. Every founder of a monastery also had the right to demand a corrody for one of his kinsmen, or any other whom he chose to appoint. The right must have been often abused, for one of the Articuli Cleri (9 Edward II) dealt with the question. The King is petitioned to refrain personally, and to prevent other great men, from demanding corrodies and pensions or from sojourning in religious houses and thereby impoverishing them: and a legal remedy is provided. Whether the evil was checked thereby may be doubted.

At Christ Church, Canterbury, in the fourteenth century, the King, by gradual encroachments, had come by custom to nominate three corrodiers. Protests seem to have been made without any great success. In 1318, when Edward II wished them to receive John Griffon in their house "with the same exhibition as Thomas Cottyng had during his life," the prior and convent objected that they were grievously burdened with sojourners and exhibitions, heavy fees and numerous aids and demands. "Whence it comes that we are obliged to pinch ourselves in our diet, and to restrict the hospitality and alms which we used to practice before we were so oppressed." But, whether at that time or a little later, John Griffon got his corrody[1]. On his death, the prior and convent again protested against the nomination of a successor. On this occasion they pleaded that they were landowners in a county surrounded on three sides by the sea, and were therefore greatly impoverished already by their duty of guarding a great extent of coast. In 1337, Edward III yielded so far as nominally to surrender his claim, but none the less continued to fill vacancies as they occurred. Under Richard II, the house at last obtained relief[2]. The King resigned his rights, and they, in return, guaranteed to celebrate with great solemnity the festivals of the Passion and Translation of St Edmund, King and Martyr, making especial mention of Richard's name in the Collects. The mediaeval civil servant could hope, if not for presentation to a good living as a pension after his years of service, at least for a corrody. The case of the poet Hoccleve is probably the most familiar. In 1424, after 37 irksome years of clerical

[1] J. B. Sheppard, *Literae Cantuarienses* (R.S.), I, p. 43.
[2] J. B. Sheppard, *Canterbury Letters* (C.S.), p. vi.

work, versification and hoping for preferment, "votre tres humble clerc, Thomas Hoccleve de l'office du prive seal," being then about 56 years of age, was granted by the King and the Privy Council such sustenance yearly during his life in the Priory of Southwick, Hants., as Nicholas Mokkinge, late master of St Lawrence in the Poultry, had received. He had waited long for his corrody, for in 1389 Henry IV had granted him £10 a year for life, or until the King should promote him to an ecclesiastical benefice without cure of souls worth £20 a year[1]. Minor benefactors, also, might find the monks' appreciation expressed by means of a corrody without anything in the nature of a formal sale. John Gower, to quote the case of another poet, was a considerable benefactor to the Priory of St Mary Overey, Southwark, during his lifetime. He was granted a lodging (*hospicium*) which included an oratory, within the priory. Here he lived with his wife until his death in 1408, leaving various sums to the prior, canons and servants of the house by will[2].

Secondly, the grant of corrodies was often one of the means adopted for the endowment of hospitals or almshouses. Thus at St Albans on the occasion of the burial of the Abbot William (1235), the keeper of the convent of St Mary des Prez, founded by Abbot Warin (1194) for leprous nuns, appeared with a claim that according to the orders of the founder, the nuns ought to be given a corrody on the decease of each abbot since Galfred up to the number of 13, which had never been done. The claim was examined and approved and the corrodies were given[3]. Kilburn Nunnery was endowed in the same way[4]. At St Albans, again, a female recluse at St Michael's was entitled to a corrody from the cellarer.

Then again a monastery might be burdened with the payment of a corrody as a punishment for some offence. An example will be found of this in the case of St Albans at a date between 1260 and 1290. One of the household of Edmund, the King's

---

[1] F. J. Furnivall, *Hoccleve's Works* (Early English Text Society), I, p. xxvi and refs.
[2] G. C. Macaulay, *Complete Works of John Gower*, The Latin Works, pp. xvii–xix.
[3] *Gesta Abbatum*, I, p. 305.
[4] Dugdale, III, p. 427. So, too, was the nunnery at Thetford. Dugdale, II, p. 117.

brother, was received by the monastery less respectfully than he liked. His complaint was passed on by the earl to the King, who forthwith ordered the monastery to provide one of Edmund's men with a corrody for life.

Then, as Dr Hunt points out, the corrody was not infrequently used as a means of paying wages, or attaching some workman or professional man to the monastery. Dr Hunt quotes an instance in 1316 of the attachment of a plumber to Bath Priory, who, being a villein, was manumitted in order to allow him to quit his holding, and then granted a corrody by the monks to do the convent's work. Cases of this kind are not uncommon. In 1349, the Prior and Convent of Christ Church, Canterbury, retained counsel in the same way. Master Richard de Vachan, LL.D., was guaranteed for his "laudable service" past and future, sustenance in meat and drink becoming his rank, every year till the end of his life, and a suitable furred robe, "such as he had from us this year." He was also assigned a chamber, "to wit, the solar nearly built opposite the New Hall of the infirmary, to the east," and was to be allowed a squire, three grooms, and three horses at the expense of the house[1]. Another instance which has come under my notice provides for the payment of a musician to "thump the organs"[2] and teach the choirboys, and to instruct any of the monks who wish to learn the art of organ-thumping.

Closely allied with grants of this kind are the numerous cases in which corrodies are given as part of the stipend of the vicar of an appropriated church close at hand, or of a chantry priest attached to the convent church. It was probably the frequent use of corrodies in this way which led by the later part of the Middle Ages to the inclusion of corrody-holders in the ranks of those liable to ecclesiastical taxation, whether for King or archbishop[3]. Lastly, as Dr Hunt also mentions, the corrodies were not infrequently granted out of true charity—generally as a provision for some servant who had grown old in the convent service.

[1] J. B. Sheppard, *Literae Cantuarienses* (R.S.), II, p. 293.
[2] "Pulsare organa"—the word used elsewhere is "tundere." I have unfortunately mislaid the reference, but a similar agreement in the case of Buckland Abbey will be found in Dugdale, v, p. 712.
[3] See, for example, the Register of William Gray, Bishop of Ely, 1474-5, *Ely Diocesan Remembrancer*, 1910.

Even where a sale was made, doubtless the effect was not always bad. The purchase of a life-annuity must at times have been of benefit to both parties. But to apply Dr Hunt's statement that "these sales were probably rare" to other houses than Bath, would seem to be going too far. It may indeed be granted that the cartularies show but few instances where a sale is mentioned, and even that the cases in which it is possible to trace some *quid pro quo* other than cash, whether work of a servant, or the duties of a chantry priest, or the gift of lands by persons who wished to live within the convent walls, are at least as numerous as those in which we are left guessing as to the reason why the corrody was granted. The cartulary of Merton Priory, for example, mentions 37 corrodies; two of these were royal presentations; 13 were granted to chaplains and clerks, and eight to servants; three were given in consideration of the resignation of land; one was sold; and in 10 cases no record is made of the reason for the grant. The Eynsham cartulary records 26 corrodies, two of which were royal presentations; four were granted to chaplains and clerks, and 10 to servants; six went in settling suits or obtaining resignations of land; one was sold, and three are left without cause stated. But it is in the compotus rolls, and not in the mere record of the corrody in the cartulary, that the true effects of the corrody might have been seen. The absence of any mention of payment in the document proves nothing, inasmuch as cases where grants of land were made in return leave no trace on the terms of the corrody. The receipt of a sum of money paid for a corrody would doubtless go straight into the compotus roll, the terms of the corrody alone into the cartulary[1]. Once again the fragmentary nature of the accounts as we possess them, the curtness of the entries and the absence of continuous detail conspire to prevent a satisfactory statement from these sources as to the extent to which corrodies were sold, and the general success or failure of the monastic officials in estimating the

---

[1] It is rare, I think, to find a corrody in which any mention of the sum received is given: it does not, however, follow that nothing was received. Thus at Merton a corrody was granted to a citizen of London, Roger le Furbur: no mention of any equivalent appears in the document, but another charter shows that he gave a piece of land to the house (Heales, *Records of Merton Priory*, pp. 120, 137).

expectation of life. The Durham rolls help us little, beyond showing (unless indeed the accounts are over-abbreviated) that it was possible for a great monastery to get along without selling corrodies at all, for there is only one mention of such a sale in the whole of the accounts. The other printed accounts which I have inspected, while showing traces of the sale of corrodies, in some cases, to a large extent, notably at St Swithun's, give no chance whatever of seeing how long the recipients enjoyed them.

It is therefore necessary to fall back upon other evidence; and this upon the whole is distinctly unfavourable as to the effects of the corrody and the frequency of sales. The complaints made, the attempts to prevent the raising of large sums in this way without the cognisance of some outside authority, all point to the conclusion that this, like most other ways of anticipating income, was a dangerous expedient. Abbot Hugh of Eversdone, at St Albans, for example, received by the sale of corrodies in the monastery £1077, and in the cells £1000. The money, like that raised by many other means, went simply to maintain his own splendour, and must be reckoned a dead loss to the convent. At Meaux, again, during the terrible difficulties of the sixteenth century, the corrody is very much to the fore. William, the sixteenth abbot, sold two for £50: and another "pergrande corrodium" to a burgess of Hull, his chaplain and his servant, for £60. His successor John sold eight corrodies for £130: and part of the work of recovery effected later in the century was a buying-in of these corrodies, pensions, and similar grants; a fact which may be taken as showing the utility of the method to stave off a crisis, but is hardly encouraging as to the successful estimation by the monks of the chances of life. The same expedient was tried by the German towns.

From the thirteenth century the towns had issued ("sold" as it was called) annuities for life or for perpetuity, in ever increasing number, until it was at last found impossible to raise the funds necessary to pay them[1].

If the townsmen, experienced in the details of business, failed so completely to manage this system, the sale of corrodies by the monks is hardly likely to have had better success.

---

[1] *Encyclopaedia Brittanica*, eleventh edition, vol. VI, p. 787.

As early as 1222 it had been found needful to institute some outside control over the grant of corrodies: the Council of Oxford ordered that no prelates of religious houses should sell, or grant gratis, corrodies to clerics or laymen unless urgent necessity demanded it and the diocesan's consent was given[1]. The episcopal registers are full of repetitions of this prohibition. Similar facts to those cited above, and the frequent complaints of the monastic chroniclers as to the burden laid on the house by such grants, together with the praise lavished on abbots who managed without them[2], leave the impression that the system was much open to abuse, and I include it therefore among those financial expedients which aimed only at anticipation of revenue[3].

We may now turn to the means at the disposal of the religious houses for a permanent expansion of their yearly income. Bequests continued to a greater or less extent down to the period of the Dissolution. The most frequent occasion was the burial of some person within the precincts of the monastery, a payment being made for the privilege. Already by 1215 the Lateran Council could say that when a knight or a clerk enters a house of religion or chooses to be buried among the religious, even though he leaves nothing to the house, "difficultates ingerunt et malitias, donec aliquid muneris manus contingat eorum": and there are still to be traced miserable squabbles which show that the assertion was not utterly vain. But the bequests seem usually to have been obtained without difficulty. It was well for the houses to keep on good terms with the great men around them, and we find in the episcopal visitations advice that this should be done. But for the most part the stream of donations was apt to slacken, and other means had to be sought of adding fresh income.

One of the main ways was to stimulate the piety of the people around, and consequently the offerings made to the monastery.

---

[1] Wilkins, *Concilia*, I, p. 591.

[2] Thus it is recorded of Abbot Whethamstede of St Albans, as a thing worthy of remembrance and admiration, that in the course of his extensive building operations he cut down no woods, granted no corrodies, pledged no jewels and gave much from his own purse. (J. de Amundesham, II, p. 267.)

[3] Bishop Grandisson's opinion of the utility of the corrody may be gathered from a document of 1356 (*Register*, II, p. 1157) in which he warns all his archdeacons not to allow corrodies to be sold without his leave, as experience shows that they lead to debt and a decrease in the number of monks.

This might be done by the exhibition of relics. Thus, when Abbot John of St Albans (1195–1214) had got into difficulties with his building operations, he sent a preacher with relics through all the land of St Alban, and several dioceses, together with a certain clerk who had been raised from the dead through the merits of St Alban and St Amphibalus[1]. The hopes raised at Meaux by a miraculous crucifix, and their disappointment, are well-known. In 1351 Frithelstock Priory got into hot water with Bishop Grandisson for building a chapel against the bishop's injunctions, their motive, according to the bishop, being greed. The chapel was intended as a place for pilgrimage, and equipped with an "image"—possibly some such miraculous figure as that of Meaux[2]. A similar end was attained by getting from the Pope, or the bishops, privileges of indulgence. Thus when it was necessary to rebuild the nunnery of St Mary des Prez, a bull was obtained in 1256 granting to all the penitent and confessed who helped in the work a remission of 40 days' penance[3]; and a second bull of the same year granted to all true penitents who visited the nunnery on the Feast of the Virgin and within eight days following, a further remission of 40 days' penance[4]. The extent of these indulgences may be seen from a proclamation of Durham (before 1244) pointing out the advantages to be obtained by contribution to the building fund. The Pope, the Archbishop of York, and two Bishops of Durham, the Bishops of Carlisle, Lincoln, Galloway, St Andrew's, Dunkeld and Glasgow had all granted indulgences to the truly penitent who helped. In theory, it should be noted, the penitent was only entitled to the indulgences of the bishop of his diocese and archbishop of his province, together with the papal grants: in practice the restriction was ignored[5]. In addition, a long list of monasteries had promised to sing masses and recite psalters, which, together with those which Durham itself offered, made a total of 7332 masses and 4000 psalters[6]. Between 1235 and the middle of the fourteenth century, Durham received no fewer than 55 of these indulgences, most of them granting 40 days' remission

---

[1] *Gesta Abbatum*, I, p. 219.
[2] Hingeston-Randolph, *Register of John de Grandisson*, II, p. 11.
[3] Rymer, *Foedera*, I, p. 606.   [4] *Ibid.* I, p. 614.
[5] Canon Wordsworth, *Yorkshire Archaeological Journal*, XVI, p. 375.
[6] *Rites of Durham* (2nd edition), p. 148.

of canonical penance[1]. In the later Ely registers as, for example, that of William Gray, however, it is remarkable how few were granted to the religious houses, the vast majority go to private individuals who have met with misfortune.

Then also there were various speculations on which the monks were not averse from embarking. One kind of these must frequently have been of benefit to all parties, namely, the purchase of mortgages, or an engagement to become responsible for the payment of some person's debts in return for a pecuniary consideration. One interesting example of this kind is found in the case of Tewkesbury[2], where at some date after 1199 the abbey entered into an agreement with Robert le Bigod whereby he gave them in fee-farm all his land of Godrington, they paying him 2s. a year to bear all demands thereon except the "foreign service." In return the monks gave him 84 marks and two palfreys to redeem his body from the prison of King John wherein he had long been straitly confined. But a more general type of transaction was a payment of debts to the Jews or other usurers. Thus at Tewkesbury, at some time between 1421 and 1442, the monastery acquired all the lands of Jordan Wace in Bristol by paying off 26 marks debt "tam in Judaismo quam alibi" for which the lands were pledged, and receiving Jordan and his wife into the monastery with a corrody for life apiece[3]. The invaluable Chronicle of Meaux records six similar transactions on the part of the monastery between 1160 and 1269, three at least involving very considerable sums of money. Occasionally a monastery is to be found investing in the lands of some crusader. The Chronicle of Meaux records one curious case in which the house, in order to obtain possession of a legacy, made itself responsible for the bringing up of a boy. But the greatest, and the most widely used, method of all was the appropriation of churches. All through the centuries under consideration it went on unceasingly. The monks, as has been said, were the chief offenders, though the bishops were not clear of blame. Appropriations were sought upon almost every occasion conceivable: for the rebuilding of a monastery destroyed by fire, for the maintenance of hospitality, for the maintenance of

[1] *Rites of Durham* (2nd edition), p. 159.
[2] Dugdale, *Monasticon*, II, p. 78.　　　[3] *Ibid.* II, p. 77.

scholars at a University, for the monks' or the abbot's "mensa," for the increase of the convent's numbers, for almost every possible side of monastic life. The excuse was invariably poverty. How far the excuse was true it is often difficult in any given case to say, how far the remedy was the only applicable one, impossible. There were cases where it was clearly untrue: at the very time, for example, when churches were being granted to St Albans for the improvement of the convent beer, the abbot was actually adding large sums from other sources to the possessions of the monastery. The commission issued in 1256 to the Bishops of Llandaff, Lincoln, Salisbury, Coventry and Worcester as to the simoniacal acquisition of churches has already been cited[1]. We may add an earlier case in which an appropriation was revoked by the Pope—that of the Church of St Keveran, Cornwall, appropriated to the Abbot and Convent of Beaulieu on a plea of needing money to support hospitality[2]. They had, according to the Pope, £1000 a year in rents, and were in a "desert" place with little or no hospitality to exercise. Moreover, "revelling in the goods of the monastery which could support many more monks, they have turned the said church into a grange, and admit scarce a single guest." One instance may be noted in which the Pope even opposed a petition for appropriation backed by a royal request. In 1372 a reply was sent through the papal nuncio to the King's repeated wish that the Church of Hemynburgh should be given to Durham, in which the Pope summarises the history of that house[3]. The revenues of Durham, when the church was transferred to the prior and convent, supported 150 canons and beneficiaries. Since that date four abbeys had been converted into priories, in each of which there used to be 24 monks: they now contain only 15 between them. Two other monasteries have also been added, each with 15 members: now they have 10 between them. Thirteen churches have been appropriated. There are now only 56 received monks at Durham, who when they go out travel with three or four horses, and spend more on their food and clothing than befits men of religion. The nuncio is to inform the King of these facts, and if he still insists upon the appro-

[1] *Calendar of Papal Letters*, I, p. 155.
[2] *Ibid.* I, p. 155. [3] *Ibid.* III, p. 117.

priation, to ask what the vicar is to have, and how many monks are to be added[1].

These, it may be urged, are exceptional cases: and certainly there are few instances to be found in which an appropriation is so plainly stigmatised. But when there is kept in mind the persistent evils of the system, the cases in which the expenses of obtaining the appropriation absorbed the profits to no small degree, the evidence already given as to mismanagement and waste and the facts (to be considered in the next chapter) as to the general material standard of living which the religious houses maintained, the thought inevitably suggests itself that this method of increasing their revenues might have been denied to the monks with great advantage to the reputation of all concerned. One fact by itself is significant. The Cistercians in the early days of their Order were forbidden the possession of churches.

The present chapter seems the most suitable place to say what little it is possible for me to say upon a subject which has as yet appeared but little in these pages—the economic condition of the nunneries[2]. For, so far as it is possible to pierce the obscurity which hangs far more deeply about the history of these houses than over that of the monasteries, the story seems, save only in some few rich houses, to be one which centres round the under-endowment of a population tending rather to increase than to diminish, and in which the part played, so far as finance goes, by those whose business it was to watch over the well-being of the nunneries, is to try to check the tendency of the expedients which the nuns adopted, to break down the monastic seclusion to which they had devoted themselves. The general poverty of the nunneries seems incontestable; the persistent attempt of bishops and synods was to keep down the number of the nuns instead of insisting upon the necessity for raising it, as in the case of the monks; and the characteristic

[1] One more particularly flagrant case may be cited. In 1309 at St Augustine's, Canterbury, the head of the house gave a feast to 6000 guests at a cost of £287. In 1310 came the appropriation of two churches, and before 1350 three more were added. (Dugdale, I, pp. 139, 144, 147.)

[2] The following pages represent simply a confirmation from the original authorities of theories already put forward, and backed by fuller evidence, by Mr G. G. Coulton.

features of the nuns' own financial expedients were established in the face of an almost unbroken official disapproval.

The meagre endowment of the generality of the nunneries shows itself even at a glance: an inspection of the lists of grants given in such a work as Dugdale shows that except in a few cases few nunneries could count upon an income comparable to that of the average monastery. It is difficult to obtain figures for the English houses, but the state of affairs in the province of Rouen in 1255–8 may give a valuable analogy. In the diocese of Rouen itself, monasteries with a total population of 548 had an income of £34,837 tournois, or £63$\frac{2}{3}$ per head. In the same diocese nunneries with a total population of 220 were endowed to the extent of £5310, or only £24$\frac{1}{10}$ per head—not much over a third of the monk's income. In the other diocese of the province 586 monks had an income of £36,905, or £62$\frac{9}{10}$ per head; while 203 nuns had only £3020, or a little under £14$\frac{2}{5}$ per head[1]. That things were not very much different in England two facts alone will show. It will not have been forgotten that from the scope of the Taxation of Pope Nicholas were excluded "nuns, and other regular persons whose ecclesiastical rents and incomings are so meagre and slender that they cannot be supported from them, but have of necessity to beg publicly for their sustenance." The prominence given here to the nunneries is itself significant, but it becomes doubly so when we notice that out of the 18 Cistercian nunneries mentioned in the 5th volume of Dugdale's *Monasticon* six make no appearance in the taxation at all, while the rest appear with incomes valued at the smallest of figures, in some cases only at a little over £1. Everything goes to show that, with few exceptions, the endowments of the nunnery were as a rule quite small.

But on the other hand, the difficulty was to keep down the number of nuns to something that could be fairly said to be in proportion with the scanty revenues at their disposal. The episcopal registers reveal it as the constant effort of the bishops to prevent the veiling of fresh nuns. It is perpetually provided that no more are to be admitted without the consent of the bishop (a proviso which I have only noticed in two cases when monasteries were in question). There is not infrequently a number

[1] See also pp. 179–80.

laid down which is not to be exceeded, or even to which the convent must be reduced, and it is clear that the bishop's permission was not lightly given to an increase of numbers. As to the reason of this there can be but little doubt. The mediaeval convent provided an easy way of getting rid of incumbrances—of providing with least trouble for a daughter, a sister or a ward: and on the other side there was the temptation to relieve for a while the continual stress by accepting a fresh inmate for the sake of her dowry. A word might have been said as to this practice when dealing with the monasteries, for it was not unknown among them: but it seems to have been especially prevalent among the nuns. It was much reprobated by the authorities, who regarded it as simony. It was denounced, without special reference to the nuns, by the First Lateran Council; by the Council of Oxford (1222), which forbade as an evasion the practice of demanding on pretext of the poverty of the house an extortionate sum to clothe the new inmate; by the Benedictine Provincial Chapter at Canterbury (1222); by Gregory IX, who said that a gift might be taken if offered but might not be demanded (a proviso easy of evasion), and who declared, moreover, that nearly every nun was stained by this kind of simony. The Benedictine Chapter of Bermondsey (1249) prohibited it: so did Innocent IV in his recension of Gregory's Constitutions (1253); and, to conclude, the Benedictine Chapter of 1444 spoke of it as leading to the rejection of very suitable men and the admission of incapables (*idiotas*), and prohibited the taking of anything more than was necessary to provide the novice with dress and bedding. The difficulty was therefore inveterate[1]. As to the reason for its prevalence among the nuns, once more the invaluable Register of Odo Rigaldi may be taken as a guide: it is there very noticeable that the nunneries which disregard the archbishop's injunctions, or which petition most eagerly for leave to admit new members, are those which are most deeply in debt.

A few words must indicate the nature of the special means which were adopted by the nunneries to cope with the difficulty. There can be but little doubt that the practices of keeping schools

---

[1] Yet, in the later fourteenth century, it was clearly regarded as quite normal. Truth, in *Piers Plowman* (B text, Passus 7), advising merchants as to the charitable use of their wealth, bids them "marien maydenes, or maken hem nonnes."

and of taking paying guests (or to use the word used in one of the English visitation records, "perhendinauncers")[1] were a direct consequence of this continual economic stress, and that both established themselves in the face of a steady opposition from the visitors, fearful lest thereby the quiet and peace of monastic life should be disturbed and its true object missed. Once again the Register of Odo Rigaldi may be appealed to as the strongest support for these views, giving as it does a fuller continuous information for a whole series of nunneries than any other mediaeval document yet printed. In every case where educational work is going on, or boarders being taken, the house is in debt: in every case the injunction is given that no one is to remain in the house save those who intend to become nuns: the few houses which are well off have neither schools nor boarders. Whatever evil consequences the general poverty of the nuns may have had, it was in the main to this struggle against debt that the educational work which they did must be attributed.

---

[1] Dugdale, *Monasticon*, v, p. 207.

CHAPTER VI

THE MATERIAL COMFORT OF MONASTIC LIFE

IT will be remembered that, in the consideration of monastic expenditure, there was set aside for future treatment the question of the amount of revenue absorbed by the maintenance of the monks personally, and the general consideration of their maintenance of the physical asceticism which characterised early monasticism, and was one of the features which won for it the admiration of the best mediaeval minds and personalities. This question of the material comfort enjoyed by the monks is not so unconnected with higher considerations as it might seem. It is really a matter of importance to determine whether the monk adhered to the hardness of life which characterised the monastic Rule from the first and which with every revival of monasticism assumed its old prominence again.

St Benedict rejected the wilder forms of self-torment which characterised the monasticism of the East. But it can hardly be assumed from his Rule that he contemplated any life for his Order much easier than that of the Italian peasantry of his day. He left many things to the discretion of the abbot, but he probably did not expect that the discretion of the abbot would materially alter the standard of life which the Rule contemplated. Yet for the Benedictine Order, as a whole, such a relaxation took place, and was defended on the score of the abbot's independent authority. The Cistercian movement was in the main a revolt against local custom and a return to the letter of the Rule, possibly over-stringently interpreted, but closer after all to its spirit than the ordinary Benedictinism of the day. The story of the discussion in St Mary's, York, which ended in the foundation of Fountains[1] gives a dramatic expression of the points at issue. On the one hand were the prior and his reforming associates, "weary of the din of the city, sighing for the desert, for toil with their hands, for the pottage of the prophets." On the other was Abbot Geoffrey, old, conservative, "honest and

---

[1] Dugdale, *Monasticon*, v, p. 292 *et seq.*

good," but over-simple and unlearned, pleading that he could not in his abbey change the "ancient rites and wonted customs" held throughout the world. The prior appealed to the Rule itself, and contrasted the customs of the house.

When some go to the church, others go away by times after collation to trifling amusements and useless garrulous gossipings, as though insufficient for the day were the evils thereof, unless the night too had its evils provided.

He spoke, too, of

the unworthiness (*insolentia*) of their food, the sweet and solemn changes of their drink, the costly fineness of their clothing....We wax fat on the labours of others, and the whole world is not enough for our evil mind.

The popularity of the Cistercians bore witness to the world's belief that they interpreted the Rule aright. It was not an easy path that the monk professed to tread. It would be idle to expect all to attain to the heights of saintship in this respect, and we must be prepared to make allowance for a certain declination from the austerities practised, to take an example, in the early days of the Cistercians. But none the less, the ideal was there, and profession was made to seek its attainment. Mediaeval thought and feeling respected the effort; and the reverence with which the monks were regarded, and their consequent spiritual influence, must have been affected by their recognising or ignoring the duty which they had taken upon themselves.

It is, then, a matter of real importance to see what went on in this direction. One man at least in the time of Edward II wrote down his thoughts for us in the tongue of the people[1].

Religioun was first founded duresce for to drie,
And nu is the moste del i-went to eise and glotonie.
Where shal men nu finde fattere or reddere of leres
Or better farende folk than moncks, chanons and freres?
In uch toun
I wot non eysiere liff than is religioun.

All know what Chaucer saw. His portrait of the monk who rode to Canterbury is as vivid as the rest of that wonderful gallery:

What sholde he studie and make himselven wood,
Upon a book in cloystre alweye to poure,
Or swynken with his handes and laboure

[1] T. Wright, *Political Songs* (C.S.), p. 329 *et seq.*

As Austyn bit? How shal the world be served?
Let Austyn have his swynk to him reserved.

. . . .

I seigh his sleves y-purfiled at the hond
With grys, and that the fyneste of a lond;

. . . .

He was not pale as a forpyned goost,
A fat swan loved he best of any roost.

What most men of the Renaissance and the Reformation thought
of the matter cannot be better expressed than in the ribald old
song which Scott quoted, or perhaps invented:

The friars of Fail, they drank good ale
The best that e'er was tasted,
The monks of Melrose made gude kail
On Fridays when they fasted.

But the men of the Reformation, it will be said, were parties too
deeply interested to have their word taken as historical evidence,
even had controversial methods been cleaner than they were;
and Chaucer was that chartered libertine, a satirist; and the
writer of Edward II's reign was a pessimist. It is after all to the
records left by the monks themselves and those who, sympa-
thising with their lives, made friendly efforts to aid them in
pursuing their ideal that we must go for a settlement of this
question. Remembering that luxury and comfort are relative
terms, and that the standard of life has varied enormously, let
us turn to the bald facts of our authorities.

We may begin by noticing the relaxation which shows itself
in the Cistercian Rule on the question of eating flesh. The
original Cistercian Rule, following the Rule of St Benedict,
prohibited the use of flesh entirely, with an exception only in
favour of the sick. The same prohibition is found in the Rule
as revised in 1256, and seems to have been in force at least
theoretically until 1335. Benedict XII then issued a privilege
allowing the Cistercians to eat meat in the infirmary, and by
invitation of the abbot in his own lodgings. By the middle of
the fifteenth century further relaxations had taken place. The
eating of meat was still not allowed in the refectory, but a special
room was usually set aside for the purpose; and except in seasons
of fasting, it was usual to eat flesh three times a week, namely,

on Sunday, Tuesday, and Thursday. The amount of meat consumed in one of these Cistercian abbeys, when the end was not far away, may be seen in the case of the Abbey of Whalley. Here Dr Whitaker calculates that the average yearly consumption late in the fifteenth century was as follows. At the abbot's table, 75 oxen and cows, 80 sheep, 40 calves, 20 lambs and four porkers; in the refectory and other places in the house, 57 oxen, 40 sheep, 20 calves and 10 lambs. The guests and servants of the house had their share, but for a house of about 20 members the allowance seems large[1].

The example of the Cistercian monks in this respect is the more interesting because their Rule represents the last definite mediaeval revival of the original monastic severity in this respect. We may compare with interest the much earlier case of the Augustinian Priory of Bolton[2]. The larder here in 1305 provided 38 oxen and nine fat oxen killed "against Easter": during the summer 40 cows and two calves, 51 pigs, 26 sucking pigs, 23 sheep and seven carcasses which were bought at York, besides goats, fowls and other similar provisions. That is to say, a house consisting of about 15 canons and some 24 servants consumed on the average each week about one and three-quarter oxen, one pig, half a sucking pig, half a sheep and other flesh. The difficulty in these cases, and in all others like them, is to say how much should be allowed for hospitality. But everything goes to prove that extreme laxity prevailed in this respect. The process which has been traced in the Cistercian houses was a mere repetition of what had already taken place in the Benedictine houses. The letter of the Rule was evaded and its spirit ignored by a recourse to the discretion of the abbot who had the power of relaxing the stringency of the law.

The system will best be seen by a consideration of the regulations laid down in 1293 by William de Colerne, Abbot of Malmesbury[3], who definitely regularised this relaxation with the object of checking the favouritism which had hitherto been shown. The system was simple: as with the Cistercians the abbot allowed a certain number to dine, not in the refectory,

---

[1] *History of Whalley*, I, p. 132.
[2] Whitaker, *History of Craven*, p. 461.
[3] *Regist. Malmesbur.* (R.S.), II, p. 382 *et seq.*

but in a special chamber called the "misericord" where meat was allowed: and, moreover, the abbot might extend his hospitality to such members of the monastery as he chose. William ordered the matter thus: whenever meat might be eaten (that is, except when the Church ordered a fast) half of the monks were to dine in the refectory, and half in the misericord, so that each monk dined in the misericord and the refectory alternately. From this reckoning, however, were excluded those dining at the abbot's table and those in the infirmary. Thirteen monks at least were to be in the refectory each day, and those dining in the misericord were not to get a double allowance by receiving the food served in the refectory. Three courses were to be served in the misericord for dinner and one for supper, the prior receiving as much as two monks. The reading aloud at dinner prescribed by the Rule was to be observed, "garrulitates et scurrilitates" being avoided.

Such was the general Benedictine system: and it is worth while noticing how the restrictions were whittled down. The Provincial Chapter of Northampton (1338)[1], which accepted the Statutes of Benedict XII, also collated and revised the already existent statutes and introduced certain modifications, one of which touched upon this use of the misericord. The rule was that half of the convent should remain in the refectory: this restriction was classed with certain others as "gravis et difficilis": the emendation was introduced that only half of those actually in the convent should remain in the refectory, and that from these should be deducted (as at Malmesbury) those in the infirmary and those in the company of the abbot, and, moreover, the obedientiaries, as long as they were occupied with the business of their offices. No such limit was set as there was at Malmesbury to the number who must dine in the refectory, and it would be interesting to know how many as a rule actually remained. In the end, as the Provincial Chapter of 1444 shows, it was a common punishment to make a man dine in the refectory for a certain number of days continuously[2].

Enough has been said upon this subject to indicate the laxity which showed itself in this direction. What as to the other evidence as to the standard of monastic comfort? For St Swithun's,

[1] Reynerus, Appendix, p. 102.   [2] *Ibid.* p. 128.

Winchester, there has been preserved a series of kitchener's accounts which give the actual food eaten on every day in a series of weeks covering practically every season of the year. The document is most interesting in every way, but far too long for citation. A couple of days' expenses will illustrate the ordinary week-day fare, apart from vegetables, bread and beer. As fairly typical of the winter diet, other than on fast days, may be given the account of the 20th November, 1492:

	s.	d.
Moile (bread soaked under the roasting meat) . .	o	7
140 Eggs	1	2
Tucket (haggis) as entrée	o	1
Beef	3	o
Pork	2	o
Sowse (pickled pigs' feet and ears) for ministrants	o	3
Entrée of sub-prior and hordarian	o	6
	7	7

For the summer diet may be taken the 27th May, 1493:

	s.	d.
Meat for Batir	o	4
250 Eggs	1	3
Isynges for entrée (perhaps pickled salmon) .	o	2½
Sew (pottage) for supper	o	6
Beef	3	4
Mutton	1	8
Calves' feet	o	1½
Entrée of sub-prior as ministrant . . .	o	10
Hordarian's do. . . .	o	2
	8	5

Making all due allowance for fast days, it will probably be agreed that Dean Kitchin's words are fully borne out.

The Diet Rolls show that, though the bills of fare are somewhat monotonous the terrible sameness of an entirely unchanging diet from week's end to week's end was not felt at St Swithun's....It is probable that this monastery enjoyed a considerably better diet than was to be found elsewhere. Taking the general condition and level of food throughout the country, the brethren did not fare amiss even in the hungriest times; in those days it was given to but few to have "their meals regular": the husbandman's dinner was less plentiful, less choice, and less varied than theirs.

Dean Kitchin calculates the daily allowance of meat alone at about a pound and a half per head. "We may conclude that, rough and coarse as the living may have been, there was plenty of it, and in sufficient variety for health."

On the question of dress, it has already been pointed out by M. Jusserand[1] how the councils bear out Chaucer's satire, especially as to the dress of monks when travelling. He quotes the Council of London (1342) which

reproaches the religious with wearing clothing fit rather for knights than for clerks, that is to say, short, very tight with excessively wide sleeves, not reaching the elbows but hanging down very low, lined with fur or with silk.

They wore the beard long, rings on their fingers, costly girdles, purses or bags whereon figures and arabesques were embroidered in gold, knives which resembled swords, boots red or chequered in colour, shoes ending in long points and ornamented with slashes; in a word all the luxury of the great ones of the earth. The Council of York (1367) dealt with the same matter, more especially the wearing of short clothing in place of the monks' robe when on journeys. To these instances cited by M. Jusserand may be added the instructions given by Gregory IX to the Cluniacs a century earlier, which also deal with this same question of the dress and equipment for riding, and, directing that the dress of the monks should be seemly, restricts its value to 30s.—probably of the standard of Tours, or the equivalent of 7s. 6d. sterling of that date. The dress of the Augustinian canons at Bolton of practically the same date (1317) cost nearly twice this sum; 15 were clothed for under £10, or 13s. 4d. each[2].

Again, eighty years after the first example quoted by M. Jusserand, the Benedictine Provincial Chapter at Westminster was dealing with this same question of dress. Uniformity of dress, in shape and colour, is ordered to be observed. The excessive length of the frock sleeves is noticed: often they reach the ground: henceforth they are not to reach over the hand beyond half an ell. The shape of the hoods and riding-habits is to be uniform: and that fine cloth " de Worseto," held fitter for a knight than a monk, is totally forbidden both to abbots and their subordinates.

At practically the same date (1406) the chamberlain's rolls at

---

[1] *English Wayfaring Life* (1892), p. 115.
[2] Whitaker, *History of Craven*, p. 465.

Eynsham allows us to see the general amount spent on the dress of one of the monks there. The average is about 15s. a head a year. The materials are say (or serge), burnett, silk, black cloth, linen and linsey-woolsey[1]. What the general equipment of the monk was like it is possible to see from the list of things which, in accordance with the Rule allowing the monasteries to demand that each novice should provide his own outfit, the Ely novice was required to bring with him[2]. The "necessaries" were as follows: two "cannae," one mattress, two pairs of blankets, two pairs of straylys, three coverlets, one "furytpane," one "blew-bed" of say; one cowl and a frock, one black furred tunic, one black plain tunic, two white tunics, one black furred amice, one plain amice; one girdle with a pouch, and a penknife, tables, a comb, and needle and thread in "le powch"; one small girdle for nights; three "paria staminorum" (linsey-woolsey shirts); four pairs of breeches with "brygerdel" (an undergirding) and points, two pairs of soled hose (*caligae*), four "paria de le sokks," two pairs of boots, one for day and one for night; one "pilch," three "paria flammeole" (flannel shirts?), three "pulvinaria" or bolsters, and one white cap for nights; two towels, one dirty-clothes bag or "pokette," one shaving-cloth; one goblet (*crater*), one "*ciphus murreus*" (probably a mazer), and a silver spoon. The equipment sounds sufficiently elaborate as a list of necessaries; when the novice's outfit was on such a scale, it is hardly surprising that it was worth while making him find it himself.

In dress and food, then, the monk must have stood well up in the social scale: nor was he without other comforts which would vary the monotony of his existence. Apart from the entertainment provided by the minstrels and mummers who make so large a figure in the Durham account-rolls, and whose performances may have diverted the prior's visitors alone, the monk of Durham had a fair chance of an annual holiday: for the prior, when at certain seasons of the year he retired to one of his manors for his "*ludi*" (a relaxation to which the cells subscribed

---

[1] H. E. Salter, *Eynsham Cartulary*, II, p. xci.

[2] Rev. D. J. Stewart, *Ely Cathedral*, p. 23. "Straylys" is glossed as "a coarse kind of sackcloth" (A. Jessopp, *Visitations in Diocese of Norwich*, p. 263), and as "blankets" (Durham Account Rolls). I learn from Mr Coulton that the word is applied to rough frieze or cloth not made up. For "cannae" I can make no suggestion.

and which evidently implied a good deal of feasting), he took some of his monks with him: and in 1408, when the fund appropriated to this purpose was applied to the reduction of the convent debt, the monks were sent four at a time to stay for three weeks at Finchale Priory[1]. Nuns clearly had considerable liberty of going to stay with their relations, a practice which must have helped the finances considerably. Bishop Grandisson in 1329, after ordering the Abbess of Canonsleigh not to allow the nuns to go without his leave to any place whence they cannot return in the same day, grants them leave to go and visit their relatives or friends if they are properly attended by "honest and elderly ladies" (honestis et senioribus dominabus) and do not stay away above fifteen days: ten years earlier Walter de Stapeldon ordered that the nuns of Polsloe were not to visit their friends except once a year, and were not to stay above a month[2]. But in every house there was always the relaxation of the periodic bleedings, a medical safeguard which clearly was turned into a holiday.

Here, too, there must be discussed the maintenance of one side of the monastic organisation which hitherto has been passed over in silence, namely the communistic system which lay at the base of everything. The individual monk made abjuration of all personal property; and this, as Gregory IX reminded the religious[3], was absolutely irrevocable; not the abbot, nay, not even the Pope might allow a monk to have private possessions; "quia abdicatio proprietatis, sicut et custodia castitatis, adeo est annexa regulae monachali ut contra eam nec summus Pontifex possit licentiam indulgere." None the less, there is evidence to show, if not the breakdown of the system, at least that in the period under consideration it was extremely difficult to get it observed, and that certain relaxations were sufficiently common. The persistent repetition of denunciations of "proprietary" monks, and the persistent prohibition of any private income, are sufficiently remarkable. Turning once more to the succession of articles of the English Benedictine Chapters of the thirteenth,

[1] *The Priory of Finchale*, p. 30.
[2] Hingeston-Randolph, *Register of Grandisson*, I, p. 514; *Register of Stapeldon*, p. 316 *et seq.*
[3] Matthew Paris, *Chronica Majora*, III, p. 505.

fourteenth and fifteenth centuries, the monastic reforms of several Popes, and similar documents, we get the following series of decrees bearing on the point. Innocent III in 1215, followed by the Council of Oxford (1222), orders that no monk is to have anything of his own; or to dare to hold at farm any church, manor or possession of his monastery; and that those entrusted with the clothing of the monks are not to give them money to equip themselves but to furnish them with what is needful, and receive back the old clothes for the use of the poor or for other needs of the house. The Benedictine Provincial Chapter of 1225 repeats the prohibition of private property. The reforms of Gregory IX, as laid before the Benedictine abbots by the legate Otho in 1238, add a prohibition against leasing the manors or other possessions of a monastery to a monk. Once a year all proprietary monks are to be excommunicated, those unrepentant are to be expelled, and those whose sin is discovered only at death are to be punished by burial in a dunghill. The Cluniac Statutes as reformed by Gregory IX and Nicholas IV contain provisions for the punishment of proprietary monks by excommunication. The English Benedictine Chapter of 1249 repeats that proprietaries are to be excommunicated once a year. Innocent IV's Benedictine reforms practically follow those of Gregory IX. The Constitutions of Benedict XII (1337) let us see the evasions which were sometimes employed. They make special provision against those monks and "conversi" who buy rights, possessions or annual payments either in their own or in another's name, and deliver animals to be fed by others, and engage in "multos contractus diversimode tanquam negotiatores." If such cases are found, the property is to go to the monastery, and the offender is to be incapable of holding any office in the house. Once more it is repeated that victuals, clothing, and all other necessaries must not be given by a payment of money, but in kind. It is remarkable that the Benedictine Chapter held at Northampton in 1338 to promulgate these edicts held that this last prohibition was too severe, and added the proviso, "Ex curialitate tamen et pro specialibus [spices], aliisque minutis necessariis, sine quibus ipsos monachos esse non convenit, et pecuniam recipi et dari est permissum." In 1422 the Provincial Chapter found it necessary to repeat that this order of Benedict XII about the provision of food and clothing must be firmly observed; that if monks paid a visit to their friends or relatives, honest seculars were to be appointed to conduct them and bring them back, to whom was to be given a certain sum of money for their expenses; that no monk was to have in his custody any silver cup, jewels, or books without an indenture of which one part was to remain in the hands of his superior; that offence against this decree was to be reckoned as "proprietas"; and that when a monk's clothes wore out, he was not to keep them, but to hand them over to the proper official.

That the danger was a real one, the necessity forcing those in authority to repeat persistently these prohibitions is sufficient evidence. But certain relaxations of the strict rule of poverty got themselves accepted. The instructions of Benedict XII as to the provision of clothing, in particular, were not observed. The injunctions of Bishop Gray for Bardney Abbey show the change[1]:

Also that each monk receives yearly from the common goods of the monastery only 20s. for his habit (*vestitum*) and bedclothes, and of this they have not had entire satisfaction, we enjoin upon you, Abbot —— that you cause provision and supply of this their private property (*peculium*) inasmuch as it is very moderate to be made.

The system was evidently common. Similar injunctions were laid down[2], probably in 1432, for Eynsham, where the amount allowed to each monk was 26s. 8d. The practice adopted in this house can be seen from the account-rolls.

A most interesting account of the chamberlain, for 1403 or 1404[3], shows that although the sums granted for the clothing of the monks were in the chamberlain's hands, the application of it was not communistic. A definite sum was assigned to each monk, a priest receiving a little more than the rest; a separate little account was kept for each member of the monastery, and the balance in hand of each account was carried over to the next year. Clearly the monk had some control over the way in which the money was disposed of: some with the abbot's consent made

---

[1] A. Hamilton Thompson, *Visitations of Religious Houses*, I, p. 4. The injunctions are of uncertain date, but fall within the limits 1431–36.

[2] *Ibid.* p. 54.

[3] H. E. Salter, *Eynsham Cartulary*, II, Preface.

presents to their kinsfolk, others made a pilgrimage to Canterbury, or paid the expenses of the house in entertaining their
friends. It is probable that the monks' salaries or stipends
which are mentioned in the Norwich visitations were applied
in the same way. The Augustinian canons of Westacre[1], for
example, complained in 1514 that they were not receiving their
stipends; that some of them were in debt because their salaries
were not paid; that the prior did not pay them the pensions due
to them. Brother Richard Auger deposed that Brother Richard
Palle, formerly prior, owed him 30s. for his salary; Brother
Thomas Symon explained that the custom of the house was for
each of the brethren to receive 20s. a year, which was placed in
the charge of one of the "sounder" members of the house, but
that this custom was not being observed. It is difficult to regard
the system as anything but a relaxation, slight but distinct, of
the rule of poverty.

Then, also, the practice prevailed of allowing pocket-money
to the monks. It shows itself at Bury St Edmund's early in the
thirteenth century, when Abbot Samson allowed each monk to
have "two shillings, if so much happened to have been given us
by way of charity"; so that it might be expended upon poor
relations or for purposes of piety. The practice in its latest legal
form is given by the Benedictine Chapter of 1444. The reception
of money gives rise to a tendency to acquire private property,
as well as to secret business and other illicit things, and also
grumbling: it is in part against the Rule: but, according to
ancient customs, so long as they are not without discretion, or
lavish in expenditure or unwise in management, "all our subjects are allowed to receive or expend money, partly for necessaries, partly for recreations": not however at will, but only
on these things, and giving a most faithful account. The account-
rolls of Abingdon show into what such a system developed.
Thus in the chamberlain's account for 1417–18 occur payments
to the abbot (£2), the prior (16s.), the sub-prior (12s.), each
priest (10s.), and each non-priest (7s.) for spices on the Feast of
the Nativity of the Virgin. Further payments were made at
four other seasons of the year, with the result that each priest
received from the chamberlain £1. 16s. 8d. a year (say some £22

---

[1] A. Jessopp, *Visitations of the Diocese of Norwich* (C.S.), pp. 101–5.

modern) and each non-priest £1. 7s. Other smaller presents appear in the treasurer's accounts. Much the same system prevailed at St Swithun's, Winchester, where the chamberlain's roll shows that in 1417 each brother received 13s. 4d. in four instalments; and according to a sacristan's roll of much later date (1536–7), presents were due from this office as well.

At Durham in 1409 the secretary alone distributed £24. 9s. among 31 monks, and other obedientiaries also gave sums: at Worcester in 1521–2, £32. 17s. was distributed from the chamberlain's office alone among 38 monks. From 1468 each monk of Westminster contributed a mark yearly to the building of the nave, which with a "recreation" or harvest-outing which they also denied themselves added from £33 to £36 a year to the building fund[1]. In 1533, the Abbot of Westminster engaged that three chantry monks should say daily mass for the well-being of Henry VII, his queen, their ancestors and their descendants. They were each to be paid £5 over and above such "findings, profits and rewards" as were received by every monk not holding office in the abbey[2]. A single man, to-day, fully provided for, and with some £60 a year at his disposal, could hardly be said to be without private property.

Examples may be quoted which indicate that even more marked laxity in the observance of this side of the Rule might pass unnoticed, or even with the permission of the authorities. In 1385 Brother John de Thornton, a monk of Ely, was so heavily burdened with debt, that he was licensed by the bishop to celebrate an annual in the cathedral church for five years, and to receive six marks yearly for his labour[3]. In 1338 Bishop Grandisson found that the "officia" of the obedientiaries at Tavistock Abbey, and the property belonging thereto, had long been farmed out to some of the monks of the abbey at prices below their true worth ("a longis, ut audivimus, retroactis temporibus sub certis prestacionibus annuis fuerunt monachis nonnullis dicti monasterii, licet ad ampliores sufficerent, dimissa"). More remarkable still are the entries from the Treasurer's roll at Abingdon in 1383–4, already cited[4]. Peter Craundon, ex-cellarer

[1] Rackham, *Nave of Westminster*, pp. 32–3.
[2] Dugdale, *Monasticon*, I, p. 279.
[3] *Ely Episcopal Registers*, Register of Thomas de Arundell.
[4] See p. 47, above.

and ex-kitchener, pays off a debt to the monastery of £1. 6s. 4d. and still owes £16. 15s. However the debt was incurred, individual poverty cannot have been well observed in a place where, according to the official accounts, one of the brethren was expected to produce a sum of over £18, or something like £200 in modern money.

Finally, it is possible, in some cases, to give the actual figures showing what was considered a fair maintenance for a monk. These cases, though few in number, may serve to give a clearer idea of the standard of comfort reached than can be gathered from the facts mentioned above. It is not possible to use the monastic accounts here, since due allowance cannot be made for the amount spent upon servants and guests. The most valuable documents for the purpose are those recording the addition of fresh monks and the sums granted by benefactors for their maintenance. Although a fair number of these are to be found, most of them tantalisingly mention a manor or some other piece of property without giving its annual value. The remainder, however, give some guide as to the cost of feeding, clothing and housing a monk.

The starting-point is best taken from one of the Cistercian houses in its early days when the enthusiasm of the lately created Order was still in full flow. Waverley, the first English Cistercian house, was founded in 1128. At some date, either in the reign of Richard I or John, a bequest was left to the house for the maintenance of one monk in addition to those then in the convent. Its amount was 13s. 4d. a year[1]. It may be taken then that for this sum a monk could be maintained, fed, and clothed for a year, since the expense of housing would not be much. About forty years later (at some date between 1235 and 1239) a bequest for the same purpose was made to another Cistercian house, the Abbey of Meaux[2]. In this case the bequest was the site of a mill, and the convent paid the donor £5 a year for it during his lifetime. Most probably, then, the income from the land was about £5, and the cost of maintaining a monk at Meaux was over seven times what had been considered necessary at Waverley forty years before. It will be remembered that the

[1] Dugdale, *Monasticon*, v, p. 238.
[2] *Chronica Monasterii de Melsa*, II, p. 51.

Council of Oxford in 1222 had fixed for the first time the minimum portion of a secular vicar at 5 marks (£3. 6s. 8d.): the vicar would have heavier expenses to meet than the monk, inasmuch as, even if a house were provided, he would have to bear some of the burdens of his church, synodals, the archdeacon's procurations, and so on.

Another Cistercian house gives us an estimate for the support of a monk towards the close of the thirteenth century. The Church of Whalley was, after much difficulty and expense, appropriated in 1298 to the Abbey of Stanlaw: and the monks thereon moved to Whalley and there built a new abbey. One of the conditions of the appropriation was that twenty monks should be added to the foundation, though this seems never to have been done[1]. The abbot, being confronted with a demand for increased taxation by the Chapter of the Order, presented a petition trying to prove that they would not be much to the good through the appropriation. In this petition, the support of the twenty extra monks is reckoned at 5 marks each annually, or £3. 6s. 8d. This, it is noticeable, is the same sum as was provided for the stipend of each of the seven vicars of the chapels under the Church of Whalley. An increase of these proportions, it seems fairly clear, represented a substantial rise in the standard of living. In 1328-9, Bishop Grandisson found Tywardreath Priory deep in debt. He ordered, therefore, that, until the debt was paid off, each monk should be allowed only 15d. a week, or £3. 5s. a year, for the necessities of life. But he evidently considered that that sum was liberal, for, finding in 1333 that the house was still in debt, he cut the allowance down to 8d. a week, or £1. 14s. 8d. a year.

One more instance may be got from Meaux at the close of the fourteenth century, by reason of the balance-sheets drawn up by Abbot Thomas Bolton in 1393[2]. A total obtained by taking the item "common expenses," and assigning to the monks a portion of the wine purchased in the same proportion as that borne by the monks' expenses to those of the abbot's chamber and the guest-hall, amounts to £160 and a few shillings. This does not include the wages of the servants, but it does include

[1] Whitaker, *History of Whalley*, I, p. 176.
[2] *Chronica Monasterii de Melsa*, III, pp. lxix–lxxviii.

the entertainment of such guests as fell to the share of the abbey, and the keeping of the house in repair. We must consider, however, that produce to the amount of £150 was consumed by the house in addition to the above sum. If we allow two-thirds of this sum for the food of the servants, the expenses of the guests and the repairs of the house, we shall probably be over rather than below the mark. The maintenance of the 26 monks, apart from the wages of their servants, the entertainment of their guests and the repairs of their house, may be stated at £210, or practically £8 a head—roughly equivalent to £104 a head in modern money.

To turn to the Benedictine houses, Thomas Prior of Durham in 1235 confirms the ordinance of Prior Bertram that on an increase of the revenues of Durham and Coldingham from the churches of "Lodoney" two monks should be added to each house for every 20 marks increase[1]. This puts the expense of maintenance at £6. 13s. 4d. With this we may compare the provision made in 1344 to add five monks to Walden Abbey[2]. A manor worth £100 was bequeathed for this purpose; but as the monks were to be added during the lifetime of the tenant, who was only to pay a rent of 50 marks, it may be taken that the latter sum was, for the time being, held sufficient for the purpose. This again allows £6. 13s. 4d. per head. With this may be compared the contemporary commons allowance of the scholars of Balliol and the fellows of University Hall, which amounted to 12d. a week, or £2. 12s. a year[3]. Going on another 150 years we reach the case of Bath, where, in 1500, £10 a head was being spent[4].

An interesting document of Bury St Edmund's[5], dating from the reign of Edward I, gives the yearly kitchen expenses for the maintenance of 80 monks, 111 servants (with their wages), 11 chaplains, the nuns of Thetford and the guests of the house. The total value of the corn used each week in the house, together with barley-malt and oat-malt, was £10. 9s. 9d.: the servants in the malt-house and bakehouse received 4s. 4½d. a week, and used fuel worth £1. 6s. 8d. In the kitchen, £10 a week was spent in

[1] J. Raine, *Priory of Coldingham*, p. 242.
[2] *Calendar of Papal Petitions*, II, p. 77.   [3] *Ibid.* II, pp. 16, 20.
[4] Dugdale, *Monasticon*, II, p. 270.
[5] *Ibid.* III, p. 141.

flesh, fish, eggs and cheese. The cellarer yearly provided herrings, gruel, beans, honey, nuts, salt, and peas to the value of £43.8s.8d. The abbot's portion consisted of corn, barley-malt, and oat-malt, to the extent of £11. 5s. 9d. a week; and also 6¾ oxen, 15½ pigs, 31 geese and 155 fowls, worth in all £4. 15s. 8d. Of this flesh, it should be remembered, the monks would receive their share through the practice of the abbot's invitations to dinner. The kitchen fuel for the year cost £30: the food of the prior's, cellarer's, guest-master's and guests' horses cost £60. In addition, £60 a year was spent on pittances and misericords (or extra allowances of meat and drink), robes and the cellarer's expenses. Thus the total annual expense was £1407. 11s. 2d. Once again the standard of living was clearly high for the time. If we put the number of people who shared in the monastery's expenses at 250, to cover the nuns and the guests, and reckon the servants as receiving equal quantities with the monks, which was certainly not the case, the expense per head is about £5. 14s.

Tabulated in terms of pre-war money, the figures stated above run approximately, thus:

	12th cent.	13th cent.	14th cent.	15th cent.	16th cent.
Waverley	£13. 6s. 8d.	—	—	—	—
Meaux	—	£90	£104	—	—
Bury St. Edmund's	—	£85	—	—	—
Whalley	—	£60	—	—	—
Durham	—	£120	—	—	—
Walden	—	—	£100	—	—
Bath	—	—	—	—	£120

Finally may be noticed, as a bishop's view of what was a fitting maintenance for a monk, the following rules laid down by Bishop Buckingham in 1380 after a visitation of Eynsham[1]. The chamberlain was to receive for each monk's clothing, meat and wine £4. 6s. 8d. Each of the monks was to be provided also with salt, oatmeal, beans, white peas, butter, cheese, together with firewood and other necessaries for broth and pottage. In

[1] H. E. Salter, *Eynsham Cartulary*, I, p. xxix.

addition each received an allowance of bread and beer. We cannot do better than quote Mr Salter's comment:

> If the whole income of many a parish priest was at this time no more than £5, if a monastery like Wroxton Priory had to maintain twelve canons and pay for all repairs and wages and taxes out of an income of about £50 a year, the allowance at Eynsham must have sufficed for something more than a bare maintenance. Thirty years later the commons of the Provost and Fellows of Oriel were at the rate of only 15d. a head weekly, and those of the monks of Durham College in 1464 about 17d. a head.

All this, making due allowance for such facts as those quoted above about Wroxton and Durham College, may not point to luxury or riotous living, but it points to a sufficiently comfortable material existence. If we remember the superiority of the monastic buildings as a home, we may very well think of the monks' life as well up in the scale of comfort as it was then reckoned. Ascetic in its severity the life assuredly cannot have been as a whole. It was possible, no doubt, for the individual to make it so; but the general tone cannot have been in any way austere.

The whole truth about the monks of the Middle Ages will never be gathered even from the most complete examination of their financial management. But in the consideration of the main question which must be answered before the Dissolution can be placed in the proper light, some little advance towards an answer, it may be, is made possible by the facts which are contained in the preceding pages. The main point at issue, after all, is the use which monasticism in the later Middle Ages was making of its opportunities.

The services rendered in the earlier Middle Ages have long been fully recognised. For many centuries the ascetic beliefs which underlay monasticism were in the closest alliance with Christianity: the two were inseparably fused. While every renewal of religious enthusiasm involved a revival of monasticism, it was in the monastic organisation that an attempt was made to fix that enthusiasm and make it permanent. The monastery was, as it were, an endeavour to give a body to the incorporeal spirit of mediaeval religious fervour, to furnish a hearth whereon might be kept for ever burning the fire sent down from heaven. Nor was the effort unsuccessful. For centuries the religious houses stood representative of peace, mutual endeavour, and the things of the spirit amid the brutalities, the unending strife, the semi-barbaric materialism of the welter of tribes, and later of half-grown states, out of which modern Europe with difficulty got itself formed. It was the early monks who effected whatever relaxation of the scorn felt for manual labour showed itself in the Middle Ages. It was within this shrine that the lamp of learning was kept alight through all the violence and savagery of those unlovely times when the Roman Empire fell in ruins and when the unwieldy Frankish Empire collapsed through its own internal schisms and the wild attack of fresh barbaric hosts. It was from this refuge that there came the knowledge making possible the brilliant, if often narrow and premature, intellectual achievements of the thirteenth century. It was by the monks that the great missionary work of the early Middle Ages was accomplished. It was from these homes of the religious that there went forth the emissaries to bring within the civilising sway of Christianity the English, the Germans, the Scandinavians and last of all the Slavs. Around the monasteries, and under their protection, there sprang up in many places the beginnings of town life, with all its possibilities of quickening of intellect, and devotion to the arts of peace. Above all, at times when the Church was losing sight of its mission and devoting itself to things of this world, when secularisation threatened to smother all spiritual life, the remedy was invariably found in the reaction felt when men saw once more before them those who set themselves wholeheartedly to live what, to all mediaeval minds, was the highest life. The monks' life widened willy-nilly, and the stronger the attempt to sever all connection with the world, the stronger was this influence upon the world which had been renounced. It was not well that the ideal life should be held to be one which could be sought by but a few in the strictest segregation from their fellowmen: the consequent disparagement of the virtues attainable in everyday life was in itself an evil. But every revival of monasticism from the time of St Benedict to St Bernard did, in its own despite, add to the spirituality of the social life which it deserted: and it may well be doubted if the quickening could otherwise have occurred.

But between England of the sixteenth century and these achievements there lay some four hundred years. The tendencies of monasticism during that period, judged simply on the evidence of finance, point to little that could maintain the old reputation of the monasteries.

The essentiality of the ascetic side of monastic life has been considered. It was because of their renunciation of the world, in the ascetic sense, that the monks were able to influence the world. The defence of the endowment of monasticism can rest only upon the influence which it had upon the world at large. Few would now defend it as a mere selfish attempt to save the monk's soul: though on this side, also, the element of ascetic austerity was necessary, according to mediaeval ways of thinking. But there is comparatively little in these later years to be seen beyond a life of easy sauntering comfort. Though extravagant luxury might be absent, ease and plenty were not: if the religious houses had as a rule survived the difficulties which in large measure were beyond their power to avoid, but to which waste had unquestionably added, it had been by no consistent endurance of an austere and hard life. Large households were maintained. The dress of the religious was a subject of sumptuary regulation for three centuries. The monk lived comfortably, as comfort went then: he was provided with pocket money for luxuries, apart from those which the ordinary fare of the monasteries gave him. How the original severity of the rules about eating flesh was relaxed we have already seen. No doubt there were discomforts in the elaborate system of Church services; no doubt the individual monk did, at times, take the asceticism of his profession seriously. But, on the whole, he lived a slow and well-to-do life. The influence which monasticism had exerted on account of its asceticism was gone during these later centuries.

What of the other means of influencing the world? We have seen how soon the practice of manual labour died away. We have seen also something of the great change which took place in these centuries, leaving the monks with but little of their own property beneath their own care and management. The opportunity which had been taken in the earlier stages of monasticism of dignifying the ordinary toil of life, of passing on to the world the knowledge of agriculture or industry gained in the quietness of their lives, was progressively neglected during this later period. The burden of carrying on the monastic organisation no longer involved the contact with, and care for, those living in the world, which had made of the religious houses centres for the dissemination of civilisation. Alms and hospitality also (to put the case at its weakest) were not so much to the fore as would be expected. It was not much otherwise in the case of learning. The question of monastic education has not been discussed in these pages, and must therefore here be set aside. But everything points to a great decline in this respect. The way in which the monastic chronicles dwindle away to the meagrest entries of the accession or death of some abbot, or cease altogether, is of itself significant. The failure of the monks and friars to take part in the movement of the new learning is not without significance, for, as the history of the Counter-Reformation shows, it was due to no inherent impossibility of a union between Roman Catholicism and the types of learning so bitterly opposed at the outset.

All this meant stagnation and decay. The enthusiasm for the full asceticism of monastic life died away: there is not lacking evidence that even the pride in and love of the monastery itself which followed it was far in decline. The records of pitiful quarrels and ill-feeling which are to be found in the later episcopal visitations all tell of the absence of any quickening spirit, the presence of weariness and *ennui* which quarrels for want of something better to do. Everywhere the horizon of the monk was narrowed. The internal management of the business of the house still remained to be carried on, but many of the outside connections formed as the house grew in wealth and power were cast aside. The monks' interests were concentrated upon the convent once more, but in a very different sense from that of the early days when the walls of the monastery were a haven, wherein the ascetic fleeing from a hopeless and dying world might save himself alive. They were imprisoned now within the deadening confines where life crept slowly on from day to day, where sense of responsibility was lost, sympathy narrowed and intellect cramped. Speaking generally, the monk no longer sought his own salvation with passionate eagerness, nor used his position of superior reverence and respect to influence those with whom he came into contact. Shirking inconvenient duties took the place of renunciation; prerogative was replaced by privilege. The asceticism of the monastic life which was its strength, was also its weakness. The world admired the ascetic and called upon him to lead it and to serve it: and the effort to respond was fatal to the ascetic life and to the religious ardour which had been identified with it.

The narrower question of the Dissolution is that of the means whereby it was carried out. The wider question is whether, on the whole, monasticism had anything further to give to England. The period which we have been considering was not, of course, the only one when monasticism was in decline. It had been in decay, for instance, during the ninth and tenth centuries. It had shown itself capable of persistent revival: it has shown itself capable of revival abroad at sundry times during the course of modern history. But England, in common with the Teutonic peoples in general, was moving away from mediaeval Catholicism towards Protestantism. The monasteries were called upon to justify the possession of their endowments by showing what use they were making of them. They were called upon to show what good was coming to the world by reason of the possessions which had been given to enable them to get as near as they could to their ideal of the Christian life. If they could not make reply to the question, that they were to the best of their ability leading that life, or if they could not show that, having set aside part of that ideal, they were as far as human frailty allowed doing active and positive work among their fellow-men, there was not much more to be said. That the work of spoliation was cruel, bunglingly done, productive of misery and crime, is all very much to the bad. But that the monasteries were on the whole useless—useless in the sense that they were not justifying their possession of great wealth, privilege and dignity—is an argument which an inspection of the documents from the financial point of view tends, so far as it goes, to confirm. From the mediaeval ascetic point of view they were not deserving of approval: from the modern point of view they were doing little which could not be less extravagantly done by men un-hampered in their social work by an obligatory rejection of social ties. The days when monasticism had stood almost alone for spiritual life, learning, peace and lawfulness were over. The monks were not strong enough to uphold the old view of life in the face of the new opinions: they could not persistently develop and maintain the sides of their life on which men of the new beliefs looked with approval, save in the face of a public opinion ever jealously on the watch. It is by reason of such facts as these that the Dissolution must explain itself as other than the result of credulity, poltroonery and ingratitude in the English nation: it is on these lines that, taken in the main, it must justify itself. The facts about monastic finance may yet, upon full investigation, plead strongly towards its defence.

APPENDIX A

THE CLUNIAC HOUSES

1262–1279

IN the following pages will be found tabulated the information given as to the financial condition of the English Cluniac houses contained in the pages of Sir G. F. Duckett's *Visitations of the English Cluniac Foundations*. It is valuable as giving both the number of monks and the debt of the houses, but unfortunately contains no information as to the income of the monasteries concerned.

I. Number of Monks and Laybrethren.

	Statutory No.	1262		1245–6		1279	
		Monks	Lay-brethren	Monks	Lay-brethren	Monks	Lay-brethren
Barnstaple	—	—	—	—	—	6	—
Bermondsey	24	32	1	20	—	18	—
Bromholme	25? 16?	—	—	16	—	—	—
Careswell	3–6	—	—	—	—	4	—
Castleacre	26	—	—	32	—	35	—
Clifford	11	—	—	—	—	9	—
Derby St James	3	—	—	—	—	3	—
Exeter St James	2	—	—	—	—	2	—
Farley	20	—	—	18	2	18	—
Horksley	2–3	—	—	—	—	5	—
Linton	32	22	2	27	4	25	—
Lewes	35	—	—	—	—	50	—
Mary [St] of Holme	—	—	—	—	—	3	—
Monks-Horton	8–13	—	—	12	—	13	—
Montacute	34	25	—	20	—	28	—
Northampton	25–30	34	—	30	—	25	—
Pontefract	20	16	—	—	—	27	—
Prittlewell	24	—	—	15	—	14	—
Thetford	22?	22	—	24	—	22	—
Wenlock	40	34	—	40	3	35	—

II. Debts.

	1262			Various			1275–6			1279		
	£	s.	d.	£	s.	d.	£	s.	d.	£	s.	d.
Barnstaple	—			—			48	13	4	48	13	4
Bermondsey	177	6	8	—			666	13	4	1533	6	8
Bromholme	—			—			120	0	0	—		
Careswell	—			—			40	0	0	nil		
Castleacre	—			—			504	0	0	1133	6	8
Clifford	—			—			—			66	13	4
Derby St James	—			—			—			6	10	0
Exeter St James	—			—			8	0	0	20	0	0
Farley	—			—			nil			nil		
Horksley	—			—			—			66	13	4
Linton	1000	0	0	—			120	0	0	686	13	4
Lewes	nil			—			2666	13	4	2333	6	8
Mary [St] of Holme	—			—			—			nil		
Monks-Horton	53	13	4	—			—			nil		
Montacute	200	0	0	⎰ 245	6	8	193	6	8	175	6	8
				[1268]								
				⎱ 373	6	8	466	13	4	133	6	8
				[1269]								
Northampton	181	13	4	—			—			—		
Pontefract	666	13	4	2133	6	8	—			233	6	8
				[1267]								
Prittlewell	—			—			100	0	0	333	13	4
Thetford	406	13	4	533	6	8	802	13	4	—		
				[after 1270]								
Wenlock	1084	6	8	333	6	8	1000	0	0	866	15	4

APPENDIX B

THE PROVINCE OF ROUEN
1248–1269

THE statements made on pp. 126 and 150 as to the state of monastic finance in the province of Rouen are based on the evidence contained in the register of Odo Rigaldi for a year or two only. The results thus arrived at may be compared with those of a calculation covering the 21 years for which the register yields material.

Taking for each house of monks an average of the slightly fluctuating population as recorded from time to time, we may conclude that the 162 houses visited in the province contained approximately 1832 monks: in the diocese of Rouen 952 in 90 houses, and in the other dioceses of the province 880 in 72 houses. Satisfactory evidence as to income and debt is forthcoming only for 104 houses: but, as these contained 1492 monks, any conclusions reached as to their state may be applied without much hesitation to the remainder.

The income of these 104 houses, as given by the Archbishop, amounted to 84,068 livres tournois, or a little over 56 l.t. per head of the population.

In estimating the average debt, some difficulty arises from the fact that the visitor occasionally did not record how much the house owed. If these visitations are omitted entirely, the combined average debt for the period was 28,020 l.t. If it is assumed that no mention was made of debt because there was none, the total sinks to 20,360 l.t. The true state of affairs is probably represented nearly enough by the mean of these totals, 24,190 l.t.[1] This gives a debt of a little over 16 l.t. per head, or 28·6 per cent. of the average income.

Further light is thrown on the situation by the following tables, distributing population, income and debt according to the size of the house. It will be observed, for example, that the expenditure

---

[1] This may be a slight understatement: the higher total disregards the possibility that the debt remained unchanged since the last visitation, the lower always accepts the possibility that it had been extinguished.

Population and Income (Monks)

Income per head (l.t.)	Houses of 1–10 monks		Houses of 10–20 monks		Houses of 20–30 monks		Houses of 30–40 monks		Houses of 40–50 monks		Houses of 50–60 monks		Houses of over 60 monks		Total	
	Houses	Monks	Houses	Monks	Houses	Monks	Houses	Monks	Houses	Monks	Houses	Monks	Houses	Monks	Houses	Monks
20 and less	2	6	3	53	—	—	—	—	—	—	—	—	—	—	5	59
20–30	10	46	3	34	1	22	1	31	—	—	1	56	—	—	15	158
30–40	9	26	9	123	4	96	3	99	1	48	—	—	—	—	23	276
40–50	8	29	3	41	4	95	2	69	—	—	—	—	—	—	19	312
50–60	7	32	—	—	—	—	1	31	—	—	—	—	—	—	9	101
60–70	6	26	—	—	4	102	—	—	1	42	—	—	—	—	11	159
70–80	4	13	2	36	1	23	2	69	1	50	—	—	1	62	8	153
80–90	—	—	1	11	—	—	—	—	—	—	—	—	—	—	5	153
90–100	1	7	1	15	—	—	2	77	—	—	—	—	—	—	2	22
Over 100	5	22	—	—	—	—	—	—	—	—	—	—	—	—	7	99
Total	52	207	22	313	14	338	11	376	3	140	1	56	1	62	104	1492

Population and Debt (Monks)

Debt per head (l.t.)	Houses of 1–10 monks		Houses of 10–20 monks		Houses of 20–30 monks		Houses of 30–40 monks		Houses of 40–50 monks		Houses of 50–60 monks		Houses of over 60 monks		Total	
	Houses	Monks	Houses	Monks	Houses	Monks	Houses	Monks	Houses	Monks	Houses	Monks	Houses	Monks	Houses	Monks
10 and less	21	83	11	157	8	200	2	69	2	92	1	56	—	—	45	657
10–20	11	37	5	71	2	47	5	169	1	48	—	—	—	—	23	324
20–30	9	53	4	50	2	46	2	68	—	—	—	—	1	62	19	327
30–40	4	15	1	19	1	23	1	30	—	—	—	—	—	—	5	38
40–50	5	15	—	—	1	22	1	40	—	—	—	—	—	—	7	64
50–60	1	2	1	16	—	—	—	—	—	—	—	—	—	—	3	64
60–70	—	—	—	—	—	—	—	—	—	—	—	—	—	—	—	—
70–80	—	—	—	—	—	—	—	—	—	—	—	—	—	—	1	16
80–90	—	—	—	—	—	—	—	—	—	—	—	—	—	—	—	—
90–100	—	—	—	—	—	—	—	—	—	—	—	—	—	—	—	—
Over 100	1	2	—	—	—	—	—	—	—	—	—	—	—	—	1	2
Total	52	207	22	313	14	338	11	376	3	140	1	56	1	62	104	1492

per head must have varied greatly from house to house. As against 493 monks maintained on 40 l.t. or less per head, 312 lived in houses with an income providing from half as much again to twice as much, and 274 in houses which could afford even more. Debt was apparently rather more uniform. A debt of 10 l.t. or less—well below the average of 16 l.t.—accounts for 44 per cent. of the total population: the number with a debt per head double the average is less than 10 per cent. of the total.

The 18 nunneries visited had, on an average, 602 inmates: in the diocese of Rouen 295 in 11 houses, and in the other dioceses of the province 307 in seven houses. Satisfactory information as to income and debt is available only for 11 houses, with 462 inmates. The total income of these houses was 11,039 l.t., or a little under 26 l.t. per head—less than half the corresponding figure for the monks. Information as to debt is rather uncertain; many visitations yield no evidence, and the average total may therefore be as high as 4363 l.t., or as low as 2345 l.t. The mean of these sums, 3354 l.t., gives a debt of a little over 7 l.t. per head. The proportion of debt to income is just over 30 per cent., a proportion only a little higher than that of the monks.

The following table of population and income emphasises the comparative poverty of the nunneries. An average income of 20 l.t. or less accounts for 60 per cent. of the nuns as against 3·8 per cent. of the monks, while the highest income per head was less than half that of the monks. The comparative insignificance of small houses of nuns is the most marked feature of the distribution of population: 54 per cent. were in houses of 50 inmates and over, as against 7·9 per cent. of the monks.

No table of debt is necessary for the nuns: in only one case did it exceed 10 l.t. per head.

Population and Income (Nuns)

Income per head (l.t.)	Houses of 1–10 nuns		Houses of 10–20 nuns		Houses of 20–30 nuns		Houses of 30–40 nuns		Total	
	Houses	Nuns	Houses	Nuns	Houses	Nuns	Houses	Nuns	Houses	Nuns
20 and less	—	—	2	31	—	—	1	34	3	65
20–30	—	—	—	—	—	—	—	—	—	—
30–40	—	—	1	11	—	—	—	—	1	11
40–50	—	—	—	—	—	—	—	—	—	—
Total	—	—	3	42	—	—	1	34	4	76

Income per head (l.t.)	Houses of 40–50 nuns		Houses of 50–60 nuns		Houses of over 60 nuns		Total		Grand total	
	Houses	Nuns	Houses	Nuns	Houses	Nuns	Houses	Nuns	Houses	Nuns
20 and less	2	89	—	—	2	123	4	212	7	277
20–30	1	47	—	—	—	—	1	47	1	47
30–40	—	—	—	—	—	—	—	—	1	11
40–50	—	—	1	60	1	67	2	127	2	127
Total	3	136	1	60	3	190	7	386	11	462

APPENDIX C

THE BURSARY

THE following list completes the various references to bursars, treasurers or receivers which I have encountered in addition to those given in the text. In most cases the information is similar to that given above, or fragmentary. In the fourteenth century the office is mentioned in the case of St Albans (Dugdale, *Monasticon*, II, p. 209); St Mary's, York (Miss M. Sellers, *York Memorandum Book*, I, p. 27); Thorneye Abbey (*Register of Thomas de Insula*, summarised in the *Ely Diocesan Remembrancer*); Newstead Abbey (S. Raine, *Register of Archbishop Grey*, S.S., p. 210); Selby Abbey (*ibid.* p. 327); Whitby (*Chartulary*, ed. J. C. Atkinson, S.S., pp. 555 *et seq.*, 632; a specimen of the bursar's roll, 1394–5, is given; in 1320 the bursars had been restricted to the receipt and payment of money, the external business of the house, hitherto attached to the bursary, being transferred to a cellarer); Tavistock Abbey (F. C. Hingeston-Randolph, *Register of John de Grandisson*, visitation of 1338, II, p. 889 *et seq.*; *Register of Thomas de Brantyngham*, visitation of 1373); Plympton Priory (*Register of John de Grandisson*, II, p. 956); Gloucester, St Oswald (W. Brown, *Register of Archbishop Giffard*, S.S., visitation of 1250, pp. 203 *et seq.*); Bury St Edmund's (Dugdale, III, p. 167); Ramsey Abbey (Miss N. Neilson, *Economic Conditions on the Manors of Ramsey Abbey*, p. 22). A record of the statutes and constitutions of the Cistercian Order made in 1667 for the monastery of the Blessed Virgin in Wilhering includes an undated "Modus Visitandi," which instructs the visitor to inquire whether there are more "bursae" than that which is common to the convent. The bursar is to give full account to the visitor of the value to the community of the various sources of its income. (*Studien und Mittheilungen aus dem Benedictiner-Orden*, Vol. XVIII, 1897.)

INDEX

Abbot, papal confirmation in exempt houses, 26, 102–4; separate establishment, 27; sole legal representative of house, 28, 35; claims on funds of house, 49, 52, 53; control of obediences, 54; relations with Chapter, 54–60; autocratic powers, 62, 128; nepotism, 129; difficulty in choice of, 131

Abbot's Langley, rapid change of incumbents, 77

Abingdon Abbey, fragmentary accounts, 5; monk paid for work on windows, 15; separation of abbot's income, 28; obediences, 31; sacristan's account (*1396*), 36; ex-obedientiaries' debts to house, 47, 165; treasurer in charge of reserve fund, 48, 52; abbot draws on funds, 49, 53; burial dues, 85; payments to monks at university, 106; hospitality, 112; pocket-money, 164

Accounts, complexity of, 37, 63–7; bursary intended to simplify, 43; legislation as to, 58, 66; clerks paid to keep, 132; failure to present, 133

Albans, St, Abbey, monk as stone-cutter, 15; monks holding office, 15, 30; abbot's barony, 28; obediences, 31; bursary, 33; responsible for abbot's debts, 53; stone coffins, 55; hospital endowed, 55, 133; protest against quarterly accounts, 67; doubtful use of church patronage, 77; cost of papal confirmation, 102, 103; failure to provide students, 107; hospitality, 112; financial difficulties, 120, 127; Pope forbids loans to King, 127; abbot's nepotism, 129; case of peculation, 130; business incapacity of abbot, 131; official-general, 132; loans raised by obedientiaries limited, 133; leases at nominal rents, 138; corrodies, 141, 144–5; relics used to raise funds, 146; appropriations to improve beer, 148

Albon, Abbot of St Albans, patronage under, 77

Alien Priories, special difficulties of, 22

Alienation of lands without convent's consent, 57

Almsgiving, 112–17

Annuities, sale by German towns, 144

Appropriation of churches, 76–91, 147; for limited period, 78; bishop's control of, 80; statutes and petitions on, 80, 83; papal mandate of inquiry, 81; maintenance of fabric, 88; monastic and other, 89–91; pensions to cathedral authorities, 89; proposed, to maintain students, 106, 109; to promote lawsuit, 109; corrody as part of vicar's stipend, 142

Articuli Cleri, 140

Augustinian Order, *see* Benedict XII; valuation of English houses prohibited, 71

Baldwin, Archbishop of Canterbury, interferes in business management of cathedral priory, 39

Balliol College, Oxford, scholars' commons allowance, 168

Bardney Abbey, bursar's functions, 43; appropriates pensionary churches, 78; financial difficulties, 120; clothing system, 163

Barnstaple Priory, financial difficulties, 121

Bath Priory, reorganised by Bishop King, 135; retains plumber by corrody, 142; cost of monk's maintenance, 168

Battle Abbey, fails to provide scholars, 107

Beaulieu, cell of St Albans at, suppressed to maintain university students, 108

Beaulieu Abbey, Pope revokes appropriation, 148

Bec Abbey, income not scheduled, 133

Belvoir Priory, rapid reduction of debt, 134

Benedict, St, Rule of, obediences mentioned in, 32; on position of Chapter, 55; degree of asceticism enjoined, 153; on meat-eating, 155

Benedict XII, Pope, reform of Augustinian statutes, 22, 57, 58, 59, 105; valuation of monasteries

Nicholas IV; decline of numbers in English houses, 22; financial difficulties in England, 120; visitor on veracity of English members, 62; population and debt of English houses, 176

Coldingham Priory, cost of maintaining monk, 168

Colerne, William de, Abbot of Malmesbury, rules for use of misericord, 156

Confirmation of abbot, papal, expense of, 102–104

Conversi, *see* Lay Brothers

Cornworthy nunnery, lady lodges in, 125

Corrodiers, as element of population, 19

Corrody, 139–47

Cost of maintaining monk, 166–70

Craundon, Peter, monk of Abingdon, in debt to house, 47, 165

Croyland Abbey, servants employed, 14; corrodiers, 19; case of nepotism, 130

Debt, before Black Death, 119–28; rapid reduction of, 133; expedients to reduce, 136–49

Dennis, monk of Norwich, holds several obediences, 132

Dilapidation, 60

Dower, on entering religion, 151

Drayton, Nicholas, monk of Abingdon, paid for work on windows, 15

Dress, *see* Clothing

Durham College, Oxford, monks' commons allowance, 170

Durham Priory, obediences, 31; bursar, 43; inaccuracy of Taxation of Pope Nicholas, 72; decline in offerings at shrines, 74; mortuaries, 87; coal-mining, 92; university students, 106; no corrodies sold, 144; indulgences, 146; Pope's reasons for refusing appropriation, 148; holidays, 160; pocket-money, 165; cost of maintaining monk, 168

Durham, Rites of, 43

Edward II, claims to appoint corrodier, 140

Edward III, claims to appoint corrodier, 140

Eggleston Abbey, losses through Scots raids, 128

Elnstowe, 61

Elstow nunnery, bursars appointed, 41

Ely, diocese of, monastic and other appropriations, 89

Ely Priory, novice's outfit, 160; monk paid to celebrate annual, 165

Ely, St John's Hospital, secular appointed master, 132

Erdynton, Peter, monk of Eynsham, university expenses of, 106

Ertwode, appropriated church served by monks, 79

Estates, leased out in fourteenth century, 11; farmed out to monks, 165

Esteney, John, Abbot of Westminster, holds obediences, 132

Eversdone, Hugh de, Abbot of St Albans, expense of papal confirmation, 102; introduces leases at nominal rents, 138; sells corrodies, 144

Evesham Abbey, difficulties with lay brethren, 9; servants employed, 13; corrodiers in, 19; cellarer's functions, 46; abbot to meet debts of obediences, 49, 50; misgovernment of Abbot Norreys, 56, 61, 101; papal privileges as to abbot's confirmation, 103; failure to maintain scholars, 107; hospitality abused, 111; alms, 114; financial difficulties, 119; debt rapidly reduced, 134

Evil Times, On the, poem, 117, 154

Exemption from episcopal authority, 62, 63, 101, 102

Exeter, diocese of, pensions to Chapter from appropriated churches, 89; monastic and other appropriations, 90; state of houses before Black Death, 121, 165, 167

Exeter, St James' Priory, financial difficulties, 124

Eynsham Abbey, servants employed, 15; servants pay for posts, 18; monks holding office, 33; position of cellarer, 48; disposal of property without bishop's license, 61; cost of visitation, 98, 99; payments to monk at university, 106; case of nepotism, 130; corrodies, 143; dress, 159, 163; cost of maintaining monk, 169

Eyton, pension paid by rector to nunnery, 78

Felley Priory, bursar appointed, 43

Finchale Priory, alms, 114; Durham monks spend holidays at, 161

Forde Abbey, dilapidation at, 121

Fordham Priory, financial difficulties, 121

For EU product safety concerns, contact us at Calle de José Abascal, 56–1°,
28003 Madrid, Spain or eugpsr@cambridge.org.